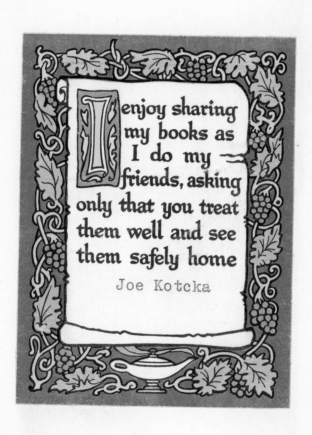

I enjoy sharing my books as I do my friends, asking only that you treat them well and see them safely home

Joe Kotcka

RUSSIA REVISITED

BY LOUIS FISCHER

RUSSIA REVISITED

*A New Look at Russia
and Her Satellites*

BY LOUIS FISCHER

DOUBLEDAY & COMPANY, INC., GARDEN CITY, N.Y., 1957

Library of Congress Catalog Card Number 57–9503
Copyright © 1957 by Louis Fischer
All Rights Reserved
Printed in the United States of America
First Edition

CONTENTS

PART I

RETURN TO RUSSIA:

A Personal Account

CHAPTER 1

At Home in Moscow

The saddest thing about journalism is that there is no substitute for being there; absence compels the journalist to be a historian. Twenty days in Moscow. Only twenty days, but they sufficed to breathe life into the dead body of material on the Soviet Union which I had gathered since I left the country in 1938. Post-Stalin Russia, in particular, became a reality.

My visa allowed me eight days. After my arrival I pleaded for an extension and received ten days more, then two days more. I decided to spend them all in Moscow, where I had resided from 1922 to 1938 (with intervals for trips to America, Europe, and the Middle East) and where, therefore, I hoped to meet old friends and make new contacts.

I had promised myself, before returning to Russia, to go with an open mind and an open heart and not to seek support for previously expressed views. This was to be a new leaf, or a new book, and I would not care if what I learned upset or modified earlier ideas. I wanted information, not confirmation. I wanted to look at Russia in the perspective of the thirty-four years since my first visit.

My purpose, as I planned the trip, was to study human beings and the Soviet system in terms of human beings. I intended to devote little time to exhibits, excursions, factories, galleries, and so forth. In fact, I devoted none. But the number of Soviet citizens with whom I had frank, revealing conversations both in their homes and elsewhere far exceeded my most optimistic expectations. Personally the entire experience was heart-warming, professionally very rewarding.

The nonstop Finnish airliner circled over Moscow two hours and twenty-five minutes after leaving Helsinki. The moon was full and the morning star rising rapidly. The city looked as the usual western city does from the air—an area of electric brightness. Strings of prominent red lights outlined a tall building which, I learned later, was the new university.

Once on the ground we encountered the traditional and comforting Russian disorder. As the plane lowered its steps foreigners and Soviet citizens were already waiting there to greet incoming passengers. No air hostess or airlines official led us into the air terminal. We straggled in individually.

A large oil painting of Stalin hangs in the first room. It shows him, idealistically, in white jacket against a blue background, standing alone on a vast brown newly plowed collectivized field, although, as Khrushchev said in his famous secret speech to the twentieth Communist party congress in Moscow on February 24, 1956, "The last time Stalin visited a village was in January, 1928. . . .", before collectivization.

The customs examination room lacked the usual long counters. Luggage was simply piled in a heap on the floor. With some difficulty I finally got an official's attention. He wanted to see the foreign currency I carried but did not count it and gave me a paper registering the total as I stated it. My three pieces of baggage were not opened. In the twenties and thirties the contents of all baggage underwent meticulous examination, with special scrutiny of every scrap of printed and written matter. I asked an older customs officer whether, as in the past, my typewriter and camera would be noted in my passport. (This then made it legal to take them out of the country.) He said, "Formerly we did that, not now."

The Intourist (Soviet Foreign Tourist Agency) auto was late. In the small waiting room stood a larger-than-life bronze statue of Stalin. Some people were sleeping on the wooden benches. A woman in headkerchief swept the stone floor with an old-style broom of thin twigs.

Finally the driver arrived and we started off on the eighteen-mile ride along the broad well-paved Kiev Highway to Moscow. It was nearing midnight. I asked the driver about himself. He was thirty-one; son of a worker; lived in a small room with his wife and a daughter five years old. There being no bath in the home they went once a week to the public baths. Yet as we entered town he proudly pointed to the giant new housing blocks around the university. Others were in the process of construction. "For the professors," he said. The university itself looked like a huge birthday cake with lighted red candles waiting to be blown out.

Muscovites were queuing for the last autobus. We passed the Park of Culture and Rest and crossed the Moscow River Bridge to enter the Red Square, impressive in size and silence. Near the Kremlin wall, which forms one side of the square, stands the Lenin Mausoleum, and in the moonlight I could discern the name of Stalin which had been added under that of Lenin. Inside, next to Lenin, I thought, lay Stalin, officially denounced bungler and murderer. Why had he been put there, and when would he be removed?

The next morning saw my first efforts to communicate with Russians. Not knowing whether old friends had moved or died, I wished to consult the telephone book. There was none in my room at the National Hotel, none in the hotel office; the telephone operator said she had none.

The Moscow telephone directory was a political publication. One appeared in 1937; the next was delayed till 1951, for many thousands had been purged in the intervening years and a new telephone book would, by omitting their names, officially confirm their end. The most recent directory was

published in 1954. By withholding the telephone directory
the National Hotel presumably hoped to erect an additional
obstruction between non-Russian-speaking foreign visitors
and Soviet citizens. But a six minutes' walk up Gorki Street
brought me to the central post office where one dilapidated
1951 directory lay on a table for all to use. The 1954 edition
was not available.

Happily I found the names, addresses, and telephone numbers of several friends. I did not call them, however. I remembered how in 1937 a Soviet guest whom we knew well quickly
fled from our apartment when the phone rang and the Moscow operator told me that Paris was on the line. In that black
era even the most indirect touch with the outside world drove
Soviet citizens into justified panic, and in 1938 the number
of those who dared visit or invite me had dwindled to near
zero. Unaware to what extent this condition persisted, I now
decided not to telephone. I assumed my telephone would be
tapped.

Imagine then arriving at an apartment without prior notice
and ringing the bell; the door opens and there stands a close
friend whom I had not seen for almost nineteen years and
who had never expected to see me again. I must have been
like an apparition from another planet. Exclamations, kisses,
and tears; "It's a miracle, it's a miracle," they cried as he,
his wife, and I held one another in a single embrace.

I never had a warmer welcome anywhere. All evening,
from seven-thirty till midnight we talked about our families,
friends, experiences, problems—and, of course, drank endless
tumblers of hot tea with lemon and strawberry jam. It was
intimate, moving, revealing. How they suffered before World
War II, during the war, and until several months after Stalin's
death in March, 1953, nobody can describe.

I spent five evenings in that apartment during my twenty-
day stay. They wanted me to come but not to telephone; a
visit to my hotel was unthinkable. Another family enter-

tained me three times, and two others twice. Altogether I visited fourteen apartments and had prolonged, frank conversations in them with thirty-six persons, middle-aged and youthful. Nearly all of the latter were members of the League of Communist Youth (Komsomol). One friend—an elderly engineer—had returned in 1954 from eighteen years in the Arctic concentration camp of Vorkuta. Only two of the thirty-six telephoned me or permitted me to call them; both were prominent and felt politically secure. Most of the others said they would have been afraid to receive me a year ago. But the de-Stalinization following the twentieth Soviet party congress in February, 1956, introduced some relaxation, and "if things continue this way," a woman said at her dinner table, "we may yet enjoy freedom." My very presence in the Soviet Union despite fierce attacks on its policies seemed to them a favorable portent and a promise of further liberalization. Some heard of those attacks from recently rehabilitated Siberian exiles. Concentration-camp inmates were better informed than Muscovites.

In addition to the Soviet citizens I visited at home, I had a remarkably uninhibited half hour's chat with Anastas I. Mikoyan, Deputy Prime Minister of the Soviet government and member of the Communist party Presidium (or Politburo), and at least sixty conversations, which I invariably turned toward personal and political topics, with taxi drivers, Intourist chauffeurs, hotel personnel, and others. It was easy, moreover, to have discussions with people one met by chance on the street, in shops, in restaurants, and elsewhere.

One afternoon, for instance, I came down the hotel corridor and was about to enter the waiting elevator when the floor lady, who had her desk at the landing (she kept the room keys and supervised miscellaneous services like laundry, the delivery of newspapers, and mail), asked me politely whether I wouldn't pay an accumulation of bills for pressing, dry cleaning, and washing—28 roubles in all. I searched in my pockets, found 20 roubles, apologized, and promised to pay the balance soon. A pretty Russian woman inside the elevator had watched the scene with a smile, and when I joined her there she said, "And with us everybody has money."

"Listen," I commented, "please don't tell fairy tales. Certainly, some Soviet folks earn plenty of money, but others don't, and even those who do cannot buy the clothing or rent the apartments they badly need."

By this time we were in the hotel lobby. "Nevertheless we don't complain," she asserted.

"That's the trouble with this country," I exclaimed. "You don't complain. If you had complained, if you had been able to protest, you wouldn't have undergone the horror of Stalin for twenty-five years." (I always spoke as freely in Moscow as I would in London, Paris, New York, or anywhere.)

"That was," she said.

We were now standing at the corner of Gorki and Mokhovaya Streets, perhaps the city's busiest crossroads. "Millions of victims succumbed to the Stalin regime," I argued vociferously, "and you brush it all off lightly with 'That was.'"

"What could I have done?" she pleaded. "A word of criticism meant death or at least banishment. But it is not so today."

"Try criticizing Khrushchev," I jested.

She laughed and I laughed and we parted.

This woman was not a partisan of the Soviet system, she was a patriot, and she wanted to praise and be proud of her country, especially in converse with a foreigner. That attitude, I found, was not uncommon.

On my second day in Moscow the sun shone brightly and I sallied forth into the Red Square to take photographs. The name of the square is prerevolutionary; red in Russian means beautiful too. It is not really beautiful, it lacks the grace and artistic proportions of Rome's Piazza Navona or the majesty of the Place de la Concorde in Paris. But it possesses grandeur, a vast emptiness, like old Russia's, and all its features (the fantastic St. Basil's Church with its bunched varicolored steeples and domes shaped like pineapples, onions, and beets; the squat, somber marble mausoleum; the Kremlin wall; and the GUM department store) seem remote from and unrelated to one another.

I had no sooner entered the square and taken a stance at a spot from which I hoped, ambitiously, to encompass the entire space when two Soviet men approached me, and the one carrying a FED camera asked what light exposure I was using. I told him but added that my film had been bought in America. He admired my new made-in-Britain light meter; the Soviet meters, he volunteered, were inexact. Answering questions he said his camera cost 500 roubles; he and his friend worked in a television-manufacturing plant in Voronezh. They had come to Moscow to iron out the factory's technical difficulties. Their TV apparatus was as good as the East German, but he did not know the American brands. "How large is the screen there?" I indicated the different sizes. "And how are general conditions in America and what are the relations to us?" he inquired. I answered objectively, then reversed the same questions.

"Conditions have improved," he said. "We already have enough food. Clothing, however, is bad, especially in lesser cities like Voronezh." He and his buddy were wearing very old suits, the collars and lapels of which were literally disintegrating, and broken-down shoes.

"What about the political situation after the twentieth party congress?" I probed.

"Oh, infinitely better," he affirmed. "In 1949 I attempted to photograph the Red Square and was shooed away by a militiaman. Photographers were often arrested. Now anyone can take pictures of the mausoleum, the wall, the inside of the Kremlin, the river embankment, et cetera." And in fact Soviet

and foreign amateurs and professionals were swarming all
over the place.

"Have you read Khrushchev's speech on Stalin's misdeeds?" I asked.

"Yes," he replied, "the Letter of Khrushchev! It was read
to us in the factory and party members as well as nonparty
people heard it."

"Nevertheless," I said, "you see Stalin's face in many places
and his mummy is over there on display."

"True," he agreed, "but, as Comrade Khrushchev explained, the change must be gradual. We have an electrical-
equipment factory in Voronezh which was named after Stalin
but no longer is. Until recently I would not have been standing here talking to a foreigner. We need to know more about
the outside world. Above all, there must be no war." On this
prayer we shook hands fervently and went our separate ways
to photograph the sights.

I took 252 photographs in Moscow. In the old days they
would have had to be developed and printed within Russia
so that the authorities could see whether a forbidden object
was recorded. This time I snapped everything I wished, including military personnel—once immune to the camera—and
kept the undeveloped films till I reached London. With perhaps a dozen exceptions, the photographs show people; they
were my uppermost interest, and I photographed all of them
in the heart of the city where well-dressed citizens are likely
to be more numerous than in the poorer outlying districts. I
also traveled by metro, trolley bus, autobus, taxi, tram, or on
foot to peripheral sections of the city, either to visit homes
or observe pedestrians and traffic and see the variety and
prices of goods on sale. I could not have been trailed or followed; and, what is really significant, the friends whom I
visited were not worried whether I was or not.

How do living conditions compare with 1938?

As the national showplace and center of power, Moscow

has always enjoyed privileges. Its officeholders crave the best for themselves and their city and can usually channel more commodities into the shops and more roubles into the municipal exchequer. Big provincial towns like Leningrad, Kiev, and Tiflis are known to live at least 20 to 30 per cent under Moscow standards; the descent to smaller urban centers is steeper.

Studying the photographs, rereading the copious diary entries I made several times a day, and rethinking the entire experience now, I have no doubt that Muscovites are better clothed than eighteen years ago or at any time since the 1917 revolution. Top marks for apparel go to the army officers—and their womenfolk. But though most men's suits are miserably tailored, the male species in general is not badly decked out; and, following Bulganin, Malenkov, and other leaders, who apparently must also lead in fashions, many men wear neckties and felt or straw hats instead of the once ubiquitous proletarian cap. Bad clothes used to indicate proper—that is, lower—class origin and were therefore a political asset. Perhaps they were merely making an ideological virtue out of a material deficiency. Since then, however, someone on high must have decided that a bourgeois appearance does not induce a bourgeois mentality. (Or does it?)

The women of course outstrip the stronger sex stylistically; they have to, for though legally free and equal, the majority are slaves to their jobs, husbands, children, and households, and usually show the signs of their unequal burden. Nevertheless, lipstick is rare and make-up rarer despite its low cost and fair quality. A university student told me it would never occur to her to wear lipstick in class.

(P.S. The moment I arrived from Moscow in Prague I realized how drab and shabby Muscovites looked by contrast. The texture of Soviet clothing is shoddy, the dyes dull, the styling at least a decade out of date. And Prague is a sartorial slum compared to Rome, Paris, or London.)

The Soviet food situation has also improved. The supply of bread and cake, wine and vodka, sugar, candy, and ice cream, domestic and imported butter, cheese, and margarine, and fish, fresh or canned, especially the latter, is—with seasonal variations—plentiful in Moscow and adequate elsewhere. The official press, however, admits shortages of meat and milk ("Already," *Pravda* wrote on August 3, 1956, "many cities do not feel any shortage of milk or dairy products"). Nor is the shortage remarkable in view of the fact that private peasants slaughtered and ate or sold their cattle before being propelled into the collectives during the late twenties and early thirties. Since then, moreover, livestock in the collectives has been neglected. A farmer will tenderly tend his own calf, but will he get up on a freezing night to care for a sick animal that belongs to the collective? The figures which Nikita S. Khrushchev, with startling and characteristic disregard of the resultant shock, published in September, 1953, on the reduction in livestock compared with 1928, when collectivization commenced, and compared with wartime tsarist Russia in 1916, obviously mean fewer animal products per person today. This conclusion is confirmed by the astonishingly lifelike wooden replicas of chunks of beef and dead ducks and chickens in the windows of Moscow meat stores (I used to admire them in the thirties) and the poverty on the hooks, shelves, and refrigerators within.

Walking down Moscow's Kuznetski Most, I saw a crowd on the pavement and peering over their heads I discovered a table with a heap of withered little apples on it. "What are they selling?" a passerby asked. "Apples," I replied. She joined the queue. Many women, and men, carry shopping bags whenever they go out on an errand or to work. You can never tell what might turn up. The majority of food stores are ancient and tiny and even the biggest, all old, are too small and packed tight with buyers.

The availability of food, clothing, and household articles

being uneven, with one part of a city getting more than others, one city more than another, and towns more than villages, spending entails much traveling. I heard of a woman who came hundreds of miles from Saratov on the Volga to Moscow to buy furniture. In a dress shop on Kirov Street in Moscow at least half the waiting customers were peasant women in headkerchiefs who had probably brought in the milk on their backs that morning. Peasants also buy food in town. Bad quality is a further contribution to overcrowding in stores. A woman who acquires a pair of shoes which wear out in four months soon appears once again in the queue. All Soviet statistics for quantity must be cut down drastically for poor quality.

In the late 1920's, when political criticism was still permitted and published, the Trotskyists complained at party conferences about the plague of queues and attributed it to high policy. "A passing phenomenon," the Stalinists retorted. It seems to be a permanent feature. The Soviet Union is the land of unending queuing—for food, clothing, transportation, etc. This condition is due to urban overpopulation in consequence of expanding industry and bulging bureaucracy, to inefficient distribution and antiquated sales methods which flourish under the state monopoly of trade, and to sporadic supply bottlenecks. All of these, in turn, spring from one basic cause: neglect of the needs of the individual which is both traditionally Russian and typically totalitarian. The same circumstances explain why housing in all cities, Moscow included, is intolerable.

A printer's assistant whom I visited in her Moscow home—one small room which she occupies with her husband—said to me, "I work an eight-hour day, and incidentally our shop is in the basement while the fat bureaucrats occupy the upper floors. I get an hour for lunch. It takes me an hour to reach my job and an hour to return. That makes an eleven-hour day. Add two hours, or more, for food shopping. Then when,

quite exhausted, I finally come home I have to cook dinner
on the primus in a communal kitchen with five other house-
wives."

The most depressing aspect of Moscow is the faces of its
people. In them I could read the history of the Soviet Union
without falsification: almost forty years of hardship and
strain for the older generation, and fewer years, of course,
for younger men and women; but even teen-agers and children are harassed and overburdened by the officially admitted and decried educational speed-up and, often, by the
difficult conditions at home. The price which the Soviet people paid to beat the mad Hitler's legions and meet the mad
wishes of Stalin is Everest-high. Probably no great nation in
history has suffered so much so long at the hands of its own
government. It needs rest and appreciates the least measure
of relief and relaxation.

CHAPTER 2

New Look, Old Form

The best news I heard in the Soviet Union is that there are no political arrests. I asked all my Soviet friends and acquaintances, as well as numerous foreign diplomats and journalists, whether they knew of any persons arrested by the secret police. "Not in the past year," they replied—except in Tiflis after the March, 1956, student riots there.

"The nightmare is over," a Moscow university professor said. The nightmare was no dream, it was a reality from 1917 to 1954, and even on into 1955. In the thirties the mornings were rare indeed when our maid, who had gone down at dawn for milk and met other maids in the queue, would not bring back the black tidings that "So-and-so was taken away last night by the NKVD from Apartment 17"; or, "They came for our upstairs neighbor at 2 A.M." Such information always spread quickly and spread fear; that was the planned result. The secret police pounced on its victims suddenly and what it did with them later long remained a secret; but no attempt was made to limit the ripples created by each arrest. They deepened the terror.

On my recent trip to Moscow, a Soviet journalist explained to me that "In every city and region, the NKVD used to be given a quota of arrests. Then the city was divided into sections, each of which had its quota. Further, streets and houses had their quotas." Nobody could elude the frightening effect.

In that era, visiting foreigners sometimes asked, "Why should such-and-such a person have been arrested?" But the question was irrelevant. The NKVD seldom concerned itself with political sins. It rarely had evidence of crime. The reason for the arrests was the psychological impression they produced. Once behind bars, the prisoners usually wrote out and signed the confession dictated to them by the investigator and thus implicated others who were in turn arrested.

In 1937 a neighbor who was a government official waited to be arrested. He had no sense of guilt, but his little bundle lay ready—a shirt, a change of underwear, a bar of soap, and a toothbrush. He waited for the NKVD agents; he waited nervously and, in a way, impatiently. One night they relieved the tension by carting him off in the Black Maria. Every Soviet citizen had a built-in barometer which foretold the weather changes around him. If an office colleague was arrested he knew what to expect: the colleague would probably confess and he would be next.

Why did they confess? Khrushchev himself has helped unravel the puzzle. "In the main," he asserted in his speech on February 24, 1956, "and in actuality, the only proof of guilt used . . . was the 'confession' of the accused himself, and, as subsequent probing proved, 'confessions' were acquired through physical pressure against the accused . . . no longer able to bear barbaric tortures, they charged themselves (at the order of the investigating judges-falsifiers) with all kinds of grave and unlikely crimes."

Not only were ordinary citizens and rank-and-file Communists tortured in jail. The same fate overtook the highest party officials. Thus Khrushchev revealed that Robert I. Eikhe, a deputy member of the topmost Politburo, "was arrested April 29, 1938, on the basis of slanderous material . . . A second declaration of Eikhe has been preserved which he sent to Stalin October 27, 1939. In it [he wrote] 'The case is as follows: not being able to suffer the tortures to which I was submitted by Ushakov and Nikolayev—and especially the first one—who utilized the knowledge that my broken ribs [broken in earlier tortures] have not yet properly mended and have caused me great pain—I have been forced to accuse myself and others . . .' On February 4, Eikhe was shot. It has been definitely established now that Eikhe's case was fabricated . . ."

Khrushchev affirmed that Stalin himself supervised the "cruel and inhuman tortures" and the "terrible maltreatment" practiced by the Soviet secret police. Stalin, Khrushchev stated, "said the Academician Vinogradov should be put in chains, another should be beaten. Present at this congress as a delegate is the former Minister of State Security, Comrade Ignatiev. Stalin told him curtly, 'If you do not obtain confessions from the doctors, we will shorten you by a head.' Stalin personally called the investigative judge, gave him instructions, advised him on which investigative methods should be used; these methods were simple—beat, beat, and once again, beat."

On occasion, however, the stick (or lead pipe) and carrot were used. As an illustration, Khrushchev named "Comrade Rosenblum, party member since 1906, who was arrested in 1937 by the Leningrad NKVD." After "terrible torture during which he was ordered to confess false information concerning himself and others" he was summoned to the offices of Leonid Zakovsky, the NKVD chief, and told that his services were required in court as a witness. "You yourself," Khrushchev quoted Zakovsky as saying, "will not need to invent anything. The NKVD will prepare for you a ready outline . . . you will have to study it carefully and to remember well all questions and answers which the court might ask. Your future will depend on how the trial goes and on its results . . . If you manage to endure it, you will save your head; we will feed and clothe you at the government's cost until your death."

That the number of arrests, banishments, and executions ran into tens of millions nobody in Moscow now doubts; Khrushchev's address contains the basis for this widely accepted estimate. The heavy sword of Damocles hung over everyone's head and whether it fell to crush out a brain might depend on luck or a whim or a personal relationship. In Moscow, in 1956, Ilya Ehrenburg, the prominent Soviet publicist and novelist, told me he had been editing the literary heritage of Isaac Babel, a talented Russian writer. "Babel," Ehrenburg said, "was friendly with the wife of Yezhov and that saved him." (Yezhov ruled the Soviet secret police during the slaughter of 1937–38.) "When Beria succeeded Yezhov in 1939," Ehrenburg continued, "Babel disappeared; he died in a concentration camp."

In December, 1956, a well-known Soviet author, on a visit to the capital of a Communist country, was asked why Boris Pilnyak, a prominent novelist, had been executed in the 1930's. "But for an accident," he replied, "Boris Pilnyak would be sitting here and you would be inquiring why I was shot."

Pure chance played a big role. The secret police did too much to do it well, and since it was itself constantly purged the efficiency of police agents occasionally failed to measure up to totalitarian requirements. That explains why one army officer is alive today. It was summer, in the thirties, and the rest of the family had gone to the country. One night a knock at the door awakened him. He could not mistake its meaning. Nor, therefore, could he refuse to submit. But as he walked toward the door he was suddenly paralyzed with fright. He could not move. His whole life flashed through his mind, and he stood there, immobile. "Our chaps must have been here before us and taken him away," he heard a voice say on the other side of the door. Then two men descended the stairs. The next morning the officer went to work as usual. Nothing happened. In fact he soon received a promotion.

A woman writer said, "You know, it sounds very cruel but it's true, the war actually came to us as a relief. Though rivers of blood flowed we could understand the reason why. No one ever understood the reason for the purges. Well, thank God, it's over."

I learned in Moscow that Michael Borodin, ex-Chicago Russian who led the revolution in South China in the mid-twenties, had been executed on Stalin's orders; two brothers of Lazar Kaganovich were "liquidated" while he sat in the Politburo; Solomon Lozovsky, former Deputy Commissar of Foreign Affairs, was shot; Ivan Maisky, able Soviet ambassador in London before and during the Second World War, who spent two years in a concentration camp, had been rehabilitated; ex-ambassador to Belgium Eugene Rubinin was back in Moscow after ten years in a camp; General Stern (Grigorovich) and General Shmushkevich, almost the sole survivors of a gallant and devoted band of Soviet military and diplomatic officials who helped the Loyalists in Spain, have recently returned from Siberian exile. Thousands of others were home again from slave labor in the Arctic wastes. It seems the camps themselves are gradually being liquidated. The once proscribed works of several executed Soviet authors were being published. The Sherlock Holmes stories are again available in Russia. No, Conan Doyle never became a Soviet citizen, but during the insane era of Stalinist "spy" hunts it was decreed that detective stories were "harmful"; they might interfere with the work of the secret police. For many years Stalin proscribed John Reed's *Ten Days That Shook the World*—although Lenin wrote a laudatory introduction to the Russian translation in which he said he had read it twice—because Stalin received no mention in this book about the Bolshevik revolt in 1917. Now Soviet magazines have begun to print excerpts from it.

So "the nightmare is over." Soviet citizens cannot tell how long the surcease from arrests will endure. They feel cautious but are hopeful. One would think they ought to hate the political system responsible for the massacres and mass terror. Some do. Most are grateful for its new moderation.

Having visited Moscow I understand the sharp divergence of world opinion about the post-Stalin era. Since Stalin died in March, 1953, foreign experts have argued whether and to what extent the Soviet Union has changed. Some assert that all is the same; some that much is different; and some that *plus ça change, plus c'est la même chose*. My own conclusion might be expressed in a paradox: there have been no basic changes in the Soviet Union, but essentially conditions are different.

The forms of the Soviet system remain unaltered, and it is the forms that one observes from the outside or superficially inside. In form the Soviet Union is a one-party dictatorship whose masters wield unlimited power. No democratic institutions have been introduced. No constitutional provision would prevent the party Presidium or federal cabinet from decreeing another Stalinist slaughter. Individuals enjoy no inalienable rights; rulers are subject to no legal checks and balances.

However, the perceptible, palpable curbing of the secret police, the cessation of political arrests, and the rehabilitation, posthumously or in the flesh, of numerous police-state victims constitute a decisive improvement for Soviet human beings. That is what one senses inside in free discussion with them. The citizen's built-in barometer reads: fair, or fine. He is praying for sun. He knows, nevertheless, that weather is often unpredictable, and he accordingly hesitates to make a false move into the political open air. Only the exceptional person—the student in particular—gives public expression to his despair or bitterness or envy. Most mind their step. Dissatisfaction exists, for every Kremlin admission of past evil provokes resentment. What can the Soviet citizen feel as he holds in his hand a fine novel by Bruno Yasensky or a collection of the brilliant essays of Mikhail Koltsov who, he now knows, were executed though innocent? He can only be conscious of the injustice and the irreparable harm. To this extent the revelations of Khrushchev and the reinstatements and rehabilitations which have followed his secret speech made matters much worse for even the most supine, bandwagon Communist; the atrocities of the regime are today documented and proved.

But what can he do? The decades of Stalin's horrors are not easily forgotten. They created a docile population. The present rulers are therefore confident. When any sign of unrest manifests itself they pull in the reins. They also allow some people to let off steam. The leaders are still in the driver's seat and the masses are still in harness. All's well with the Kremlin as long as there is no economic catastrophe at home and no cataclysm abroad. But to judge by their words and acts the heirs of Stalin do not mistake the nation's compliance for enthusiasm or its brooding silence for happiness.

CHAPTER 3

Moscow and Madison Avenue

Even the Soviet citizens who receive a foreigner in their home instruct him not to send letters or eagerly desired gifts from abroad. A little less fear does not mean much more freedom. Certainly the nation enjoys no freedom from propaganda. "The flaming sword" of the secret police has been sheathed, but the voice and hand of the almighty state are everywhere.

For well-nigh forty years the brain of the Soviet individual has been assaulted, punched, pushed, and squeezed out of one shape and into another by the dictatorship. If the result is a loss of resilience and receptivity nobody will wonder. A Moscow resident said, "What I want most is to come home after work and shopping, lock myself in, and read a good book, preferably a classic." There are few places to hide from the government's attention.

To be sure, every country engages in propaganda, and so do private business firms. But there is a revealing difference between Madison Avenue and Moscow. New York's Madison Avenue—symbol of high-powered publicity and big advertising—caters to other men's vanity and sells other men's goods. Its skillful operators must sometimes laugh at their own gyrations and exaggerations. But Soviet supersalesmanship is not something external or secondary; it is of the very essence. Muscovite propaganda is the heartbeat of the sys-

tem. The legendary Potemkin villages were designed to fool
an empress during one trip. Soviet "Potemkin villages" seem
to fool the designers (or at least some of them), who spend
huge sums of money and even distort the national economy,
while harming human beings, in order to dazzle their fellow-
citizens and foreigners. "Madison Avenue" is propaganda
about works. Moscow sometimes damages the works for the
sake of propaganda.

When Moscow's renowned Bolshoi Ballet arrived in London late in 1956, the Special Correspondent of the *Manchester Guardian* paid tribute to its technique, yet emphasized "its remarkable lack of taste and imagination in the
matter of decor. The style tends to be at once out of date and
shoddy. But," he continued—and here he unconsciously characterized the Soviet approach to many aspects of life—
"compensation for lack of taste and inventiveness is provided,
lavishly, by the immense scale of the productions and the
massive use" of machinery.

Incapable of combining bigness with beauty the Soviets
substituted bigness for beauty. What they fail to achieve by
skill they try to attain through mass. Quality is sacrificed to
quantity. If finesse and art cannot impress, weight and dimen-
sions should. In part, this probably reflects the enormous ex-
panse of the country and its planned isolation from healthy
influences abroad; in part, its vast natural resources. But more
than anything else it stems from the government's unparal-
leled power, uninhibited by public control or protest, to indulge in expensive lavishness in the midst of poverty. Told
that the people were clamoring for bread, Marie Antoinette
is said to have said, "Let them eat cake." Taking bread to
mean the comforts and even necessities which the regime
could not supply, Stalin gave them wedding-cake skyscrapers
and grandiose projects—circuses instead of bread.

Communist gigantomania, which is love of the massive
rather than the magnificent, the irrational rather than the

functional, derives from a need to impress. Every totalitarian state yields to the temptation of conspicuous construction. Its taste runs to Stalinallees, displays, parades, and façades.

Opulent stage settings and dramatic presentation were traditional in Russia. The Bolsheviks retained them on the stage and applied them to politics and economics. Under tsarism, and now, the palace exists side by side with the hovel.

The Soviet government is preparing to build a Palace of Soviets in the Lenin Hills area of Moscow. Its history goes back more than two decades when Stalin ordered the razing of the great white-walled, gold-domed Orthodox Cathedral of Christ the Saviour that towered over the city. In its place he intended to erect a mammoth convention hall which, with a tall statue of Lenin on top, would be the highest building in the world. Enormous difficulties were encountered in laying the foundation in Moscow's quicksand subsoil, and work was finally suspended in 1941. But on August 25, 1956, the Council of Ministers of the Soviet Union announced a competition for a new architectural design of the Palace. The structure, according to the official statement, is to include a hall measuring 46,000 square feet with 4600 seats; two chambers, each 15,000 square feet in size, for the Council of the Union and the Council of Nationalities which constitute the Supreme Soviet and approve the acts of the Soviet government; a salon, with an area of 41,000 square feet, for state banquets and receptions; and offices, washrooms, committee rooms, and so forth, covering 64,000 square feet. The total floor space of the Palace rooms is not to exceed 360,000 square feet. Outside, there will be parking lots, capacious approaches for cars and processions, and a huge plaza to accommodate open-air gatherings.

The new Foreign Office is twenty-nine stories high; the new university's tower is thirty-four stories high; four other Moscow buildings are crowned with equally ugly "skyscraping" superstructures. Their height creates a special water-pressure problem and necessitates special fire-fighting apparatus. After Stalin's death the government prohibited such imitative monstrosities.

But the Palace of Soviets, whatever its shape, will be a costly colossus. Moscow completed a stadium with 106,000 seats in 1956. Stalin is gone, but gigantomania marches on.

Soviet citizens hardly approve of this phenomenon at their expense. A Moscow engineer estimated that dwellings which house ninety thousand persons would be wrecked to create the open spaces and approaches around the Palace of Soviets. "And the materials and labor that go into the Palace could give us apartments for tens of thousands who now live very badly," he added in a whisper.

"With so much space, why do they build up into the air?" a taxi driver exclaimed as we passed the Foreign Office. I inquired how he lived. "One room, fourteen square meters," he replied. (140 square feet.)

"And how many in the family?"

"Myself, my wife, a daughter of thirteen, and a boy of seven."

"Excuse me," I said, "we are both grownups. Would you mind telling me how you manage with your family life in such circumstances?"

He shook his head sadly. "Yes," he sighed, "it is a problem. The bed must not creak and we must not talk or make any noise."

I was in a limousine with a Soviet driver employed by a foreign embassy. I put the invariable question: "How many square meters?"

"Five." (50 square feet.)

I looked back. "That's about the size of this automobile," I suggested.

"That's right," he confirmed. He had no children. His wife worked. They could afford a bigger home but cannot get it.

During my Moscow stay there was a run on the bookshops

for a new statistical handbook, the first in many years, entitled *The National Economy of the U.S.S.R.* On page 243 this official publication revealed a remarkable phenomenon, a steep drop in the birth rate. The number of children born to every thousand inhabitants was 47 in 1913, 44 in 1926, 31.7 in 1940, 26.5 in 1950, 26.8 in 1951, 26.4 in 1952, 24.9 in 1953, 26.5 in 1954, and 25.6 in 1955. This is not surprising. Two parents and two children is as much as any one-room apartment will accommodate.

I visited a room occupied by a boy of twenty, a boy of ten, and their father and mother. The older son slept behind a wooden screen, the younger one on the couch. There was a narrow bed that blocked half of the two-panel entrance door. Where the fourth person slept I could not imagine, for what with two cupboards for dishes, food, laundry, etc., and a dining table, a desk, and four chairs, there just was no space for it. The family shared the bathroom, lavatory, and kitchen with five other families each of which had one room.

Right in the heart of Moscow, and in the outskirts, one sees innumerable pre-1917 one- and two-story houses from which the outside plaster has crumbled away exposing the crisscross wooden slats. Some outside walls are buttressed with logs to prevent further buckling. In a courtyard one minute's walk from the British embassy a wooden board on the wall of a small, three-story brick house gives the surnames of the twenty-four tenants. Judging by the size of the house it could not have more than twenty-four rooms. Its windows are askew, the rickety stairway has a revolting smell, and winter frosts followed by thaws have broken off parts of the brickwork. My search for friends took me into many houses like this. Most of them lack bathing facilities. Nearly all, but to be cautious I will say the majority, of the workingmen I consulted told me they used the public baths. One morning the floor waiter in the National Hotel was too hoarse to engage in our usual over-the-breakfast talk; he had visited the baths the evening before and caught cold. In the outer rim of Moscow women draw water from street wells.

Friends have an apartment on one of the big Moscow boulevards. I first visited them there twenty-nine years ago. I saw them there on my recent trip. Nothing has changed. The same staircase filled with the stench of age-long dirt; the same chipped steps; on the fourth floor, the same cracked door; the same apartment corridor crowded with folded beds and tall wicker baskets storing unseasonal clothing; the same unattached seat and deep rat hole in the lavatory; the same crowded conditions in each of the five one-room and my friends' two-room (for five adults) subapartments of the communal apartment. Children race through the corridor where women carry pots and kettles from the kitchen to their tables; a neighbor plays the gramophone; another has the radio on; the third is singing. A single improvement: in the common kitchen they cook with gas.

This is a prerevolutionary house that has stood up well these many years with an occasional painting but few repairs. In another house the repairmen had arrived, started work, left for six weeks, returned for a month's activity, gone away again, and are now back to do another stint of undetermined length. For eight months the residents have lived as in a bivouac. Cold weather was commencing; if the repairs were not finished before winter they would be interrupted till spring.

For sentimental reasons and to make comparisons I went to 15 Sivtzev Vrazhek—an eight-story block of apartments consisting of several sectors, each with its own entrance. When the construction of the house was completed in 1936, our family moved into Apartment 68. We had three rooms, kitchen, lavatory, bath, and balcony. That was what I wanted to see. Early one evening I entered the vestibule, dimly lit by a weak electric bulb in the ceiling, inserted the elevator key, which hung from a string, into the door slot, opened the door, pushed No. 3 button, and rode up. The bell of our former apartment had disappeared, so I knocked. No response. Since it was a rather strange errand (I would have to explain that I had once lived here and would like to see the premises again), I waited several minutes and knocked again. No answer. I knocked a third time. From the rear sector a man appeared and said, "Nobody in. The sixteen tenants of this sector have been evicted. Here everything is rotted." On the ground floor I found the door to an apartment open. The inner walls, the floors, and the ceilings had been ripped out. The entire apartment was being rebuilt—and the house only twenty years old! A striking example of how quantity erases quality.

Two years ago the American embassy in Moscow took over a newly erected building for offices and employees' residences. Already many inside walls are cracked. The roof leaks, and rainwater has made abstract paintings on ninth-floor ceilings. The structure looks as though it had been in use at least a decade.

Why ten-story apartment blocks when, at least in Soviet conditions, they are more expensive and difficult to build, service, and repair? Because they were designed to make an impression, to divert attention from the abounding hovels.

The bulk of Moscow's population lives in pre-1917 dwellings which have been getting abnormally heavy wear because many private apartments originally occupied by a single family are now communal apartments occupied by four, five, or six families. A much smaller percentage of Muscovites inhabits homes built by the Soviet regime before the Second World War; some of these are still good, others resemble slums. Since 1945 the Soviets have modernized their construction methods (the metal-pipe scaffolding and huge lifting cranes I saw in 1956 were unknown before 1938) and put up a large number of big houses along the river quays, in the outskirts, and in the center of town. I was a guest in several which make an excellent impression. My hosts, who belong to the new upper class, had apartments of four to five rooms with all the necessary conveniences. But half a million would seem a gross overestimate of the number of privileged persons in these new quarters. The remainder of Moscow's seven million inhabitants are miserably or inadequately housed.

Discussing the housing problem an ambassador said, "Moscow would have to run very fast to stand still," for it is doubtful whether new construction provides space for the natural increase in population, the migration into the capital despite sincere government efforts to stop it, and those evicted when public edifices and parks are planned or when streets are widened or when state bureaus expand and proliferate.

Crowded homes affect family relations, sex, studies—everything. It frequently happens that a divorced Soviet couple must continue to live in the same room, and sometimes a third person, the new spouse, joins them, because no alternative living space is available. In the central Moscow post office on Gorki Street and in the branch post office on Kirov Street hundreds of persons are seated at large tables during any hour of the day or evening writing letters; presumably they have more privacy and quiet there than at home.

Given the buoyant industrial development of the Soviet Union after 1928, urban overcrowding was unavoidable. The early growth of capitalism in Europe and America produced similar effects. But much suffering could have been prevented had the Communists been as interested in the comfort of the individuals as in the might of the state.

However, since the basic principle of dictatorship is in fact state power, not personal convenience, Moscow builds a Palace of Soviets (when it has halls where banquets, assemblies, and mass meetings have been taking place) and the new Lenin Stadium for 106,000 spectators (when there is already one for 70,000) although human beings live six in a room without plumbing.

Nor is this situation confined to Moscow. In the town of

Frunze, only 19 per cent of the 1955 plan for house construction was fulfilled. An article in the Moscow *Izvestia* of September 1, 1956, datelined Stalingrad and signed by two writers, describes conditions in several small towns near by. One "has a single tea room which enjoys an unenviable reputation; in it are filth and dirt and bad food. In the unpleasant cinema it is suffocating in summertime and cold in winter.

"Who is at fault? Naturally the local officials. They dream of big Palaces of Soviets and stadiums—like in capital cities—and don't want to repair the club for homeless waifs or the public bath house . . ."

Of course the country models itself after Moscow where all the wise men sit.

Another article in *Izvestia*, bearing the title "Why It Is Uncomfortable to Live in a New House," begins: "Kharkov. 19 Danilevsky Street. A person crosses the street and enters the new, beautiful eight-story house. The elevator is again not working. He has to walk up to the sixth floor, dangerously supporting himself by the shaky bannisters." The occupant of the apartment has to use a hammer so as to turn the key and open the door for his guest. Inside, plaster drops from the ceiling. "There is no water. It rarely reaches the top floors." Accordingly a meeting of the residents and builders was summoned. "It reveals," writes the *Izvestia* journalist, "what are the results of the absence of technical and architectural supervision of the building process, haste, lack of coordination between the contractor and the subcontractors, bad construction materials, and also an irresponsible attitude toward approving the finished house. Striving to speed up the approval of the house for some kind of holiday, the commission of approval and the architectural constructional inspectors often reconcile themselves to big imperfections. True, they extract a pledge from the builders to remove these imperfections by a definite date. But such pledges, as a rule, remain a dead letter."

Speeding up the opening of a building "for some kind of holiday"—usually November 7 or May 1—is the confirmed Soviet way: "On the anniversary of the Great 1917 Revolution, 100 new apartment houses were completed in Kiev"; Madison Avenue-Moscow propagandizing itself at the cost of the population. Over the years, the newspapers have complained about this practice thousands of times. But some psychological deficiency impels the Communists repeatedly to convince themselves. Some inner distrust forces the Soviet system again and again to trumpet its unfinished achievements.

Izvestia gives further details about 19 Danilevsky Street: a leaking roof, "already rusted" metalwork, rickety balconies, "peeling paint on window frames, cracks in the walls . . . and much more." At the meeting where residents' complaints were aired, the chief engineer explained that "We build tens of houses and cannot examine and check every one of them."

The occupants of 27 Stalin Avenue in Kharkov held a similar meeting, according to the *Izvestia* contributor, and protested that the walls of their new house were too hollow to allow the hanging of a picture or a clock. "There's no point in converting a living room into a museum," the contractor replied.

"The plumbers," the article continues, "destroy the work of the carpenters, the electricians ruin the work of the plasterers." One cause of the trouble, says the correspondent, is the system of extra compensation to the building workers for economizing in the use of materials. So, he says, cement "is mixed . . . with more sand. Economy is certainly necessary, but not to the detriment of quality." In the twenties and thirties I read, and quoted, many such articles in Soviet journals.

The Moscow *Literary Gazette* of August 25, 1956, throws light on another facet of Moscow's Madison Avenue mentality. A journalist reports from the Donetz coal basin: one mine manager complains that "we are not fulfilling the plan

because we haven't enough people, housing is difficult." A
second manager tells the journalist, "We have no place to
house people . . ." A third: "The miners are leaving. I cannot
provide even a married man with a room." But the *Gazette*
reporter learns that many new homes had been erected for
miners. What happened? Residents arrived from the neighboring town of Stalino armed with "orders" from the highest
authorities for rooms in the new dwellings. The mine management protested to these usurpers and argued that they should
have remained in their former homes.

"Ah, yes," they reply, "we would have stayed where we
were, but then the flowers . . ."

"What flowers," the miners exclaim.

"Well, the flowers in the square in front of the district party
headquarters."

"But there was no such square."

"There wasn't. Now there is."

A park for the party building. Another façade. Behind it
miners and others dwell in sardine-box squalor.

To the enormous price the Soviet nation has paid for its
great victory over Nazi Germany and for the cruelties of
Stalinism must be added the high cost of the continuing fol-
lies of façade-ism and, of course, the very big bill of the do-
everything state.

Communist regimes, in Russia and outside, constantly
seem to be trying to prove a thesis, to demonstrate the supe-
riority of their ism, to overtake or outdistance somebody.
Communism in practice is the most competitive, show-off
system ever devised. The Soviets and their satellites speak of
their achievements, which have, in many places, been considerable, in a tone of breathless wonder and endless self-admira-
tion as though nobody else had ever built cities, factories,
and dams, or widened streets, increased production, and har-
vested a good crop, and as though these same things might

not have been done in their own countries without them and with fewer human sacrifices.

Soviet leaders might do well to travel abroad incognito, with a moderate measure of objectivity or humility in their luggage, and walk the streets and see, for instance, how Holland, small and deficient in soil and natural resources, has rebuilt her economy since the war so that, despite the loss of rich Indonesia, she is better off than before; or to West Germany which rose from the rubble by dint of hard work and able management; or to the garden of Israel where will power and ideals have moved rocks and fructified sand; or to prosperous little Austria; or wealthy Switzerland; or northern Italy; or to America. The experience might lend Soviet propagandists a sense of proportion and teach them that a good deal of their people's toil has been wasted in carrying the heavy burden of an inefficient industrial and agricultural system. It is largely to prevent such disillusioning discoveries that few Soviet citizens are allowed to travel abroad.

CHAPTER 4

Revolt

The propaganda noise that thunders through Soviet life jams the still small voice of truth, faith, and art, and leaves the people uninspired and bored.

Stalin said, "The press is the sharpest and strongest weapon of our party." This slogan, displayed at newspaper stands, invokes the cynical comment that the sharpest weapon has become very dull indeed. Day after day after day the Moscow *Pravda* and, following it, every other daily, exhorts readers to action. In harvest time, for instance, front-page editorials repeatedly insist that the crops be collected on time. But what can the millions of Muscovites, reading these sermons as they hurry to office, store, or factory, do about harvesting? They can refuse to read the editorial. Certainly the peasants do not read *Pravda*. The harvest is undoubtedly Russia's most important single economic operation, but one would have thought that a material incentive for the man on the farm would be more effective than a verbal shower every morning for persons completely removed from agriculture.

Another day the *Pravda* editorial shrieks that the seasonal fish catch on the Volga has been unsatisfactory, and spurs the fishermen to fulfill the plan. In the far North and Siberia, timber cutting is lagging; the party Central Committee has adopted a resolution admonishing the lumber industry to do better; Moscow editorials drive the point home to their urban readers.

Soviet newspapers are as unappetizing as regurgitated dishwater and as exciting as the minutes of last month's meeting of the board of directors of a zipper factory. I asked my friends how much of the press they read. They take one or two dailies and scan the headlines in order not to miss any significant development. But they skip the exhortations, the monotonous, synthetically enthusiastic, cliché-ridden announcements from industrial enterprises that they have over-fulfilled the plan, and the telegrams about the milkmaid in Tula who extracted 35 per cent more milk per cow than last year.

Flying from Moscow to Prague, the plane stopped at Vilna (now called Vilnius) for refueling. My neighbor bought a paper and later gave it to me. While reading, I sensed that the woman across the aisle was eager to see it. I handed it to her and watched. Her eye moved rapidly over the first page without stopping at a single item. Then she turned the four-page sheet inside out and spent considerable time on an article entitled "The Approach of Mars," which filled the lower half of page two. The next page apparently did not interest her. Page four, generally reserved for foreign news, occupied her for about five minutes.

Nor do people believe what the papers print. A Muscovite said, "If I want to know what is happening in some part of the Soviet Union I try to speak to someone who has been there. I would like to do the same about foreign affairs but I rarely meet foreigners."

When a report on the United Nations or a conference of the Big Four foreign ministers devotes five-sixths of its space to the Soviet spokesman's speech and the rest to paraphrases of all the others interspersed with such words as "he alleged" and "he vainly attempted to create the impression that . . ." some readers at least see through the obvious technique of

distortion by selection. Little dishonest tricks are perpetrated
—like the monthly *International Life* buttressing an argument with a quote from "the prominent British religious personality, H. Johnson," an artful disguise for Mr. Hewlett
Johnson, the Dean of Canterbury, known by some as "the Red
Dean." Or, to give the impression that public opinion abroad
is on Russia's side, the Soviet press will cite editorials in little-
known foreign Communist dailies without indicating that
they are Communist.

Statements in the press often conflict with the reader's own
experience. It contributes nothing to faith in the veracity of
Pravda (which means truth), for example, when one of its
authors charges that "reactionary" writers abroad "invent
tales about 'the persecution' of Jews in the socialist state." Soviet Jewry suffered concretely and acutely from that persecution, and their fellow-citizens were aware of it. If *Pravda*
wants the evidence it can be found in a Warsaw Communist
paper which printed the names of the Jewish poets, novelists,
editors, theater producers, and others shot in the Soviet Union; *Pravda* itself published additional data on the subject.
Fortunately the horror ended several months after Stalin's
death, but the wounds and memories (and anti-Jewish unfair
employment practices) remain.

Readers who lose trust also lose interest.

The teaching of history in Soviet schools and its presentation in Soviet journals is in a state of utter confusion. Scholars
who wrote one thing a few years ago are reversing themselves
today. The history of the Stalin period must now be completely rewritten, and pupils will have to unlearn what they
studied and begin anew. The past of tsarist Russia is also
undergoing revision. Ivan the Terrible became Ivan the
Fourth in Stalin's time. Now he is again Ivan the Terrible.
He has been "rehabilitated" and is his former self again. On
a hint from on high, teachers taught that Catherine the Great
was responsible for the greatest successes of the Russian Em-

pire. After the Communist empire builder died, Moscow discovered her deficiencies. Peter the Great, whose face was lifted because Stalin saw himself as Peter's modern incarnation, has been cast back into feudal purgatory by recently unfettered historians. The poor schoolchildren don't know what to think; their teachers are bewildered; and authors of textbooks are afraid to put pen to paper.

A dead hand lies heavily on all creative processes in the Soviet Union. "The twentieth party congress," writes *Pravda,* "sounded a serious alarm over the retarded state of literature." The same article laments "the grayness, dullness, colorlessness of many books . . ."

A Moscow woman who loves literature confessed that she sometimes leaves the Moscow Art Theater before the end of the performance. In the 1920's and 1930's this would have been sheer sacrilege; the Moscow Art Theater was probably the world's greatest. Yet "Now," the Soviet *Literary Gazette* mourns, "its box-office queues, which did not disappear for decades, are gone." In general, the Moscow theater was the best anywhere. Russians delighted in it because the drama on the stage lifted them out of the drabness of daily life. The lift is no longer there, and they feel its absence. "How few," sighs a writer in the *Literary Gazette* of June 14, 1956, "have been the real plays and strong emotions in our theater in recent years." Soviet drama, he declares, has become "intolerably dull."

Satire and humor, in which few Communists distinguish themselves, is of such poor quality that "the departments of satire and humor have disappeared from the pages of our thick [monthly] literary magazines," says the Moscow *Literary Gazette.*

The Soviet cinema, once the envy of good producers in all countries, has likewise deteriorated, and the Kremlin knows and says it.

Under Stalin, praise of Soviet art was mandatory. Minor

faults, to be sure, were occasionally admitted, but the dictator's dictum that even the worst in the Soviet Union excelled the best in capitalist nations gave wings to Soviet conceit; Russia did not need to take lessons from the West.

This nonsense has vanished. Not only is the deplorable condition of Russian art frankly avowed, it stimulates "hot, passionate disputes," writes a *Pravda* contributor. "Not for a long time," he adds, "has the artistic world witnessed such social liveliness."

Opposite opinions on art and literature are tolerated. Valentin Katayev, the novelist, lauds a Soviet painter who has learned from Matisse. *Pravda* takes him to task on the ground that Matisse was a "decorationist"—an impressionist guilty of "characteristic rejection of realistic forms." A few years ago such a shaft from the central organ of the Communist party would have silenced and hurt Katayev. Today the dispute continues to rage.

Soviet publications now feel free to acknowledge the gradual, and then precipitous, decline of Soviet art and literature in the twenty-five years of Stalin's absolute reign. But in attempting to analyze its cause and to prescribe a new course they reveal the real dilemma of the Soviet Union's present stage of evolution; it becomes clear that a little liberty, doled out by government chiefs, cannot solve problems born of unfreedom. This is true of culture as well as politics.

To explain the crisis in all fields of artistic effort, Soviet writers seize upon Stalin's personal despotism or "the cult of personality" as it is officially translated. "The cult of personality," *Pravda* states, "seriously harmed the development of our literature and art and, in the creative sphere, spawned such pathological phenomena as kowtowing, varnishing [of the truth], and parade pomposity." On the same note, at another time, *Pravda* wrote, "The cult of personality introduced traits into creative activity which are alien to the art of socialist realism . . . [it] led to the production of works which falsified and twisted the role of the popular masses in history."

But is this the reason? Or does it conceal the reason? Soviet assertions inadvertently supply a clear answer. For example: David Zaslavsky, a regular contributor to *Pravda*, condemns the humor of *Punch*, and of American magazines which he finds even worse, because their aim is merely to make people laugh. Then he declares, "Our satire has an altogether different function. It is an effective instrument of the party and the Soviet nation against everything which hinders socialist construction and socialist culture."

At the autumn of 1956 Biennale de Poésie in Knokke-le-Zoute, Belgium, Pavel Antokolsky, a Soviet poet and the chief Russian delegate, said poetry should contribute to "peace among nations." "Peace" means Soviet foreign policy. Poetry is politics. That is why Boris Pasternak, the greatest Soviet poet, stopped writing verse and for many years supported himself by translating Goethe and Shakespeare.

Pravda recently asserted, "Our art must be saturated with the spirit of the struggle for Communism, must fill the hearts of the people with zest, and develop socialist convictions. This is not beyond the power of the Soviet artist armed with the ideas of Marxism-Leninism . . ."

Small wonder the Soviet people find such art dull. It is art not for laughter, or pleasure, or the greater fulfillment of man, but for the fulfillment of another five-year plan and the greater glory of the party-state. The Kremlin admits that the personal glorification of Stalin in word, paint, stone, and metal—at his own behest—was an abomination. Yet it still instructs writers on the purpose and style of their work. If it was wrong to force creative artists to serve "the cult of personality," it is no less destructive to ask them to serve the cult of the party, dogma, institution, or program.

The result is boredom. Almost the worst thing I discovered in the Soviet Union was that life had become boring.

The Soviet social system, having ceased to be revolutionary, is conservative. Stalin killed the revolution by killing off the revolutionists. But the same effect would have been achieved by the dictatorship's insistence on obedience and orthodoxy in thought and action. Communism is conformism. Soviet civilization is an ant civilization, in which there is nothing new except the size of the ant heap. Quoting authority—whether Stalin or Lenin or Marx—is not conducive to reasoning, thinking, experimentation, or excitement.

Boredom and conformity produce protest, especially—but not only—in youth. So does inequality.

One evening, after I had ordered dinner in the restaurant of the National Hotel, a man came in and sat down at a table one removed from mine. He was obviously a Soviet citizen (one could tell from the quality of his clothes and his very wide, sailor-like trouser bottoms) and obviously hungry and grumpy. But the waitress did not come. He looked around at me, shrugged his shoulders and lifted his eyebrows in a gesture of impatient disgust, and said, "Will she ever appear?"

I assured him she would and suggested that he meanwhile move over and keep me company. He sat down in the chair opposite and complained about the long delay.

"In America," I said, "we attach importance to time; here you don't." I made this remark not because of its profundity or complete accuracy; I merely wanted him to know I was a foreigner. Had he been afraid of the contact he might easily have excused himself and returned to his table. That is what he would have done in the latter part of the Stalin era and, probably, until 1955. Instead he stayed throughout the meal.

Over the borscht I mentioned an article I had read in the morning paper about rowdyism and juvenile crime in Soviet cities and villages. "It is not really crime," he volunteered. "We spoil our children. The older generation suffered so much so long that we try to give our sons and daughters every possible enjoyment, and of course they are spoiled."

Soviet delinquency resides in two classes: the rich youth,

and the disgruntled poor. My dinner partner referred to "the golden youth"; others call them "the jet set," suggesting fast living. In Moscow's streets and restaurants they are distinguishable by their fine clothing in tight, British Teddy-boy or American zoot-suit style, and the crew cuts or Tarzan coiffeurs of the male teen-agers, and the conspicuously flashy dress of the girls; clearly an effort to escape from the pervading drabness. They ape foreign ways, even addressing one another in English or Latin, and have acquired an encyclopedic knowledge of jazz. Many American visitors have had to reply, "Sorry, I never heard of him," when accosted by a jet setter interested in the latest hits of a bandleader in the U.S.A. This too is an escape—across the Soviet border, a step toward the West.

The behavior of the upper-class fast set in the Soviet Union may be bizarre and profligate but it is neither violent nor vicious. Yet it worries the authorities so much that they are discussing its most embarrassing manifestations in public. Thus the *Komsomolskaya Pravda* of August 15, 1956, revealed that the son of Minister of Foreign Trade Kabanov and a son of Minister of Heavy Engineering Petukhov had been arrested for staging "drunken orgies" with the daughters of an air force lieutenant-colonel, an army major-general, and a secret-police colonel. These children of the mighty, the report stated, stole from their parents and friends to pay for "forbidden delights." Subsequently the three girls received one-year sentences for burglary.

When I alluded to this episode, my dinner companion hinted gently that it was perhaps a youthful translation of the lavish living at the Soviet social summit. Palatial villas, hunting lodges, private railway trains, beautiful automobiles, and great feasts are not conducive to austerity in those who can manage, by fair means or foul, to avoid it. Nor does the acceptance of privileges and the wielding of power by fathers promote idealism in any but the exceptional sons.

"Of course you know," I said to the Russian, "that we have considerable juvenile delinquency in America. In the main our youth is healthy; that is surely true of Soviet youth too. But the pressure to conform always breeds rebels."

"Yes," he agreed. "I have read in our journals about juvenile delinquency in the U.S.A. Our writers, however, attribute it to capitalist decadence. Yet now it exists in a socialist country."

"Maybe this proves," I ventured, "that your country is not socialist. More important—as I see it, certain global social climates or atmospheric pressures produce similar results irrespective of isms or ideologies. The revolt of sons against fathers and mothers is a universal phenomenon which no iron curtain can bar. Also, youth, like colts, are irked by harness and the whip, and I imagine that here the harness is heavier and the whip sharper."

He said nothing.

(During the silence I thought of two pieces of information that had come to me in Moscow: between symphonies a famous Soviet composer writes music for the films in order to earn a living; many inventions lie unused for years in Russia because of management inertia and resistance to innovation. Delinquency is not the only phenomenon that does not respect the iron curtain.)

The richer the Soviet delinquents the more their manners and misdemeanors approximate those of their western contemporaries. But even after the wild oats have been sown—and on into old age—onerous duties, ubiquitous grayness, political claustrophobia, no room of one's own, and the ineluctable din of propaganda drive many Soviet people through all the escape hatches into alcoholism, gambling, inertia, and mental disease. A Communist friend of mine who cut timber for eighteen years in an Arctic concentration camp developed iron muscles and broken nerves; released from captivity, he takes drinks and drugs, and, to prevent a complete crackup, he clings to the stale slogans and dogmas of three decades ago when I first met him.

"Why don't you give a passport to Paul Robeson?" he demanded.

"Keep quiet, you fool," his wife shouted.

"Coming from you, after eighteen years' confinement, the question is funny," I replied. "Perhaps we should organize a committee in New York or London to get you a Soviet passport," I suggested facetiously.

"God forbid," he exclaimed.

"He will soon convince himself that he was never in a camp," a Young Communist whispered in my ear.

The ex-lumberjack seemed to be trying to save his mind by an unthinking orthodoxy which would blot out the passage of the decades.

Apart from these stresses in Soviet society, professional crime also exists, but its extent is unknown, for the government withholds the information. Of late, however, the press and radio have given prominence to amateur criminality or rowdyism; Russians call it hooliganism. This was defined, and denounced, at a Moscow meeting on October 10, 1956. "Hooliganism," the radio report of the assembly stated, "is a crime against public order and public security. A swinish attitude toward women and disrespect for neighbors must and will vanish."

Addressing the gathering, Assistant Prosecutor-General Boldyrev begged Muscovites to support the militia (civilian police) in suppressing hooligans. His appeal was seconded by an official of the Ministry of Interior, which supervises the civil police. "Our experience," he affirmed, "shows that a small crime always leads to a bigger one. It all begins with somebody showing off, at first playing innocuous card games, then comes ochko [twenty-one] for money, smoking, and lastly the discovery of alcoholic beverages. The blind love of some parents prejudices their reaction to this unsavory conduct, and they begin to see the light only after their children find themselves in the dock." He ended by urging citizens to "preserve the honor of Moscow."

Minsk, the capital of Byelorussia, is one city of many that has already taken measures to cope with a situation resembling Moscow's. The extent of Minsk hooliganism may be judged from a statement of a police official to *Pravda* that workers, students, and clerks have been organized into auxiliary militia brigades which "actively participate in maintaining order in parks, public gardens, clubs, cinemas, workers' housing settlements, and residential districts." Brigade members, he added, stand guard all evening and night at bus and tram stops. Nevertheless, he complained, hooliganism had not yet been eradicated; sometimes citizens "protect disorderly elements."

Sometimes, apparently, the police do too. *Pravda* reports the receipt of many letters to the editor criticizing the courts and militia "for their liberalism toward debauches." *Pravda* also states that hooliganism is rife on collective farms.

Such manifestations of social illnesses are new neither in the world at large nor in the Soviet Union. What is new in Russia is their extent, depth, and growth, and the way they defy countermeasures. Apparently the Communist system is all-powerful except in face of circumstances which it creates and nourishes. Unfreedom and the awful feeling that one has no control or influence over the conditions of life (or over the inaccessible mortals who have) feed frustration, cynicism, and a yearning for pleasure and power—power to dominate and hurt. A national atmosphere of bullying breeds bullies. A society which cuts the individual down to a convenient size finds him avenging the operation.

All this is revolt, not revolution; a personal protest, not a political program. It would have been silly to ask Soviet citizens whether they wished, or intended, to overthrow their government. The very idea would be frightening and fantastic.

Stalin's two and a half decades of tyranny showed that the party and the Politburo, the army and the proletariat were powerless because he enjoyed a monopoly of power. His demise caused a diffusion of power at the upper level but not to the people. And only those who have power can affect politics directly and in the short run. It is not that the Soviet nation has no love of democracy; it has no means of achieving it. Elections are controlled, there is only one party, and all other organizations, whether political, educational, economic, social, professional, or for sports, are dominated by the state.

Some day a change may come through the gradual growth of material well-being or a struggle for supremacy in the leadership or a shift in international affairs. This is a broad arena where speculation can run riot.

The nature of the Soviet system is such that its basic alteration would cause serious and prolonged dislocations which frighten thoughtful Russians. I was dining at the home of a famous Soviet writer I knew in the 1930's; we were alone and he spoke frankly and critically about conditions; he had lived in Europe and mastered several western languages; the denial of freedom in Russia hampered his work. He is not a party member. Yet when I said that the only antidote to residual Stalinism was liberty, he flung his arms high and wide and exclaimed, "For heaven's sake, anything else, but not freedom." A professor used practically the same words on another occasion. Both contended that if the peasants won freedom they would disband the collectives, and the city would lack food; factory workers would demand the right to strike and participation in management. The writer and the professor saw their country's future in black-and-white terms of Communism or chaos. They dislike Communism but fear chaos. Forty years of Bolshevik rule have blotted out the other alternatives and the men with enough courage to strive for

them. This probably was Stalin's conscious goal. The task of
his heirs is easier as a result. Their attitudes toward him therefore seem to represent varying mixtures of gratitude and admiration, plus revulsion and hate.

CHAPTER 5

Three Young Communists

There is an incompleteness in the dethronement of Joseph Stalin which reflects fears, doubts, and differences in the Kremlin.

At the elevator landing of the fourth floor of the National Hotel hangs a portrait of Lenin and opposite, in marshal's uniform, one of Stalin; on the third-floor landing, again Lenin and Stalin, and the late President Kalinin; on the second floor, Lenin alone; on the first, Stalin alone; in the lobby, Stalin alone—and somber. Huge paintings of Lenin and Stalin dominate the great hall of Moscow's central post office on Gorki Street. A giant "Glory to the Great Stalin" sign decorates the main Tiflis railway station. Such examples could be multiplied endlessly. Many towns, factories, farms, and institutions are still named for him.

To be sure, innumerable likenesses of the late uncrowned autocrat of all the Russias have been removed from public places. But neither his image nor his reputation has been "liquidated" with the customary totalitarian thoroughness. And since such matters, particularly one of so paramount importance as the posthumous role of Stalin, are directed by a master baton, the fact of his rejection-retention suggests that hesitation governs the minds of Stalin's heirs in dealing with his ugly heritage.

The split approach of the leadership is matched by a split

in the public. In my Moscow experience this was exemplified by extended talks with three members of the Komsomol, or Young Communist League, Sacha, Ivan, and Sonya.

Sacha, twenty-one, tall, lean, and handsome, is studying mathematics. When I visited him in the family's one small room, father was at his job in a government office, mother had gone shopping, and younger sister was in school. After inquiring about the new university, relations between men and women students, and cost of tuition and books, I put the invariable question: Had he read Khrushchev's secret speech denouncing Stalin at the twentieth party congress in February, 1956?

"The Letter of Khrushchev," he said, "yes, it was read to us."

"You know," I remarked, "it was a speech, not a letter, and the best reason I can see for calling it a letter is that a speech would have had to be included in the published stenographic record of the congress, whereas a letter can be passed off as something unrelated to the congress and therefore not subject to publication."

"Hm," Sacha whispered, "there may be another reason of which we are ignorant."

"Well," I continued, "how do you feel about Stalin after hearing what Khrushchev had to say against him?"

"I love Stalin," Sacha asserted aggressively.

"You love the man who butchered millions before and after the war, broke up lives, and caused mountains of casualties in the fighting with Hitler!" I said.

"Stalin," Sacha insisted, "was a great statesman and he built up our country."

"And what about the millions he ordered shot?"

"Since they were Trotskyists they had to be shot."

"And Bukharin, the philosopher of Communism, popular leader, beloved of Lenin and the youth?"

"If he was harmful to the state he had to be shot."

"You have heard of Mahatma Gandhi, I presume," I probed.

"Yes," Sacha replied, "we think highly of Gandhi."

"Until 1955 you thought badly of Gandhi because you had not yet been told to think well of him. But that's not my subject at the moment. You know Gandhi and Nehru were very harmful to British rule in India and ultimately expelled it. According to your logic Gandhi, Nehru, and their Indian nationalist colleagues should have been shot."

"They were imprisoned often," Sacha argued.

"That's right. But they lived to win—which is decisive. The reason they were not shot is that the British were afraid of the Indian protest, which could be expressed even under imperialism, and, more important, because England is a democracy."

"Permit me to smile cynically," Sacha remarked.

"You think there is no democracy in the West?"

"There is for owners of property," Sacha declared.

"Have you heard of free elections in the United States, France, Great Britain, Sweden, and many other countries?"

"Yes, but we are not fooled," Sacha assured me. "Those elections are controlled by capitalists. The workers have no rights except in a socialist country."

The discussion which followed lasted for an hour in the morning and was resumed in the afternoon when I returned to see his mother. I would like to think I made an impression, or at least sowed a seed; I am not at all sure I did.

The next day I told Ivan about Sacha's "I love Stalin" and other declarations. "Your Sacha is a fool," Ivan said.

Ivan is twenty-three, the secretary of a Young Communist League unit, a physicist. His older brother was killed in the defense of Moscow against Nazi attack in December, 1941, and their parents, who were my close friends, died in Siberia where they had been evacuated as the Germans approached Moscow.

Ivan's memory of me was necessarily vague, but his father

and mother had spoken about me, and I got a warm welcome when I appeared at his apartment door without advance notice. He occupies a 160-square-foot room with his young wife, Sonya, also a member of the Komsomol, and a sweet baby one year old. After I played with the child a little it was put to bed behind a curtain suspended from a wire which cut off a triangular corner of the room. Ivan then extinguished all but one dim light. To keep the air fresh he and Sonya did not smoke (though Sonya lit up a cigarette every time she went to the kitchen to fetch a kettle of fresh boiled water for tea). We talked in low voices.

They submitted to my questions and I to theirs, and friendly affection grew up between us; in a way I was a link with Ivan's deceased parents. Conversation rolled along pleasantly and in relaxation. They were eager to have me come back and I did, twice.

In those three evenings we roamed the face of the earth. Their biggest worry was war. I explained why I thought world war had become most unlikely; it would be an atomic-hydrogen war which would destroy both belligerents; what possible gain could it bring? Nevertheless, I added, imperialism remained, and that creates tensions. The surviving western imperialisms were in retreat, witness India, Burma, Ceylon, Indonesia, Sudan, Morocco, Tunis—now free—and the Gold Coast, Nigeria, and other colonies on the threshold of independence. "Soviet imperialism, however, dominates a large part of Europe."

"How can a socialist state be imperialistic?" Ivan protested.

"Your approach is via dogma and theory," I replied. "My approach is through the facts. Did the Soviet government attack Finland in 1939?"

"That was a very unpopular war," he said.

"I am glad to hear it," I commented. "Did Russia annex Esthonia, Latvia, and Lithuania which Lenin had recognized as independent nations and with which the Soviet Union

entertained diplomatic relations for two decades? Suppose
America, France, or Britain had done something similar?
Wouldn't you have called it imperialism?"

"Well, of course," Sonya interjected.

"Shall I go on?" I inquired. "Russia grabbed half of Poland
in 1939. Stalin imposed Communist regimes on the rump of
Poland and on all the other East European nations. That is the
Soviet Empire, and it will plague you till you lose it."

Sonya poured more tea and asked whether I could bring
some illustrated foreign magazines. "Tell me," she said, "why
is there so much polio in the United States?"

I pleaded ignorance. That was not my field.

"We often hear about strikes in the United States," Ivan remarked. "Doesn't that prove that your workers are poor?"

"This query," I began, "has been put to me several times
since my arrival in Moscow. It must mean that strikes being
illegal here, Soviet people do not understand the nature of a
strike. They must regard a strike as a final act of desperation
on the eve of a revolution. Perhaps this is suggested by Russian history. But in America hundreds of thousands of strikers drive to the picket line in their private cars, own their
homes, and send their children to college. In the West workers usually go on strike because they think they can improve
their pay or because they have a grievance. Now in a socialist
country, as you would call it, a strike may be provoked by
hunger. That was the case in Poznan."

"Tell us," said Ivan, "what really happened in Poznan."

"What do you mean, 'what really happened'?" I retorted.
"Don't you read *Pravda* or *Komsomolskaya Pravda?*"

We all laughed. "No, come," Sonya said, "you know our
newspapers don't tell us the whole truth."

"Is that all?" I asked.

"We realize that they distort," Ivan admitted, "but that
realization does not help us to know the facts."

I had made a detailed study of the general strike, followed

by an uprising, in Poznan on June 28 and 29, and gave them a capsule account of it. I stressed that much of my information had come from the Polish press, which was remarkably frank though Communist controlled.

"Yes," Ivan admitted, "our press is boring. It began with Stalin and has not changed since he died. Papa used to tell us about the 1920's when the newspapers printed reports of anti-Stalin speeches by Trotskyists."

Three days later, when I came for dinner, I brought them several heavy magazines, a ballpoint pen, and a packet of razor blades. Sonya appropriated the pen. She taught school and had had her baby only on condition that she could continue to teach. She needed to work, not so much to earn money, for they employed a day maid (who went home at four to tidy up her own room and cook dinner). Partly Sonya did not want to become a housewife. But it was more than that. Russians, not unlike Germans, are in the grip of a work psychosis. It may be another form of escape, a fear of leisure, an abhorrence of idleness, or patriotism, a desire to make a contribution to the country's progress, a feeling that you cannot stay home when everybody else—and especially your husband—works. Work lends status. For that reason, maids are scarce; they prefer factory jobs and have to be lured into domestic service by good wages and concessions to their family time schedule. Sonya's maid shopped for herself while shopping for her mistress.

During dinner the baby's crib stood near the table and everything was gaily chaotic, with Sonya going back and forth from room to kitchen with pots and dishes, all of us feeding bits to the child, and taking turns at holding it. The baby was beginning to stand up and I remarked that the crib wall seemed rather low. "Don't you have a harness?" I asked.

They did not understand. I explained: straps to fasten the child to its crib or carriage. What a wonderful idea, but no such thing was available in the Soviet Union. (Every baby carriage in Prague is equipped with it.)

After dinner Sonya put the baby to sleep in its triangle while Ivan went out into the corridor for a smoke. I underscored a few more passages in a nineteen-page article by four authors in a recent issue of *Kommunist*, the party's ideological monthly, entitled "About Some Questions on the History of the Civil War." When Ivan returned he looked over my shoulder and asked what it was. "It concerns Stalin. Don't you read *Kommunist?*" I whispered.

Sonya came out from behind the curtain and nodded permissively. "He's asleep," she announced.

"No," Ivan replied, "I don't. I have too many technical journals to read. Besides the language of these party magazines is so stilted."

"I agree," I said, "but they reflect the collective leadership's thought, and this article is particularly interesting."

"Well, give, give," Sonya exclaimed impatiently.

"First," I commenced, "let me say that the article presents facts about Stalin which people abroad have known these last twenty-seven years. It deals with Soviet Russia's war against hostile domestic and foreign armies from 1918 to 1920, especially with the 1920 Russo-Polish war. That war began with a deep penetration of the Polish army into Soviet territory. Later, however, the Red forces, as you know, drove the Poles back across the frontier.

"At this point a sharp difference of opinion arose in the Soviet leadership. Lenin favored an invasion of Poland. Trotsky, the chairman of the Revolutionary-Military Council, in effect the chief of the Red army, was opposed. He contended that instead of provoking a Polish workers' and peasants' revolution, as Lenin hoped, a Russian assault would defeat itself by inflaming Polish nationalism.

"Trotsky was overruled. General Mikhail Tukhachevsky, a young military genius, directed the main Soviet thrust west-

ward to Warsaw, and, despite primitive transport, advanced
at the rate of some eighteen miles a day until he was within
sight of the Polish capital. There the Poles under Marshal
Pilsudski, aided by French General Weygand, began to offer
stiffer resistance.

"Tukhachevsky called for help. The Soviet general staff accordingly gave orders to Budenny's cavalry army, which was
operating south of Tukhachevsky in Galicia, to make a dash
toward Warsaw. Tukhachevsky's telegrams and the staff's
messages have been published abroad.

"Budenny, however, did not reply to these messages for
several critical days. Instead he persisted in what the *Kommunist* article calls 'an independent undertaking'; he continued moving southwest with a view to capturing Lvov
(Lemberg). The article reveals that Budenny's staff, dominated on the spot by Stalin, had chosen this goal on its own
initiative. As we know him now, I would not hesitate to say
that Stalin did this to enhance his reputation and political
power.

"The consequence was, the article records, that 'the western front, which had struck the chief, decisive blow at the
White-Poles in the Warsaw direction, remained unaided.'
The Central Committee of the Communist party stepped into
the picture at this juncture and instructed Budenny to pass
the command of his forces to Tukhachevsky. But, says the
article, Budenny's staff 'dragged out the transfer'. In consequence, Tukhachevsky was driven back from Warsaw, and
Russia lost the war. Stalin, it is clear from the article, shares
the responsibility for this major setback to Soviet foreign policy. Tukhachevsky, in subsequently analyzing his defeat, laid
it at Stalin's door; that probably was a factor in Stalin's decision to execute him in 1937.

"Now, Ivan, and Sonya, my purpose in dilating on the
Kommunist piece and adding my comments is to clarify the
entire process of de-Stalinization in the Soviet Union. The

article throws light on Stalin's role in the 1920 episode. But its purpose is not to get at the truth. One might suppose that the party, having burnt its fingers and hurt its reputation so badly by lying all these years in Stalin's favor, would stop lying altogether and take a new path, stop distorting history. The article, however, perpetuates the lies of the Stalin period about Trotsky and Tukhachevsky, and, in addition, substitutes Lenin for Stalin as the guiding military genius."

"Well, all right," Sonya commanded, "let's drink tea."

For a while we chatted about the season's plays and the books they read. Like many fellow-citizens they usually read novels for information regarding Soviet life; since writers are expected to be "realistic" and portray economic progress they frequently go to stay at factories or collective farms or construction projects and make these the subjects of their novels; whatever the author's bias, the reader learns something about the country.

"Have you heard the anecdote about socialist realism?" Sonya asked. I urged her to tell it.

"This goes back to Stalin's time," Sonya said. "A painter was summoned to do a portrait of a top Communist who had lost his right eye and right arm. The painter did a picture which showed him with two eyes and two arms. He was charged with formalism—and shot. A second painter, given the same assignment, portrayed the leader as he was. They accused him of being naturalistic—and he was shot. Then they called a third painter. He painted the leader's left side. He earned the Stalin Prize of one hundred thousand roubles for socialist realism. Socialist realism is selection of the good aspects and omission of the bad."

"Have you heard this one?" Ivan followed. "A Communist speaker at a meeting gave a glowing account of Soviet economic achievements. When he called for questions, a man in the audience rose and asked, 'Is this already Communism or will things get still worse?'"

It was my turn to tell them an anecdote circulating in Poland. A Pole went to a doctor and complained of being very ill. The physician examined him and reported that he could find nothing wrong. "But, doctor," the man protested, "I must be sick. I hear one thing and see another."

"Yes," Sonya commented, "there is often a gulf between propaganda and reality."

Ivan switched to a serious tone; he wanted to know my views on Marxism. Briefly I held that while Marx's methods of analysis were a contribution to social studies, they had done much harm by shifting all attention from psychological to objective or material factors. Moreover, Marx wrote a century ago when British workers did not enjoy the franchise and had no trade-union or political power. He could therefore not have envisaged a Labour government which would peacefully nationalize capitalist industries by Parliamentary act. Capitalism had changed so much in the last hundred years that Marx scarcely holds the key to its secrets. Communists make their central mistake in using him as their only guide.

But I was more interested in the fact that Ivan put the question to me when he knew my critical attitude. It reflected some doubt in his own mind, or at least a readiness to listen to another opinion on the most cardinal aspect of Communist ideology.

"You are secretary of your Young Communist League unit," I said to Ivan. "Tell me, how does the League get hundreds of thousands of its members to leave their homes and go off to the remote virgin lands of Kazakstan and Siberia to become farmers?"

"We draw up the lists," Ivan replied simply.

"No pressure?"

"No pressure is necessary," he explained. "Only occasionally a girl contends that she is about to be married or have a baby and we excuse her."

It was time to go to bed.

Forty-eight hours before leaving Moscow I visited Ivan and Sonya again. It was our third and last meeting, and we were all a bit sentimental. They had read a good deal of the two American magazines I left with them. One contained an article by Dorothy Thompson on Soviet youth, and Ivan expressed astonishment that a rich, bourgeois publication should have printed anything so friendly to the Soviets. I said author and editor were presenting the truth as they saw it. The second issue of the same journal carried an article by Dorothy Thompson on Soviet women; this, Sonya said, painted a rather gloomy picture, but a correct one.

"Listen, Fischer," Sonya added (the family had always called me that), "please don't write anything bad about our country. We want you to come back."

I was touched. "You want me to be a socialist realist," I joked. Actually I imagine her remark mingled patriotism with tenderness.

I recounted one of the morning's experiences: I had walked into the humanities department of Moscow University on Mokhovaya Street, climbed the stairs to the large reading room, and observed the earnest, concentrated faces of the students. Then I went to the antechamber to examine the cards in several drawers of the library catalog. I was appalled by the propagandistic nature of the books. As fair examples I copied three cards in the file on the United States: *The U.S. Courts, Instruments of Reaction and Terror,* by Volikov, 1950; *The Fascist Policy of American Imperialism,* by Geyevsky, 1954; *The Lie and Hypocrisy of American Bourgeois Democracy,* by Ivanov and Tovarsky (no date) . . . I turned to a fine-looking student who was making notes from another drawer. "Look," I whispered, "this is a university library, and all I find here is one-sided propaganda, no scientific works at all." I flipped over some more cards and we read them together.

"True," he said, "but would an American university library have pro-Soviet books?"

"Of course," I replied, "and probably some volumes by Lenin and Stalin."

"Would a student be allowed to take such publications home?"

"Of course," I assured him.

He returned to his work.

"You're not trying to convince us that western democracy is perfect?" Ivan observed.

"By no means," I replied. "In fact, I may have been guilty of propaganda myself. I suspect there are quite a number of American schools where pro-Soviet books would not be allowed. It is no secret, in general, that the democratic system tolerates evil. To be sure, totalitarian dictatorship breeds far greater evil than democracy. But the extent of evil is not the basic difference between the two. The real difference is that in a democracy citizens can fight evil, in a dictatorship they cannot."

Now they asked many questions about the British political system, about socialism in Sweden, about freedom in Switzerland. And when I said there was no Communism, there were no Communists in Russia or in any Communist party, the only Communism in the world was to be found in a few agricultural settlements in Israel and India where some tens of thousands of idealists voluntarily lived a life of equal work, equal compensation, and no property, their curiosity was not quickly satisfied.

Finally they spoke of themselves. "Let's be concrete," I suggested. "You want another room. In the West, persons with your income would have it. You want better clothing. You seek what the West has already achieved."

"But in the West," Ivan objected, "the means of production are owned by the capitalists, here they are owned by the state."

"Nevertheless," I replied, "everything you have told me in our three evenings together, and everything I have learned about the Soviet Union in my years of study, leads to the conclusion that the people here pay far more to the state for the use of the means of production than the American or British or any western worker pays to the capitalists. You pay more materially. In addition, you pay with your freedom and your conscience."

Sonya said, "For years we lived quietly. Now Fischer comes and stirs us up." I could not measure how much regret and how much pleasure her words expressed.

Ivan and Sonya kissed me and bade me, "Come again, come again."

Contrasting Ivan and Sonya, on the one hand, with Sacha, it appears that Sacha is securely Stalinist; he has not de-Stalinized; his mental armor is safe against the arrows of doubt and the spirit of inquiry; he is immune even to the corrosive influence of anti-Stalin revelations by his own leaders. He "loves Stalin." And in his love, at least for the present, he will be happy and serve the state effectively.

But even the incomplete de-Stalinization of 1956 shocked Ivan and Sonya into thought. Ivan's uncle, who dropped in when I was there the second evening, said, "We have been untaught to think." It was obviously not true of him, nor of his two young Communist relatives.

I left the Soviet Union with the impression, necessarily tentative, that the number of thinking citizens there—as elsewhere—is small. In any case, what could Ivan, Sonya, and their uncle do? It was different in Poland and Hungary where the still uncowed writers, seizing the opportunity offered by Moscow's de-Stalinization, and burning with a desire for national independence from Russia, started the anti-Communist landslide. In the Soviet Union, the Kremlin has everything under control, everything except possibly the incalculable future. In their struggle to capture the future, Stalin's heirs en-

joy two valuable assets: the Soviet people's love of country
(which in the satellites works against Moscow), and the
100 per cent Stalinization of agriculture—not yet attained in
the Soviet colonies. Moreover, the younger generation of
workingmen has never known, and the older generation has
probably forgotten, how to organize against an employer. In
Poznan the Polish workers knew how to oppose their state-
capitalist boss. They remembered their pre-1939 trade unions.
A Russian worker's memory would have to go back to pre-
1914, and even then the organized opposition to existing social conditions was very weak indeed.

After I left Ivan and Sonya I walked to Mayakovsky Circle
and picked up a taxi. I sat beside the driver, who seemed to
be in his middle thirties. "How do you like driving a cab?" I
quizzed.

"I hate it."

"What would you prefer to do," I pursued.

"Rob and kill."

"Now come, you're joking," I argued, "wouldn't you rather
be the director of a factory?"

"What," he shouted, "and exploit the workers."

"All right, I'm a foreign journalist. Wouldn't you like to be
a journalist or writer?"

"And tell lies?"

"You are saying that Russia is not a free country."

"And probably never will be," he submitted.

When we reached the National Hotel I offered him a tip.
Most drivers expect it. He refused it. He was clearly "a character."

CHAPTER 6

A Chat with Mikoyan

On my sixth day in Moscow I had a half-hour chat with Anastas I. Mikoyan at a reception for President Sukarno of Indonesia. A few of Mikoyan's statements were so startling that I could not decide, at first, whether to publish them. But he knew he was talking to a journalist and yet did not caution me that our conversation was "off the record" or "for background." In my quandary, I gave a summary of Mikoyan's views to a very intelligent Soviet citizen. "Maybe he wants you to publish them," my friend suggested.

Mikoyan, born in 1895, now Deputy Prime Minister of the Soviet Union and member of the Communist party's Presidium (Politburo), became a deputy member of the Politburo in 1926, and a full member in 1935, and was, therefore, for many years a close collaborator of Stalin. I had had several long interviews with him in the 1930's and also met him at diplomatic gatherings. The day after my arrival in Moscow in 1956, I wrote him requesting an appointment.

Below is the diary entry I made after the Sukarno reception:

This evening Indonesian Ambassador Palar gave a grand garden party for Sukarno attended by all the Kremlin leaders, and by masses of marshals, generals, Soviet officials, foreign diplomats, journalists, et cetera. In the embassy garden there was a long row of soft red leather chairs which culminated

in a nook where softer and bigger chairs and a sofa covered
with flowered chintz had been placed. The space between
these chairs and a food-covered table formed the hand-shaking and reception area. Kaganovich and Malenkov were the
first leaders to arrive; then Sukarno, who sat down on the sofa
between the two and talked with them through an interpreter
standing behind the sofa and leaning over toward them.
Kaganovich wore a fine blue suit and looked rather young
and well though a bit paunchy. Malenkov is not the hermaph-
rodite one suspects from photographs. He has a bulge in front
but is not blubbery; well groomed; black hair neat and
bright; particularly friendly smile when ambassadors' wives
and daughters were introduced to him. He also squared his
shoulders and turned on a special look for Soviet and foreign
cinema and still photographers. Later, Prime Minister Bulganin (pleasant blue eyes) arrived with Khrushchev—pink
face and ruddy bald head with a white fringe; mischievous
smile.

I stood this side of the food table, observing. Mikoyan came
late—fashionably dressed, his dark Armenian face handsome
despite the broken nose. The hand-shaking area was now
thickly populated with top-rank foreigners coming and going
and Russians moving from one little circle to another. I noticed Mikoyan, alone, at the narrow edge of the food table
doing nothing. I stepped up to him, gave my name, and asked
whether he remembered me. He said, "Yes, I remember, we
met before the war."

"Did you receive my letter?"

"Yes," he replied, "but there is no time for an interview,
and besides, you wrote bad things about us."

"Nothing I wrote about Stalin is worse than the contents
of Khrushchev's speech," I retorted.

"The issue is not Stalin," Mikoyan asserted.

"But Stalin made policy, and I was critical—as you were in
your speech at the twentieth party congress."

"Irrespective of what you wrote," Mikoyan replied, "we have taken a decision to admit everyone, whether friendly or hostile. We are doing a big job and you are free to see for yourself."

"How can I see for myself," I asked, "when I have a visa for only eight days."

"How much more would you want?" he replied.

"At least three weeks." I was admitted to the Soviet Union as a tourist, and tourist status entitled one to a maximum stay of a month.

"That's possible," Mikoyan said.

At this point, Leonid F. Ilyichev, the Foreign Office press chief, stepped up. (I felt sure that Ilyichev, seeing me in conversation with Mikoyan, and thinking Mikoyan did not know my record, had come over to warn him.) "Shall I say it straight?" Ilyichev said, addressing me.

"That's the way I like it," I told him.

"He's a bad man," Ilyichev said to Mikoyan.

"I appreciate your saying what you think," I said to Ilyichev. "But you will admit that there can be two opinions on many political matters."

"You invented and falsified," Ilyichev charged.

"Excuse me," I protested. "I wrote what I believed was the truth. I am a serious writer and don't invent, and you cannot prove that I have. I did condemn many of your government's policies and actions. Now I want to see whether anything has changed. Obviously I cannot see that in the eight days which end the day after tomorrow."

Mikoyan to Ilyichev: "Well, give him three more weeks. We aren't afraid. Now let's drink a toast. Where's the vodka?"

Ilyichev, his mission accomplished, walked away. I told Mikoyan I don't drink.

"Never?" he exclaimed with surprise.

"Never," I assured him. "Let's toast with Narzan," and I stretched out my arm for a bottle of the famous Caucasus mineral water. But only the Borzhom bottles had been opened. (Borzhom is another mineral water.) Mikoyan took a Borzhom bottle and poured some for himself and me; we clinked glasses. "Let's drink to the truth," I toasted.

"Good," he agreed.

"This morning," I said, "I talked with a young Communist who proclaimed that he loved Stalin. How is it possible to love a person who submitted his country to such horrors?"

Mikoyan: "Yes, many still love him; he did much for the country. It will take time to change this attitude."

"Why don't you publish Khrushchev's speech?"

Mikoyan: "It's too early. But hundreds of thousands have read it."

"The speech did not go far enough. Do you really believe that Bukharin was a wrecker and spy?"

Mikoyan: "No, I don't."

"You were one of those who used to have supper with Stalin regularly." (A group of fellow-Caucasians, including Mikoyan, Sergo Ordjonekidze, a member of the Politburo, Abel Yenukidze, secretary of the Soviet government, and Leo Karakhan, an Armenian and Assistant Commissar for Foreign Affairs, often assembled in Stalin's Kremlin apartment for a midnight supper.)

Mikoyan: "I not only ate supper with him. I was very close to him. But now and then at Politburo sessions I spoke my mind and that ended our friendship. How many people did I myself save from execution!"

"Yenukidze too saved many people and then he himself was shot. I knew Karakhan and liked him. He was shot."

Mikoyan: "Yes."

"Didn't you know this was happening? Didn't you know people were being beaten and tortured?"

Mikoyan: "Bukharin and the other Moscow trial defendants were not tortured."

"But thousands of others were."

Mikoyan: "We didn't know that. We only learned of it later. Stalin did many things without our knowledge."

"That's difficult to understand. Foreigners in Moscow knew. And these acts multiplied after 1934. It was in 1935, I believe, that the first Communist party members were executed."

Mikoyan: "Yes, that is correct. But you understand, Stalin held us in his hand. Only one escape was left to us—what Ordjonekidze did when he committed suicide. I stood before the same decision. And at the end of Stalin's life I was about to be executed. Now we have changed all this. Yet in the West we are attacked for what we did not do in those years." He spoke with bitterness.

"Now," Mikoyan continued, "we want to be left alone to build."

I expressed the conviction that a major war between Russia and the western powers was unlikely; the big bombs were our security pact.

Mikoyan: "I agree that the atom and hydrogen bombs are a deterrent. Our people certainly do not want war."

"Neither does the American nation."

Mikoyan: "Nor the American intellectuals."

"And do you think that Eisenhower wants war?"

Mikoyan: "No, we have a good opinion of him. But there are warmongers. Look at the Suez situation. The West has Hottentot morals. The Dardanelles are nationally controlled. Panama is nationally controlled, so are the German straits [Kiel]. Yet they want to internationalize Suez. I call it Hottentot morality."

"At Potsdam in 1945 Truman proposed to Stalin the internationalization of all such waterways."

Mikoyan: "Would America agree to internationalize Panama?"

"Why don't you propose it?"

Mikoyan: "Would you let Chinese ships through?"

"I don't know."

Mikoyan: "Internationalization is just a cover for imperialism, a plot to dominate small nations."

"I don't think so. The world has outlived nationalism. We must curtail national sovereignty and extend the practical functions of international organizations."

Mikoyan: "We will never agree to that. See how the big powers threaten Egypt."

"And you see how the British people oppose it. The *Manchester Guardian* . . .

Mikoyan: "The *Manchester Guardian,* yes . . ."

"And the Labour party . . ."

Mikoyan: "The party, yes, but not the leadership."

"I think you are wrong there. I have spoken with Gaitskell and others."

Mikoyan: "Look at the French socialists behaving like imperialists."

"You Communists always were opposed to socialists."

Mikoyan: "Not to all. We respect the Finnish socialists, and the Swedish and Norwegian socialists."

"The point is that the Suez Canal is a unique artery of world commerce, the throat of Eurasia, and a man like Nasser simply cannot be trusted to keep the Canal open. Nasser has barred Israeli ships. He might bar others."

Mikoyan: "Yes, but why didn't the West protest when Nasser blocked Israel's ships?"

"You are right on that." (When I got home it occurred to me that I should have said to him, "Why didn't the Soviet government?")

The Canadian ambassador passed and said to Mikoyan, "Good evening, we met in Hanoi."

"What does he say?" Mikoyan asked me. "Translate, please."

I translated. Mikoyan said, "*Da, da,*" and the ambassador moved on.

"You have been traveling a lot of late," I remarked. "To India, and Asia generally."

Mikoyan: "Yes, India. What an industrious and intelligent nation! We believe in their future. I am an Asiatic."

I thought I had held his attention long enough, and said goodbye. In parting he requested me to send him anything I wrote about the Soviet Union.

(At a subsequent, North Vietnam reception, to which I was not invited, an Asian ambassador overheard Mikoyan say to Ilyichev, "Well, what about Fischer? Have you given him the three weeks' extension?" Ilyichev replied, "The question is being examined. We will give him something." I was given twelve days more, not three weeks. "Politburo member proposes, bureaucrat disposes," the ambassador commented.)

CHAPTER 7

Why De-Stalinization?

Mikoyan is a passionate person, and he obviously hates Stalin who almost drove him to suicide and planned to have him shot. Even a commissar is not beyond human emotion. Until Khrushchev, on February 24, 1956, thrust his short dagger into the blood-drained mummy of the dead dictator, Mikoyan's speech at the twentieth party congress was the most venomous attack on Joseph Stalin.

But some of Mikoyan's colleagues had shared his humiliating and dangerous experience by the despot's side. Once Stalin actually put Vyacheslav Molotov's name on a list of those to be executed and then scratched it off. Kaganovich's two brothers disappeared, though their sister Rosa either lived with or was married to Stalin. Yet to judge by the speeches of Molotov and Kaganovich at the party congress, and by their attitudes as far as we know them, they remain Stalinists. In them, personal resentment and lust for posthumous vengeance seem under control.

Russia's political chiefs are, above all, politicians, and it is in the area of politics that one must search for the reasons why they embalmed the king and laid him in the mausoleum next to Lenin, the founder of the dynasty, for millions of awed or curious citizens to see, then announced that he was dead, allowed his throne to tilt and the effigy on it to sag, and spattered him with mud and blood, but still did not knock his head off.

Mikoyan's cry that Stalin "held us in his hand" is a valid excuse. Khrushchev's secret speech records a statement Bulganin once made to him. "It has sometimes happened," Bulganin said, "that a man goes to Stalin on his invitation as a friend. And when he sits with Stalin he does not know where he will be sent next, home or to jail." Further along in that address Khrushchev declared, "It is not excluded that had Stalin remained at the helm for several months, Comrades Molotov and Mikoyan would probably not have delivered any speeches at this congress."

In such a situation heroes would not abound. Opposition to Stalin was tantamount to suicide; even a frown of doubt by an underling, or a lifted eyebrow, might bring down a death sentence.

"Stalin," Khrushchev revealed, "evidently had plans to finish off the old members of the Politburo." As long as the whole story of Stalin's death is withheld, this sentence alone will justify lingering suspicions that the old members finished him off.

Yet whatever the truth about the tyrant's end, and despite Mikoyan's rage at western criticism of Stalin's heirs for not shortening his sanguine reign, one question refuses to be downed: Why did they not kill him long before 1953? (Why didn't the German generals kill Hitler?)

Stalin was well guarded. But one brave man could have shot him or otherwise murdered him. This is not advocacy, it is not analysis. By withdrawing legal means of opposition, tyrants have ever encouraged lethal means, and the wonder therefore is that no Soviet general, marshal, or Politburo member tried assassination.

We are here in the realm of guesses. Three possible explanations occur. (1) Stalin's collaborators were afraid to rule without him. He was skillful, shrewd, quick on the trigger, and successful because totally ruthless and ready to pay any price for victory. They were not sissies themselves, but they must have wondered who of them could do the job as well. (2) Stalin's assassination might have split the leadership, the party, and the country, and provoked civil war or at least prolonged confusion. Through terror and mythology he had made himself the one apparently indispensable agent of unity, and unity or "monolithism" is the Communist's essential creed. It justifies the annihilation of resistance. The true Communist, accordingly, must believe in the very method which may destroy him. This fetish of unity restrained the assassin's arm. (3) Stalin's co-workers saw him pushing a gigantic ball up a steep slope to the castle of their desires, the almighty state. They perhaps deplored some of his extreme means, but they favored the end, and as Bolsheviks they could not be squeamish about means. They in fact seconded his efforts, echoed his harsh views, carried out his most brutal assignments, and thus compromised themselves. They sat far out on a long limb with him, and to saw it off would not only have been a great feat, it would have tumbled them too into the abyss. Samson did something similar, but he was a giant, and blind, and in the camp of the enemy.

This discussion may have opened a path through the political thicket to clear ground where the Soviet situation can be seen in better perspective. Mikoyan said it was too early to publish Khrushchev's secret speech. This can only mean that it is one thing to let a limited audience hear the address once, and still another to make it universally available, inside Russia, to be read, reread, pondered, and debated within four walls. Dictatorship is, by definition, the rule of a tiny minority with the support of a larger minority and the involuntary, sullen submission of the majority. In such a condition, knowledge is dynamite. That is why the Soviet newspapers are so barren of information. Facts might induce thoughts. When Khrushchev, Mikoyan, Molotov, and Kaganovich descended out of the sky on Warsaw in October, 1956, the Poles revealed that they had resisted terrific Russian pressure; the entire world knew this and groped for more clues. But the Soviet public was given nothing except two simultaneous, barren official bulletins: the four men had gone; they had returned. No meat here, no basis for interpretation. A few days later a national uprising exploded in Hungary. Immediately the Soviet government recommenced jamming the BBC, which it had agreed several months earlier not to jam. In that precious interval, Muscovites told me, they relished the straightforward, propaganda-free world news relayed from Britain. But news about the anti-Russian, anti-Communist Hungarian revolution and Moscow's efforts to crush it with mammoth tanks is exactly what the Kremlin directorate must keep from the people. The rationing, funneling, and filtering of information is the primary task of any dictatorship which does not want its propaganda bubbles pricked or its national brainwashing undone. In this spirit, the Soviet leaders decided to suppress the Khrushchev speech until they were ready to go beyond the first steps of de-Stalinization.

Khrushchev's speech, and indeed Mikoyan's earlier performance on February 18, filled the democratic world with surprise and delight. For they appeared to break an idol and repair some of the damage done to truth. But it is enough to place what they said alongside of what they omitted to discover that Moscow has not succumbed to liberalism or an accession of veracity. Such juxtaposition, moreover, helps to uncover present policy. It transpires that in condemning "the cult of personality"—approved euphemism for Stalin tyranny —today's collective leadership is creating a fresh cult of anti-personality. They are blaming Stalin personally, not the Soviet system. The Marxists are refusing to submit the Stalin phenomenon to a Marxist analysis of objective circumstances.

Khrushchev's indictment of Stalin began with a quotation

from the last will and testament of Lenin, which has since been published, for the first time, in a Soviet monthly magazine. Stalin, Lenin wrote in October, 1922, "is excessively rude . . . a defect which cannot be tolerated in one holding the position of secretary-general. Because of this, I propose that the comrades consider the method by which Stalin would be removed from this position [and replaced by] a man who, above all, would differ from Stalin in only one quality, namely, greater tolerance, greater loyalty, greater kindness and a more considerate attitude toward the comrades, a less capricious temper, et cetera."

For himself, and on behalf of his colleagues, Khrushchev added further charges: "Stalin acted not through persuasion, explanation, and patient cooperation with people, but by imposing his concepts and demanding absolute submission to his opinion." . . . From 1935 to 1938, Stalin practiced "mass repression through the government apparatus . . . first against the enemies of Leninism: Trotskyists, Zinovievites, Bukharinites long since politically defeated by the party, and subsequently against many honest Communists . . . Was it necessary to annihilate such people? We are deeply convinced that had Lenin lived, such an extreme method would not have been used against many of them . . . Stalin, using his unlimited power, allowed himself many abuses, acting in the name of the Central Committee, not asking for the opinion of the Committee or even of the members of the Central Committee's Politburo . . . Of the 139 members and candidates of the party's Central Committee who were elected at the seventeenth congress [1934], 98 persons, that is, 70 per cent, were arrested and shot, mostly in 1937–38." Stalin ordered thousands of innocent persons arrested, tortured, and shot . . . "Stalin allowed the liquidation of Ordjonekidze's brother and brought Ordjonekidze to such a state that he was forced to shoot himself." [At the time of his death in 1937, at the age of fifty-one, the cause was officially stated to have been "a heart attack."] Stalin "supported the glorification of his own person" . . . he showed a "lack of even elementary modesty." In editing his own *Short Biography,* "he marked the very places where he thought that the praise was insufficient" and, after inserting, in his own hand, a piece of self-commendation, Stalin added, "Stalin never allowed his work to be marred by the slightest vanity, conceit, or self-adulation." Into the same book, Stalin wrote, "Comrade Stalin's military genius enabled him to divine the enemy's plans and defeat them." Actually, however, Stalin failed to heed warnings from Churchill, Sir Stafford Cripps, and Russian agents abroad that a Nazi attack impended, and he therefore failed to prepare for it fully; his faulty strategy in World War II led to heavy unnecessary casualties; he carried out wartime "mass deportations from their native lands of whole nations, together with Communists and Komsomols without exception."

To the above accusations in Khrushchev's secret speech at the twentieth party congress, Mikoyan, addressing the same assembly on February 18, declared that Stalin's last published work, *Economic Problems of Socialism in the U.S.S.R.,* "can hardly help us in our analysis of the economy of contemporary capitalism and is hardly correct."

Loyal to the line chalked by the Congress, others have since elaborated upon and added to these damning revelations and evaluations. They can all be grouped under the headings of mistakes and pathological mental manifestations. That Stalin was sick in the head is scarcely subject to doubt. But the Soviet attacks on him avoid the essence: that he could never have indulged his vanity, paranoia, and power lust except in a police state under his total control. Nor has any Communist leader, much less subordinate, explained that though this personally directed police state satisfied Stalin's inner cravings, it was indispensable to the establishment of the present economic system of collectivized agriculture and government-owned industry in which his heirs exult.

Khrushchev now suggests that the Trotskyists, Zinovievites, and Bukharinites need not have been shot. But he does not say they need not have been driven out of politics. On the contrary, he compliments Stalin: "Here Stalin played a positive role." The fight against these oppositionists, Khrushchev declares, "was a difficult but necessary one because [their] political line . . . actually led toward the restoration of capitalism and capitulation to the world bourgeoisie." This constitutes an apology, in Stalinist terminology, for Stalin's major political sins.

Is Khrushchev altogether correct, moreover, in asserting that the fight was difficult? It was difficult indeed so long as Stalin and his henchmen, who included some of today's leaders, engaged in political debate with the opposition. But when arguments failed, Stalin introduced the revolvers and knouts of the NKVD as the supreme intellectual arbiters, and they then won the debate with ease. The result of this intervention was the abdication of ideas and the enthronement of force. That made Stalin king, and as absolute monarch he had absolute power over every citizen, Mikoyan, Ordjonekidze, and others not excepted. Stalin's heirs retain this power, the only difference being that, as sensible and normal persons, they need not use it often.

The denigration of Stalin is shot through with these contradictions. Khrushchev excoriates Stalin for crimes against individual Communists. Is this a sudden turn to humanitarianism? He does not mention the millions of peasants who were killed and exiled in order to achieve village collectivization. He could not mention them, for collectivization is a keystone of the Soviet structure, and to put it in place some peasants had to be destroyed so that the others could be dragooned. If the new Kremlin "directing collective," as Khrushchev called his little oligarchy, were really changing course, it would make membership in farm collectives voluntary. This, however, they dare not do; the peasants would leave. Obviously, therefore, compulsion is still the Soviet government's chief weapon against eighty million peasants.

Similarly compulsion is the means by which the government runs the industries of the Soviet Union. The workingmen are not permitted to strike; their trade unions are adjuncts of the state in promoting speed-up methods and keeping wages down; they are exposed to all the evils of a mighty bureaucracy which does everything.

The four pillars of Stalinism were, and are: agrarian collectivization; state management of industry; one-party, monopoly political control; and imperialism. These continue to be regarded by the Moscow directing collective as the unalterable supports of the Soviet system (though naturally they do not call their imperialism by that name). Stalin is dead. His works live.

Russia remains a Stalinist country. Hence the difficulty of de-Stalinizing.

Then why did they attack Stalin at all?

I put this question to Muscovites. Not only did I get no satisfactory answer, the query evoked little interest; they had lost the habit of thinking in political terms. They do not know their leaders. Of all the people I talked with, only one mentioned Khrushchev. Three mentioned Malenkov: two said he was a relative of Lenin, which is almost certainly untrue but significant, for no more complimentary statement could be made of a Soviet politician; the other said he spoke French—also a tribute, and if true it would make him unique in a summit group where foreign culture is rare. To my Moscow friends, the leadership was a remote, secret world into which they could not hope to peep. "People abroad know more about it than we do," several declared. They therefore could not analyze the causes of de-Stalinization. They were interested only in its effects.

The reasons why the Kremlin condemned Stalin are manifold.

1. Stalin's heirs wished to tell the party and people that theirs was a new administration, different from and better than Stalin's. On September 3, 1953, six months after Stalin's death, Khrushchev addressed the plenum of the party's Central Committee and, breaking with the practice of stating economic changes in terms of percentages of percentages, gave exact figures showing the reduction of livestock as compared with the pre-collectivization Soviet period and with the tsarist era. Why did he do it? Not only because he revels in direct, hard hitting, but chiefly, one presumes, in order to be able to say, if and when, as he hoped, the situation improved, that the new leadership deserves the credit. He actually said so in November, 1956. It was natural for Stalin's successors to proclaim themselves a new broom; and what better method could they have chosen than to shoot holes in his reputation? Political parties in democracies do the same.

A special feature of the "new" administration was the restoration of Lenin as the chief source of Bolshevik dogma. This reversion to original doctrine, the present leadership might have hoped, would restore the early idealism of the Soviet system and therefore absorb the shock of the exposure and dethronement of Stalin.

2. Khrushchev, discussing the evils of "the cult of personality" in his secret speech in 1956, asserted that "the Central Committee of the party considers it absolutely necessary to make the material pertaining to this matter available to the twentieth congress . . . We have to consider seriously and correctly analyze this matter in order that we may preclude any repetition in any form whatever of what took place during the life of Stalin . . ." There is no good reason for doubting this explanation. All Stalin's surviving collaborators lived through years of humiliation, shame, and unrelieved fear of death at his hands. They did not want to go through the

same experience again. That is why they arrested and executed Police Chief Beria in 1953; he threatened to step into the shoes of his fellow Georgian, Stalin, and set up another one-man tyranny. After Beria, Khrushchev seemed the most likely to succeed to Stalin's eminence. As party secretary, Khrushchev would naturally play the stellar role in pulling Stalin down. But his doing so might prevent him from climbing too high up.

3. Over the years of Stalin's mass murder and blunders, many pressures were built up for the rehabilitation of his victims. Of these, pressure from the Soviet army undoubtedly was, and remains, the greatest. Russian armed forces lost many millions of dead, wounded, and prisoners in the Second World War, and Hitler penetrated further into Russian territory than any invader in Russian history. The army wanted the blame laid on Stalin. Khrushchev did that in his secret speech. Moreover, the Soviet military leadership wanted credit for winning the war. Khrushchev therefore told the twentieth congress that after "first severe disasters and defeats at the front [in 1941], Stalin thought that this was the end . . . for a long time Stalin actually did not direct the military operations and ceased to do anything whatever . . . the nervousness and hysteria which Stalin demonstrated, interfering with actual military operations, caused our army severe damage . . . during the whole patriotic war [1941–45] he never visited any section of the front or any liberated city . . . All the more shameful was the fact that after our great victory over the enemy which cost us so much, Stalin began to downgrade many commanders . . . because Stalin excluded every possibility that services rendered at the front should be credited to anyone but himself."

Between 1937 and 1941, moreover, "the cadre of leaders who had gained military experience in Spain and the Far East were almost completely liquidated," Khrushchev asserted, and he stressed the "very grievous consequences" during World War II which flowed from this mad act. The army must have urged that this be said.

Marshal Zhukov was Russia's greatest World War II leader and, says Khrushchev, Stalin did not like him. Stalin in fact once asked Khrushchev for his views on Zhukov, and Khrushchev naturally replied that Zhukov was an able general. But Stalin ridiculed Zhukov's strategy, Khrushchev reports. This was a double play: in denigrating Stalin, Khrushchev courted Zhukov, who, demoted by Stalin when the war ended, returned, on Stalin's death, first as Assistant Minister of Defense and now as Minister of Defense and deputy member of the Politburo, the highest party post ever attained by a professional Soviet soldier. Stalin, forever fearing rival power, kept the army out of and away from politics. Today the army plays a key political part.

It still has an unsettled account with Stalin: the purge of Marshal Tukhachevsky and numerous other marshals, generals, and officers (the estimate runs to thousands) in 1937, which decapitated the Red army and contributed to its poor performance in Finland in 1939–40 and against Hitler in 1941–42. The Soviet army must certainly want the big black blot removed from its record.

A second element smarting from Stalin's mistreatment are the forty million Soviet Ukrainians who constitute the largest national minority in the Soviet federation. Repeatedly in the 1920's and 1930's, Stalin purged its Communist leaders and leading non-Communists for "bourgeois nationalism" and a yearning for separation from Russia. Moscow has always been alarmed by the least sign of a surviving or reviving Ukrainian urge to independence. Stalin stamped on it ruthlessly. His successors wear a velvet glove. When Khrushchev described how Stalin had deported whole national minorities to Siberia and Kazakstan, he added, "The Ukrainians avoided meeting this fate only because there were too many of them and there was no place to which to deport them."

This again was a double-play gambit: a kick at Stalin, a cuddle with the Ukrainians. Mikoyan, in his congress speech, rehabilitated—simply by pronouncing their names—two leading Communists of the Ukraine whom Stalin had executed: Stanislav Kossior, a Politburo member since 1930, and Antonov-Avseyenko. Khrushchev rehabilitated a third, Pavel Postyshev.

Further pressures to release purged persons from prisons and camps and to rehabilitate others posthumously came from influential relatives and old associates. The logical preliminary to such rehabilitation was public criticism of Stalin's rule and denigration of his role.

4. Perhaps the biggest underestimated contribution to de-Stalinization was made by the new Soviet upper class, which consists of high government and party officials, top army and secret-police officers, writers, artists, and actors, key economic managers, important technical personnel, scientists, and top-rank professional people; they number, with dependents, between ten and twenty million persons. A Soviet friend who is one of them said, "Don't call us a class; stratum would be a better word." His mild protest echoed the official contention that the Soviet Union is "a classless society." But a sensitive, intelligent woman of sixty, who could not help seeing the perpendicular canyon between her own living pattern and that of the mass of humanity in the depths, asked me for my views on the class structure of Soviet society. This upper class or stratum (the name is unimportant when the thing is so obvious) lives well by their parents' standards, and their children enjoy the privileges which come to the offspring of the rich. But what was the use of comfort and luxury when, in Stalin's time, a knock at the door at 2 A.M. exchanged it all for a bunk in an Arctic concentration camp —or burial in an unknown grave? The upper class, including Mikoyan, Bulganin, Khrushchev, Malenkov, and their fellows, craved personal security from political persecution.

Since the present leaders perfectly understood the horror of life in the eternal shadow of death and realized how much it reduced efficiency, they gave one another and their class or stratum that tacit pledge of safety from political arrest which they knew was indispensable to the smoother running of the political and economic machine. The pledge took the form of a denunciation of Stalin's arbitrary, lawless, purge-full regime of terror. That is the implied message of the twentieth party congress of February, 1956.

5. To insure the Kremlin leaders against persecution and the rest of the upper class against perpetual harassment, the awful might of the secret police had to be subjected to control. Police Chief Beria's rapid aggrandizement of power immediately after the passing of Stalin convinced all his comrades how urgent this wing-clipping process was. The Soviet army, which hated the secret police for honeycombing it with spies and outranking it in political influence, gladly lent a hand in the arrest of Beria on June 26, 1953, and in the downgrading of his police system that brought relief at all levels. My best friend in Moscow said, "I don't know what the secret police do now. They must be studying the archives."

In Stalin's time, the secret police was the largest industrial enterprise in the Soviet Union. It employed millions of slave laborers on various economic development projects. But Russia is suffering from an acute shortage of labor in cities as well as villages, and, given the falling birth rate in both urban and rural areas, the manpower shortage is likely to last. In the circumstances, the waste of labor in concentration camps where the inmates either malingered or died prematurely was truly treasonable and had to be stopped by cutting the number of arrests and curtailing the economic functions of the police.

6. In denouncing Stalin for his crimes, the Soviet leaders hoped to exculpate themselves. They charged that Stalin

acted without consulting them. De-Stalinization, accordingly, was designed to clear the name of Stalin's heirs.

7. De-Stalinization was part of a new world outlook in the Kremlin. The Soviet directorate realized that Stalin had needlessly antagonized Tito, Turkey and Asia generally, and the western democracies. Smiles and economic and military aid to non-Sovietized nations were better suited to win friends, confuse adversaries, and increase the number of neutrals.

These seven factors were present in the Soviet situation long before Nikita S. Khrushchev delivered his famous secret address. The charges that could be leveled against Stalin had been under discussion in the Kremlin for quite some time and the supporting data were on hand. But the leadership hesitated to expose Stalin's reign for fear of the shock it would produce on the youth and others. At the twentieth party congress, however, it soon became patent that the hour had struck. Every hostile reference to Stalin's "cult of personality" found vigorous approbation among the delegates. Mikoyan's direct condemnation of the dictator evoked tumultuous applause. It is clear from the stenographic record of the congress that some leaders, like Molotov, Bulganin, and Kaganovich, still harbored doubts. Nevertheless, the decision to de-Stalinize was taken. Conceivably the failure to publish the Khrushchev speech was a concession to the doubters—as well as to the Chinese Communists who are Stalinizing China the Chinese way.

Some foreign interpreters of the Soviet scene misled themselves by equating de-Stalinization with democratization and moderation; then they disparaged Moscow for its niggardly liberal reforms. But all the reasons for de-Stalinization were political and personal. The aim was not to liberalize or to introduce democracy. The aim was to gain political advantage and personal security. Limited liberalization is merely a by-product, and, too, an indication that Stalin's terror methods are obsolete because unnecessary. Within a few hours of the despot's death at 9:50 P.M. on March 5, 1953, the government and party chiefs met in solemn conclave and adopted a manifesto, published in the Soviet press on March 7, urging the population to refrain from "disorder and panic." The men in the Kremlin would never have used such revealing words had they not been worried. They are worried no longer, so they rule with a lighter hand.

It would seem, accordingly, that inside the Soviet Union the plusses of de-Stalinization (tantamount to the replacement of one-man rule with collective rule) outweigh the discernible minuses. The Soviet Union is a difficult country to administer because all economic, political, cultural, and social functions are directed by the few hands that run the state. Published criticism of Stalin facilitates the complicated task of government by teaching the virtues of diffused responsibility. "The strength of collective leadership," *Pravda* wrote on September 6, 1956, "lies in the fact that it rests on the knowledge and experience of a wide circle of people. The collective discussion of the most important questions of party, government, and economic activities makes it possible to arrive at the most accurate decisions, avoiding all kinds of mistakes, and a one-sided approach to affairs. It is therefore necessary to conduct an insistent struggle for the enforcement of collective forms and methods of party leadership at all levels." The diffusion of responsibility, to be sure, is still extremely circumscribed. But, at least in higher party circles, even an illusory participation in decision-making must bring pleasure and a sense of self-importance after the insecurity and robot obedience of the Stalin era.

De-Stalinization has been a boon to the upper class and the leaders. But they have not turned away from the Stalin system. Therefore the question of whether they have reverted to it is not relevant. Although Stalin's most brutal methods are abandoned, the economic and political edifice he built is the goal of all Communists. It remains intact and is being reinforced. When, accordingly, Khrushchev hails Stalin as "an example of a good Communist," which he did on January 17, 1957, and on other occasions, he is not contradicting anything in his famous speech at the twentieth party congress. That historic performance accomplished its seven political and personal purposes. The rest—the scrapping of the Stalin system and the establishment of democracy on its ruins—will be a slow process in Russia. Ferment, yes. Discontent, certainly. Occasional expressions of opposition, inevitable. A palace coup at the top, say by the army, conceivable. A gradual shift to the gratification of the consumer's needs, unavoidable. But a popular revolution to overthrow the Soviet government seems quite unlikely.

Any speculation on the future of Russia—and it can only be speculation—must not underrate the submissiveness taught by the ruthless, highly centralized government of the tsars and the far more ruthless and centralized Bolshevik regime. Servility, to be sure, does not exclude resentment. In fact, they coexist. But the national memory of official severity is a harsh deterrent.

CHAPTER 8

Opium

The late Moshe Piyade, a wise old member of the Yugoslav Communist party's Politburo, in an interview on October 31, 1956, said Moscow de-Stalinized on the assumption that the process could be undertaken safely inside the Soviet Union without causing disturbances in the satellites. Piyade's plausible view suggests how badly the Kremlin understands foreign countries and how well it understands Russia.

Communist rule was imposed on the satellites between 1944 and 1948, on Russia in 1917; the difference is decisive.

Time is an important factor in politics. Compared with the 1922–38 period, when I resided in Moscow, there are fewer believers and more cynics. Party members who were once idealists are now time-servers.

One finds idealists, however, among the non-Communists. They ask questions about the outside world; they resent the paucity of foreign information in Soviet publications; they condemn the materialism of the regime. It takes inner strength and a faith in mankind to resist the tug and fleshpots of the bandwagon. A young Soviet woman told me that throughout the difficult postwar years of the repression she and seven friends, all critical of the regime—and they remain so despite de-Stalinization—shared their thoughts freely in a sublime mutual trust which was not betrayed. In a totali-

tarian country where citizens are expected to report the least
deviation from political conformity, this must stand as a victory for decency. But the young woman's relations with her
eighteen-year-old Young Communist son were strained.

Politics in a Communist country seriously complicate family life. Two teen-age boys gave their party-line mother an
uncomfortable hour at dinner arguing vehemently against
her brittle, made-in-the-Kremlin opinions. Contrariwise, the
mother of Sacha, who said, "I love Stalin," fully supported his
orthodox position, and I felt, as she did so, that she was really
trying to hold her son. His blind loyalty kept him from slipping into cynical disbelief, and her agreement was a means
of keeping him.

Soviet parents are more likely to agree with their children
than vice versa. While the children are still in the age of political naïveté, a parent hesitates to interfere with their no-
tions. For one thing, the boy or girl might, in a discussion
with playmates, say, "But my father thinks . . ." and this
could reach the authorities. Equally, many Soviet mothers
and fathers wish to protect the child's immature mind from
the tormenting psychological conflict which would arise if it
received one political line at school and in the Pioneer
(Scout) group and an opposite one at home. In such cases,
the elders usually defer to outside influences until, perhaps
in the later university years or after graduation, they decide
the son or daughter has sufficient discretion and experience
to benefit from a dissenting family voice. A family split by
politics when the children are young may be cemented together when they are employed. The adult son of a disillusioned old Bolshevik living in retirement condemned his
father's pessimism nineteen years ago, but has now quietly
withdrawn from party membership "owing to the pressure of
scientific work."

There would not be a new idea in a stack of Russian youth
magazines as big as the projected Palace of Soviets. With

few exceptions they imitate adult publications in quoting
from the proceedings of the twentieth party congress—this
will go on till the next congress some years hence—and throw
in a passage from Lenin to clinch all arguments. Most elementary journals for youngsters offer a mental diet of pure
sawdust. Two editors of the boy and girl Scouts' *Pioneer
Pravda,* who called on an author to ask for an article, received a refusal. He said, "Each of your issues is like the
others . . ." When Nina Ponomareva, the champion Russian
discus-thrower, was arrested in London on a shoplifting
charge, *Pravda* printed the story under the headline "Dirty
Provocation," and presented it as a planned conspiracy
against the Soviet Union. *Pravda's* one-sided report was read
in all classrooms. It could only teach the children to hate the
West and to hold the British judicial process in contempt.

My opportunities, necessarily limited, to talk with school
pupils and university students confirmed the impression I
had gained from reading Soviet sources that Soviet education aims to develop the brain but not the mind, to turn out
specialists but not thinking people.

One afternoon, searching for Moscow friends I had not
seen these nineteen years, I rang the doorbell of the apartment they once occupied. "No, I'm sorry," said the young
woman who answered the ring. "This is the home of so-and-
so."

I communicated my distress: I had come from America;
how could I find my friends? She suggested consulting the
new telephone book, and when I explained that this was quite
an operation, no directory being available in my hotel, and
no new one in the post office, she invited me in to see hers.
We exchanged a few polite remarks in the course of which
I learned that the woman was a nineteen-and-a-half-year-old
medical student. This, I said, interested me very much. Did
she have time to talk? She said the family was away, she felt

bored, and had plenty of time. Our conversation lasted an
hour.

After some preliminaries I put the usual question about
Khrushchev's "Letter." Yes, she had been told about it by
students who had heard it read. Did she especially remember
any part, the bit concerning Voroshilov, for instance? Yes,
Stalin suspected him of being a British spy, did not allow
him to attend sessions of the Politburo, and wire-tapped his
apartment.

"A few years ago," I said, "you were told Stalin was a
wonderful person who did only good. Today you know he
caused much suffering and killed many people unnecessar-
ily. In other words, they told you lies."

"Yes."

"Now if the government and party praise themselves will
you believe it?"

"Yes," she replied.

"But since they lied to you before, could they not be lying
to you again?"

"Not the present leadership," she insisted.

"Shouldn't you at least have a critical attitude?"

"I don't understand," she pleaded.

"You are studying Latin. A French philosopher named
Descartes said, 'Cogito, ergo sum—I think, therefore I am.'
We are human because we can think. And thinking means
choosing. You weigh evidence, you decide for yourself
whether or not what you hear is correct. You don't believe
everything anybody tells you, do you?"

"No . . . But the government is different."

"But the government told you lies about Stalin," I recalled.

"That was," she argued, echoing the party line.

"You choose between one book and another. You choose
between one film and another; you decide to wear this dress,
not that. Wouldn't it be desirable to choose your own political

ideas, make comparisons, reject one version and believe another?"

"That is all right for dresses, not politics," she declared.

Try as I might I could not break through this armor of
credulity.

A few days later I was walking down the wide Sadovaya
when I saw ahead two girls, whom I judged to be fourteen
or fifteen, in school uniform: brown dress, white collar, black
pinafore. I caught up with them and asked whether I might
photograph them to show my friends abroad. "No," replied
one of the girls, "I am so plain, choose somebody better-look-
ing." I said she had an interesting face and both would make
a good picture. "No," she persisted, "you must look elsewhere." The pretty girl remained silent. I apologized and
left them, and walked up Vorovsky Street.

In a minute they overtook me and said they had changed
their minds. I asked them to pose against a building, and
made several exposures. The plain one was the daughter of a
chauffeur, the pretty one's father worked in a government
office. They were seventeen.

Had they heard Khrushchev's "Letter"?

Excerpts.

Why hadn't it been published?

It will be.

But many months have already passed. In a democratic
country it would have been published immediately.

They could not explain why it had not been published.

"You were told lies about Stalin in the past."

"Yes."

"How do you know they are not lying to you now?"

"We believe."

The pretty girl took the offensive: "Why do so many people in America starve if you are rich and free?"

"Americans starve only in *Pravda*."

"Why do Americans explode hydrogen bombs? Do they want a war?"

"The Soviet government exploded one in Siberia several days ago, but your newspapers have printed nothing about that. Your press is not free. This explains the horrors of Stalinism. Open criticism would have saved you from them."

"Can you criticize your government?"

"Of course," I assured them, "I could write an article against President Eisenhower."

"Yes, but would it be printed?" the plain girl demanded triumphantly.

Both were studying English, and the plain one had been asked by her Pioneer group to reply to a letter sent by a boy in California who was seeking a pen pal. As we walked down the street to Arbat Square, we stopped at intersections to argue and compose the reply.

"Tell your fellow-countrymen we want peace," was their parting injunction to me.

These three young women were echoing, not thinking.

When I first arrived in Soviet Russia in 1922, a chapel containing the sacred ikon of the Iberian Virgin could be seen in the middle of the road leading into the Red Square, and on a red wall opposite the slogan, "Religion is the Opium of the People." The chapel and slogan are gone. It is the Kremlin that has been dispensing opium these many years. Innumerable minds are asleep.

"We are just coming out of ether," a woman magazine editor told me in Moscow.

She was, and there are many like her. But with the press and radio still freely distributing opium one wonders whether the small measure of de-Stalinization suffices to awaken the tired, the disinterested, and the egotistically materialistic whose taste and standards in clothes, house furnishings, art, literature, and morality are Victorian and petty bourgeois.

Soviet society is a most acquisitive, competitive society,

atomized by self-interest, the struggle for survival, the striving
for success, and by the official discouragement of all forms of
uncontrolled social organization. Democracy makes for human contacts; dictatorship for human isolation. Stalin's quarter century of despotism made friendship, trust, and personal
loyalty rare phenomena indeed. The individual was turned in
on self and family. This mentality will not change quickly.

I went to visit Mr. R., an engineer, aged fifty-eight, who is
a Communist party member. What did he say? "I earn 4000
roubles a month; receive 2400 on my pension. Here's a book
with an article of mine which brought me 25,000 roubles.
Downstairs is my Pobeda [four-seater Soviet-made car]. If the
garage were larger I would buy a Zis limousine. Recently I
returned from a two months' vacation on the Caucasus Ri-
viera. Come look at my apartment, five rooms for my wife and
myself, piano, radio, television."

I have heard such talk from New York parvenu capitalists.
The Communist engineer never mentioned an ideal. Luxuries
for the upper class are part of the opium.

I told this Communist about a mutual friend, a former high
Soviet official and party member, who had defected in 1939
and gone to Stockholm where he joined a Swedish engineering firm and became rich. But, I continued, he had never
written or said anything in public against the Soviet Union.
"So he did not slander our country," the Communist commented. "Good. In 1939 I would have condemned his act, now
I understand it. He saved his life and the lives of his wife and
children."

Khrushchev's secret speech had educated Mr. R. and made
him more tolerant of anti-Communism as long as it was not
anti-Russian. In effect he was only a Communist party member, but not a real believer in Communism. The ideal was
gone. He functioned as a cog in the great machine which
rules Russia.

In the 1920's there stood in the square facing the Moscow

Soviet (town hall) a small cement statue of a figure representing freedom, and on the pedestal was inscribed the legend, "Who does not work, does not eat," and also an article from the Soviet Constitution. In its place an enormous monument has been erected with a great marble base surmounted by the equestrian statue of Prince Yuri Dologoruki, a feudal lord who, according to cloudy history, founded the city of Moscow eight centuries ago. To me this substitution seemed symbolic of the retreat from early ideals to the present emphasis on autocratic power, from aspiration to tradition, from austerity for all to luxury for some.

Like Stalin, Stalin's heirs are pursuing the course he laid out toward national might through the expansion of heavy industries which produce steel, iron, coal, oil, machine tools (for armaments), mechanized farming, more factories, transportation facilities, et cetera, at the expense of the well-being of the bulk of the population. The Kremlin makes no secret of its purpose. In a bookstore window on the Kuznetski Most, and elsewhere, I saw an official poster with a caption, "This Will Be the Sixth Five Year Plan." Below, it gave figures for capital investment in the six Soviet five-year plans. The investment in the first plan, beginning October, 1928, was 58 billion roubles; in the second, 132½ billion; third, 131 billion; fourth, 311 billion; fifth, 594 billion; sixth—from 1956 to 1960 —990 billion. Such gigantic outlays must cause inflation and reduced living standards.

To counteract these ineluctable effects of a cruel, courageous, consistent, openly avowed policy, the Soviet regime has used a variety of instruments: terror under Stalin and the memory of it under his heirs; patriotic pride in national strength; promises of a better future for all; brainwashing to expunge thought capacity, critical attitudes, and doubts; isolation from the outside world to prevent correct comparisons; lies about other countries to distort comparisons; and, probably most important at present, the gratification of the desires of the upper class for good living and political security. The ten to twenty million persons comprising that class form a buffer, an insulating layer, between the discontent of the masses and the leadership. The upper class manages the economy, runs the government, hands out the opium. As long as it remains conservative, loyal, and willing, the Kremlin collective need not fear the consequences of the limited, controlled de-Stalinization which it has undertaken in the Soviet Union.

The anti-Russian movements in Poland and Hungary were sparked by intellectuals and students who love their countries and remember freedom. In the Soviet Union the urge to revolution is dampened by love of country and fear of too much freedom. The upper class wants the freedom which translates itself into protection from the abuses of the secret police, but not the full freedom which would wreck the present economic system by allowing peasants and workers to escape from compulsion and exploitation.

The nightmare is over, some are awakening from the ether, Hungary and Poland have been a jet of fresh bracing air, but the spell of opium is still strong.

One of the worst things I heard in Moscow was that during the 1938–39 Yezhov slaughter of state officials and intellectuals, novelists destroyed their manuscripts lest they be found incriminating. People also burned the most innocent letters. In the current mood of relaxation this is unlikely to happen. Moreover, the outside censor, in effect an agent of the secret police, has been withdrawn from the editorial offices of literary magazines, and the editor is now responsible for what goes into his journal. Debating the advisability of publishing or rejecting a piece, he might say to himself: the censor would have proscribed this; if I use it I may be reprimanded, I may even be discharged, but I will not be arrested. This consideration could, in time, make editors somewhat more daring. Even such relief in eye-dropper doses satisfies when there has been none for a generation. Besides, writers receive colossal incomes; I spoke with one who earned a million roubles annually. That too is opium for the makers of opium.

I can envisage much more liberty to Soviet intellectuals without any harm to the Soviet system. Moscow writers and professional people did not give me the impression that they intended to deviate from the official political line. They may be critical or cynical, but they will not dissent, especially in the present period of confusing de-Stalinization zigzags. The August, 1956, issue of the Moscow *Kommunist,* ideological organ of the party, stated that it had received many letters asking whether it was proper to use Stalin's works in the study of Marxist-Leninist theory. These shrewd correspondents are watching their step. The magazine told them exactly which part of Stalin's literary output is orthodox. "Stalin," it declared, "was a great Marxist theoretician." I imagine my friends shrugging their shoulders and saying, "Now I am completely befuddled." That is the right atmosphere in which to enforce an intellectual goose step.

Another article in the same issue of *Kommunist* chides an art critic named J. Grabar for defending impressionism. "He forgets the instructions of V. T. Lenin," the author reproves.

The intellectual must goose step while toeing the party line, that is, while marking time, and always "participate even more actively in life," in other words, write, act, paint, and sculpt in support of the five-year plan. The Kremlin is not liberating its servants. It can therefore give them more liberty.

Faith in the human spirit and in the great Russian tradition in literature and music impels one to hope that Soviet intellectuals will some day become restive under the yoke of party and state. The example of the writers and journalists of Poland and Hungary has produced an echo in Moscow and Leningrad. Stirrings in university faculties and among writers have come to light. But they usually stay within the bounds permitted by the authorities. The dependence is still great, intellectual independence rare. It is difficult to reverse the surgical process by which Stalin cut men down to the size of puppets.

"A state which dwarfs its men that they may be more docile instruments in its hands, even for beneficial purposes, will find that with small men no great thing can really be accomplished," John Stuart Mill wrote in *On Liberty* in 1859. That describes the state of culture in Russia nearly a century later. Art and intellect languish where man is secondary.

The Soviet Union is ruled by two men, a German and a Russian, Karl Marx and Ivan Pavlov. The Communists have of course molded Marx in their own image and allowed this ersatz Marxism to govern their politics and economics. Pavlov's influence is far more profound. Because of him, Soviet Russia has rejected all post-Pavlov psychology. He fits Marxism perfectly: conditions determine mental outlook and nervous reactions. He showed that if a dog's saliva had run often enough at the appearance of food and the simultaneous ringing of a bell, it would run at the ringing of the bell only. The Communist regime has devoted almost four decades of effort to condition men, women, and children in the same way. It has created a whole lexicon of words like "peace," "Fascism," "Wall Street," "colonialism," "socialism," "Leninist," "Communist fatherland," and "the dictatorship of the proletariat," to which the citizen is supposed to react with a prescribed degree of indignation or enthusiasm. It has also set up a chain of stimuli—fear plus material reward plus propaganda—to make the saliva flow. This monumental effort to induce a slave mentality by artificial mechanical means has succeeded far beyond the belief of anyone who loves human beings. But over the years some dogs have learned how to fool the late professor's pupils. They can make the saliva flow in public, but in their hearts they know that it is only a bell and no dinner.

The Soviet government possesses great power. That power, however, is not bolstered by faith. The Soviet system has won outer might and lost inner strength. This is part of a perceptible process of social decay. Nothing indicates that the Soviet revolution has produced a new type of human being or so modified the old type as to make him aspire to higher things, exalt his outlook on life, broaden his social vision, purify his manner of life, or induce a greater love for man or nature or art. Nothing new has been born, and the old is dull and tired.

CHAPTER 9

Power and Poverty

Soviet prices have no meaning except in relation to quality (which neither the customer at the time of the purchase, much less the window-shopper, can correctly evaluate) and to individual income. The Soviet economy is a money economy, and living depends, as everywhere else, on earnings.

Wages and salaries in the Soviet Union vary very widely, and the government is chary about publishing statistics. Nevertheless, available data help one to grope toward some conclusions.

On September 9, 1956, the Soviet government, the Central Committee of the Communist party, and the national Central Soviet of Trade Unions signed a decree fixing a minimum monthly wage of 300 to 350 roubles from January 1, 1957, onward, for workers and clerks employed in factories, construction work, transportation, and communications. "On the average," the decree stated, "the increase in wages for all indicated groups of workers and employees amounts, approximately, to 33 per cent." (In other words, they had been receiving between 225 and 264 roubles a month.) The decree declares that this 33 per cent increase will cost the government eight billion roubles in 1957. (In other words, over eight million Soviet workingmen and employees come within this lowest category. The total Soviet working class numbers forty-eight million.)

This enactment was hailed with loud Communist trumpeting. Editorials praised the government and party for their solicitude. Workers thanked the state with synthetic ecstasy. One of these was a streetcar conductor in Kiev; another, an employee in a silk mill in Tiflis; a third, a cleaning woman in Leningrad. If Citizeness Gromadskaya, the Kiev trolley conductor, ate only one egg a day and nothing more, it would cost her one-tenth of her income; if she consumed a pound of the cheapest black bread a day—normal quantity in a poor Russian diet—that alone would account for one-twentieth of her monthly wage.

This gives some idea of the low living standard of one out of every six Soviet urban workers.

Some of the remaining five-sixths do not fare much better. The Moscow *Izvestia* of October 26, 1956, reporting on the government's endeavor to reduce staffs, wrote, "Last year alone Glavmosstroi [Central Moscow Building Organization] released 6000 auxiliary workers whose annual maintenance cost forty million roubles." That comes to an expenditure of 555 roubles a month on each worker, approximately 30 per cent of which covers outlays for social insurance, social medicine, etc. The individual monthly take-home pay, therefore, is 360 roubles. A more or less compulsory investment of at least a fortnight's income annually in government loans depresses the real wage still further. And every Soviet urban worker supports one and a half dependents.

A taxi driver told me he has one room, 180 square feet in area, where he lives with his ailing wife, a daughter of sixteen, and his mother; if his fares average 250 roubles a day six days a week he earns 800 roubles a month; if he takes in more than that, he makes 1000 roubles. He also gets occasional tips.

Taxi drivers and coal miners are aristocrats of the Soviet

working class. From the Donetz Coal Basin in October, 1956, Welles Hangen of the *New York Times* reported that miners earned as much as 2000 roubles monthly—depending on how much coal they cut. Labor at the mines has been fluid since the revolution; hundreds of thousands come and flee owing to poor conditions, especially housing; even Young Communist volunteers, mobilized for the unpleasant chore, quit prematurely. Hence the extra-high money incentive.

Almost the entire Soviet proletariat receives piecework pay, which makes it most difficult to break through Soviet secrecy about the average wage. The trade unions have contrived to talk their way through long national congresses without mentioning the subject of wages.

An article in the Moscow Russian-language *World Trade Union Movement* for August, 1956, defends the lot of the Soviet workingman against an allegedly slanderous attack in the organ of the free trade unions of the West, but while it makes many affirmations about his good fortune in laboring under socialism, it gives no money figures for his wages.

The National Economy of the U.S.S.R., published by the Central Statistical Administration of the federal Council of Ministers in 1956, devotes only half a page of its 262 pages to wages, and it says nothing more than that between 1940 and 1955 the real wages of workers and employees in the national economy rose 75 per cent, while the real wages of industrial workers alone rose 90 per cent; moreover, between 1950 and 1955 the real wages of workers and employees in the national economy rose 39 per cent, and in the sixth five-year plan (1956–60) their real wages are scheduled to rise, "on the average, approximately 30 per cent."

The Kremlin must surely realize that this record of progress would carry more conviction if it were stated in roubles and kopeks. What purpose other than deception is served by giving bare percentages? Assuming that the percentage in-

creases are correct, the reason for concealing the rouble wages
can only be that they are so low.

Using scraps, hints, interpretations, extrapolations, old
data, and personal travel reports, western professional economists have toiled for years on the mystery of what the average
Soviet worker earns; their conclusions range from a low of
500 to a high of between 750 and 800 roubles per month for
a forty-six hour week.

I am content to take the topmost and probably too favorable estimate of 800. In view of Soviet prices the Kremlin
seems justified in hiding behind percentages of percentages.

(It is foolish to divide 800 by four roubles to the dollar and
come to $200 as the average monthly wage in Russia. For in
that case one would have to quote the price of an egg at
twenty-five cents, a suit of cotton pajamas at $66.75, and an
ice-cream cone at fifty cents.)

Wherever I went in Moscow I looked into shop windows
and walked into shops and recorded the prices in a notebook.
I reproduce them in the same jumbled order: women's cotton
dresses 535 roubles, 408, 492, 280, 86.50 and 108; KVN–49
television set marked down from 950 to 850; radios 1100,
2200; gold watches reduced from 1300 to 1000; vacuum
cleaners 204, 170, 300, 220; small gas refrigerator (North #2)
680; electric plate 24; electric lamp without bulb 48; baby
carriage 248, 260; child's bicycle 170; child's tricycle 125, 65;
lipstick 10.50; television sets 840 to 2200; gramophones 210,
80, 300; mouth organs 30, 40, 25; a pint of milk 1.20; women's
dresses 676, 390, 203, 612; electric kettle 99, 76.50; ice-cream
cone 1.95; silver-fox stoles 2762, 2057; men's fur caps 360, 92,
231, 70, 316; men's straw hats 45, 33; felt hats 150, 69; boy's required cap for school uniform 28.90; cloth caps 43, 32; pajamas 267; men's shirts 107, 94, 130; men's made-in-China
shirts with two detached collars 60, 68.50; cake of soap 3,
2.10; clinical thermometer 3.75; chemical contraceptives 10
for 3 roubles; vacuum cleaner 650, 495; bicycles 895, 915;

boys' bicycles 495, 434, 404; pound of butter 14.25, 14.50, 13.75; Dutch cheese 15 roubles a pound; pound of bananas one and a half roubles; one egg one rouble; a pound of black bread one rouble; a pound of white bread one and a half roubles; vodka 50 roubles a quart; pork 10 roubles a pound; tea 30 roubles a pound; potatoes one rouble for two pounds; apples 4 roubles a pound; sugar 4.80 a pound; women's kapron stockings 16.50, 22.10, and 35 roubles; women's shoes from 98 to 400 roubles; man's suit 1000 to 1500 roubles; cottage cheese 10 roubles a pound; rye bread 1.65 for two pounds; lard 13 roubles a pound; woman's knitted woolen jumpers 275, 360 roubles; and so on.

At these prices, the average wage, whether 500 or 800 roubles, spells misery, and the large below-average class numbering, with dependents, at least thirty-five million city persons, lives in dire distress. Two indices as examples: the average Soviet worker would have to spend a month's salary on milk every year if he and his dependents were to equal the average annual per capita milk consumption in Great Britain . . . The Moscow *Literary Gazette* of September 1, 1956, stated that the maintenance of each pupil in the new government-operated boarding schools would cost 1005 roubles a month.

My young Moscow friends Ivan and Sonya earned 1400 roubles a month; their rent was a negligible item. Nevertheless they could not make ends meet. Ivan's rich uncle presented him with an excellent suit (2300 roubles for the imported Czechoslovak woolens and 1000 roubles for the sewing by a hush-hush private tailor), and all summer they were guests in his wooden bungalow outside Moscow.

In Moscow one felt the harsh incongruity between the power of the state and the poverty of the people. The two are cause and effect. The government's announced policy of continuing the forced expansion of heavy industry till 1960 signifies a further grinding down of the masses so as to build

up the might of the state. This has been the undeviating
course since Stalin began it in 1928. That is why the working
class must have no free trade unions and Russia must have
no freedom. The right to protest would interfere with the government's design. The design is simple: pay the workers as
little as possible for their labor and the peasants as little as
possible for their produce and invest the difference in heavy
industry and armaments.

Throughout history, nations have accepted wartime austerity to win victory. The Soviet people, with the exception of
the upper class, have lived in involuntary austerity for almost
thirty years. I met Soviet citizens who were patriotic and others who were resigned; all felt tired. The road has been long,
the burden heavy.

Every aspect of Soviet life testifies to the high cost of Communism in terms of the citizen's health, material welfare, and
freedom. Every branch of the Soviet economy is excessively
expensive in terms of money and human effort. The reason is
always the same: the state comes first and the Communist
economic system is inviolate even if inefficient. All available
data demonstrate this truth.

The official statistical handbook says that between 1928
and 1960, Soviet production of pig iron will have multiplied
16 times, steel 16 times, coal 17 times, oil 17 times, but cotton
yarn only 2.7 times. Cotton yarn is the basis of most Soviet
clothing and household linens. Except for a few regions,
Russia is a very cold country. The handbook states that in
1955 the production of woolens per person per year was one
and a third yards. How many years would a human being
have to wait for a suit and overcoat?

The handbook gives no figures for grain production. It
merely gives percentages: 100 per cent in 1950, 97 per cent
in 1951, 113 per cent in 1952, 101 per cent in 1953, 105 per
cent in 1954, and 129 per cent in 1955. Since the annual population increase is 1.7 per cent, it is obvious that the harvest

kept pace with population growth only in 1952 and 1955; whether even in those years it sufficed to feed the country is not indicated.

But foreign economists, studying Soviet life with meticulous exactitude, catch every straw in the farmyard wind: once the Ukraine had an exceptional harvest and the total amount was stated in tons; *Voprosi Ekonomiki* (Economic Questions), a Moscow monthly, let some figures slip in its January, 1956, issue which, however, require expert interpretation. The specialists in London check their findings with those in Munich, and they with their colleagues in California and with embassies in Moscow. Their conclusions differ narrowly and a consensus emerges.

The yield per acre has risen 14 per cent since 1913 although, as the statistical handbook correctly affirms, the land in tsarist times was cultivated with primitive methods. Two million wooden plows, it says, and 17 million wooden harrows were in use, whereas in 1955 Soviet agriculture had at its disposal 1,439,000 tractors, 338,000 grain combines, 544,000 lorries, and "millions of complicated farm machines." In addition, mountains of chemical fertilizer have been applied, tens of thousands of agronomes have been sent into the villages, and countless armies of Communist organizers, agitators, shock brigaders, and Komsomol volunteers have descended on the collective farms to help in the battle for bread. Nor should one forget the oceans of ink spilled on the assumption that there can be no harvest without such moisture. With no such fuss and at far less expense, the yield per acre between 1913 and 1953 rose 29 per cent in West Germany, 44 per cent in France, 31 per cent in Sweden, and 89 per cent in Finland. In the Soviet Union a peasant produces food for himself and three to four others; in the United States a farmer produces food for himself and nineteen others.

In 1953 the Kremlin apparently realized that it was

confronted with a serious bread crisis. At that time, as Khrushchev told a Moscow Komsomol meeting which was reported in *Izvestia*, November 10, 1956, he exchanged opinions with Mikoyan "on what possibilities we had of supplying the nation with bread." The nation, then, was not being supplied with enough bread. The emergency was so great that the Kremlin, under Khrushchev's urging, launched the colossal, courageous, costly venture of plowing up eighty-eight million acres of virgin land in Kazakhstan, which is equal to the entire sown area of France and Italy and to the total harvest wheat acreage of the United States. Foreigners, and even Soviet leaders (Mikoyan was one), were skeptical about the results, but in 1956, at least, Khrushchev won his gamble; Kazakhstan produced a fine crop. Khrushchev triumphantly informed the Komsomol meeting in November, 1956, that the virgin lands of Kazakhstan, deep in the heart of Asia, had delivered to the government, in 1956, one billion poods of grain. "To supply the national population," Khrushchev said on that occasion, "approximately two billion poods of bread [per year] are necessary." This comes to ten poods or 360 pounds per head annually. Kazakhstan's new lands, accordingly, furnished half the supply. (Foreign skeptics still scoff and predict a Kazakhstan dust bowl that will blow sand into Khrushchev's political hair.) The expense was enormous in money, machines, and men; six hundred thousand volunteers were ordered into the empty lands for permanent work and several hundred thousand more for harvesting, but the government could not hesitate or delay. A bread shortage forty years after the revolution would have been disastrous.

Prior to the seeding of the virgin lands, the Soviet Union had approximately an acre and a quarter per person under grain. Yet with all the modern equipment, methods, and scientific guidance, bread was in short supply. Only one conclusion is warranted: the peasants reject collective agriculture and refuse to give it their best effort. They prefer private farming. The Kremlin knows this and is attempting to stimulate individual initiative by offering bigger financial rewards. The outcome is doubtful. The peasant is on strike against the collective farm system, especially since, of late, his private acre or half-acre plot, where he produces milk, poultry, pork, vegetables, et cetera for himself and for sale in the market, is being reduced in size or taken away altogether.

Every Communist hates the peasant, whom he regards as an anti-Communist capitalist by his very nature; the peasant reciprocates. This mutual hostility hurts production and lowers the nation's living standard. But to give the peasant freedom would cripple the dictatorship, whose maintenance and aggrandizement is the Kremlin's first aim.

Soviet enactments and acts in the last three or four years indicate a growing tendency to convert the peasant, who still enjoys some economic independence and is therefore a menace, into a proletarian tilling the land for wages. More than that, the trend seems to be to eliminate the peasant altogether. Collectivization has given rise to machine tractor stations, now employing nearly two and a half million persons, who, according to *Kommunist* of October, 1956, "ever more widely take over all the basic processes not only on the fields, where they have long since become a decisive force, but also in animal husbandry." The machine tractor stations operate the tractors, combines, and other machines, and are outside of and independent of the collective farms. Millions of peasants, in other words, are becoming redundant. There is less need for them in the village and no room for them in town. This may be an inevitable historic process, but they cannot welcome it. If they continue their slow, silent sabotage no one will be surprised.

Every year the Soviet press stresses the necessity of having all tractors in good repair before the plowing season commences, and then it gives innumerable examples where this caveat was not heeded; it urges the peasants not to neglect weeding; it warns about insufficient care of the crop and, true enough, when the crop has been cut the Moscow newspapers publish photographs showing grain piled by the roadside and rotting. The loss between standing crop and actual harvest is so high as to challenge belief; it is soberly estimated, on the basis of Soviet information, at 30 per cent. This is part of the cost of the war between Soviet state and peasantry.

Then the thefts begin. The peasant takes home some feed for his cow, hogs, and chickens—or some wheat and rye for his own consumption. "It is my crop," he reasons, "but soon the government agent will come to carry most of it away."

The collective farms are annually required to deliver to the state, for city and army, a high proportion of their agricultural produce at low, Kremlin-fixed prices. The peasant resents this as official robbery. In 1956, according to the Khrushchev speech reported in *Izvestia* on November 10, 1956, the government thus procured three billion 281 million poods of grain which, after deducting two billion poods for consumption, left an unprecedented reserve of one billion 281 million poods in the government's hands. (A pood equals 36 pounds.)

Khrushchev's reaction to this unique windfall X-rays Communist mentality and intentions. The Soviet Union, he said, was now in a position to supply grain to the "people's democracies" (Communist euphemism for satellites) which have to import it. "So," he announced with a flourish, "this year we have the possibility not only of satisfying the demands of our population and providing the required aid to friendly countries but also of depositing a large amount of grain in the government barns as a reserve. And," he added in what may be the most revealing Soviet statement since Stalin died, "when there is grain in the barns it is easier to talk with friends and it is possible to argue with enemies."

Grain is thus a chain to hold the satellites. Else why would Russia's ability to send them grain make it easier to talk to them? As Communist brothers it ought to be easy to talk to them in any circumstance.

Of even greater interest, indeed of the greatest interest, is Khrushchev's proposition that a considerable bread reserve—probably for the first time in Soviet history—makes it possible to argue with the enemy. Who is the enemy, and what does "argue" mean? Does it mean Prime Minister Bulganin's threat during the Suez crisis to hurl atomic rockets at Britain? Khrushchev spoke and Bulganin wrote in the same week.

Khrushchev returned to his pet theme on March 8, 1957, in a speech to farmers in the Krasnodar region. Urging them to produce more meat and milk, he said, "The more grain, meat, milk, and other products produced by the state farms the stronger the Soviet system will be. The growth of industrial and agricultural output is a battering-ram with which we will stave in the capitalist system."

To the Soviet leadership not only hydrogen bombs, tanks, and oil are power, bread and meat too are translated into power. The primary purpose of all policy and of all economic activity is power. Small wonder the people are poor.

The authoritative *Kommunist* for October, 1956, formulates "the basic economic task of the Soviet Union" thus: "In the shortest possible time to overtake and outdistance the most highly developed capitalist nations in production per person. That is the 'final and decisive battle' which will bring victory to socialism in its rivalry with capitalism." If more output per capita means more shoes, bread, eggs, houses, et cetera for Soviet citizens one can only bless the endeavor. But not if the first good crop provokes rocket rattling. And why the rivalry? What price victory? This does not look like the much advertised peaceful coexistence.

The Soviet national economy was always a very political economy. Economic necessity was sacrificed to considerations of politics and power. But the rising managerial class, whose spokesman seems to be Malenkov, is trying to shift the emphasis to economic matters. In five or ten years, when political bosses like Khrushchev, Bulganin, Molotov, Voroshilov, and Kaganovich, now in their sixties or seventies, will probably have left the scene, the tough-minded new generation of industrial technicians, together with the professional military men, are likely to dominate the political arena. As these personnel changes unfold—they are already beginning to unfold—it will be interesting to observe whether the soldiers will consent to foster individual welfare at the expense of national power. Today, the high cost of armaments, of the Soviet empire, and of Russia's foreign policy sharply reduces the living standard of the Soviet people.

However important the changes in leadership may prove to be, the essence is the Russian philosophy of the state. Power for the state is the key to the acts of the Soviet system. In Russian, the word for power—*vlast*—is also the word for government. To Communists, maximum power is synonymous with dictatorship. Why then dissipate the power of the government by sharing it with citizens or parliament? One of the biggest enigmas to the Soviet mind is the combination in the United States of power and freedom. Hence their facile, automatic assumption that the freedom is not real and that behind it stands the dictatorship of "Wall Street." It seems never to have occurred to the Communist chiefs that only that state is solid and efficient which enjoys the voluntary support of its people.

CHAPTER 10

Russia and the World

Nationalism and the Kremlin's love of power make it quite certain that as long as she can Russia will hold her own; this means empire. The Soviets do not propose to give back to the free world what they have taken from it.

Russia, however, does not anticipate further gains in the West. I saw in Moscow a turning away from Europe and a concentration on Asia and Africa, the Bandung world. That is where the Soviets hope to win friends and make conquests.

In the West, Moscow will maneuver, bully, intrigue, propagandize, and zigzag, but more with a view to creating trouble for the adversary than achieving notable victories for Russia. It is in Asia, home of half the human race, that the Kremlin has great expectations.

Western Europe is moving toward economic unity. Europe and America have a relatively stable economy and do not ache from wounded pride and the memory of foreign domination. Here the Communists are unlikely to catch more fish. Even the old fish seem useless; the French and Italian Communist parties, vast though their electoral following remains, have not served their purpose, which is to assist Soviet foreign policy.

Prime Minister Bulganin writes to his pen pal, President Eisenhower, and the Soviets do desire better contacts with the West. They have abandoned Stalin's stupid conceit that

Russia has nothing to learn; they want to benefit from the technical attainments of the advanced industrialized nations. Yet one has only to read the speeches of the leaders and the editorials in the newspapers (as well as the news) to sense the deep Soviet antipathy to the West. Any doubts as to the validity of this impression are dissipated by the contrasting sympathetic treatment accorded to events in most of Asia and Africa.

I have written about Soviet foreign policy for many years, but it was not till my latest stay in Moscow that I fully realized what lay at the root of the Communist aversion to the West. It is not fear of western armed might; the Russians know the West will not attack them. It is not fear of capitalism; they know their economic system can coexist with capitalism. It is fear of freedom. Multiparty democracy disturbs them; they dread its contagion. Moscow's most strenuous propaganda efforts are devoted to proving that the West is not democratic and that true freedom can only be found in the "people's democracies" and, above all, naturally, under the Russian dictatorship of the proletariat. This is now the quintessence of Marxist-Leninist education.

Moscow trusts that in Asia and Africa the rejection of the West for its imperialist sins and the desire to build new economies rapidly will lead to dictatorship. Scratch an Asian and you are likely to find a critic of the West. Many Asians, while professing democracy, show their scorn for the West which liberated them and bow adoringly before the defiant military strength of Russia and China whose rapid industrial growth, especially the Soviet Union's, offers a model which, in its poverty and innocence, non-Communist Asia thinks it can imitate with impunity. In this fertile soil, Moscow plants its seeds.

Stalin's successors have many interesting attributes, but sentimentalism is not one of them. They do not like Nehru for his handsome face or fine English style but because they think they can use him against western diplomacy and

through him ultimately wean India from democracy. More
even than Nehru they love the Nasser "monolithic" type. And
as to despotic slave-holding Saudi Arabia and Yemen, where
hands are cut off for stealing, they have a better press in the
Soviet Union than the enlightened democracies of Scandi-
navia.

Asian summit visitors are given triumphal conducted tours
through the Soviet Union which exercise a hypnotic effect.
In the case of President Sukarno of Indonesia the Kremlin
provided for his special personal requirements, and, since he
is a considerable orator, corralled crowds of a hundred thousand or more which inspired him to ecstatic, if not quite politic, eloquence. His itinerary, of course, included a collective
farm, the first he had ever seen anywhere. He arrived with
his own large retinue and in the company of numerous high
Soviet officials. Greeted by dressed-up peasants under a cere-
monial arch, he immediately made a speech, and in it declared, "The collective farm is a very good system." This rash
verdict made fine Communist propaganda.

Being unscrupulous, Moscow knows how to rouse the emotions of volatile Asians. On their visit to India in 1955,
Khrushchev and Bulganin told the welcoming masses of humanity that Goa must be Indian; Kashmir is Indian; India
is a great power; Pakistan is a tool of western imperialism;
and (in Calcutta) that Bengal made the biggest contribution
to the expulsion of the British. They said what the audiences
wanted to hear. It was all words, but it produced an effect.

In the calm aftermath of this tumult, however, at least
some sage Indians grasped one subtle reason for the Russian
courtship of their country: Moscow's rivalry with Peking.

The Soviet leaders know that behind Indian protestations
of friendship for Red China lies a dread of Peking's expan-
sionism which has already manifested itself, with no deference to Indian sensibilities, in the militarization of Tibet,

Chinese flirtations with Nepal, and a minor Chinese invasion of Burma in 1956.

When Pakistan Prime Minister Hussein Shaheed Suhrawardy visited Chairman Mao Tse-tung in Peking in December, 1956, Mao said to him, "Why is India afraid of China?" Mao's astute question was obviously designed to reassure the Pakistani. In fact, however, India is disturbed by China. The race between India and China to see who can achieve greatness first is not merely a competition between democratic and dictatorial methods of economic development; it reflects India's fears. Superficially the relations between New Delhi and Peking are most cordial. Actually India is conscious of China's southernly expansionist trend. Russian imperialism, on the other hand, has largely been directed against the West, and that enables the Indian leaders to overlook the moral issue involved. In fact, since Moscow is opposed to the Baghdad Pact and therefore to Pakistan which adheres to that pact, since Moscow, moreover, favors the Afghan Pushtanistan movement at the expense of Pakistan, India's contacts with Russia are likely to be warmer than with China.

China is no satellite. She is too big to be pushed around and too ambitious to obey. Honeyed words of eternal love and agreement notwithstanding, Communism notwithstanding, Russia is jousting with China for the upper hand in Asia. In an interview with German Chancellor Konrad Adenauer at Bonn in June, 1956, he told me something Khrushchev had said to him in Moscow in September, 1955. Six hundred million Chinese, living on a handful of rice a day and increasing at the rate of twelve million a year—that, Khrushchev declared, is a matter of some concern.

Carlo Schmid, the very cultured German socialist leader who accompanied Adenauer on his mission to Moscow, repeated a statement Politburo member Lazar Kaganovich made to him there: China needs turbines, generators, machine tools and other heavy industrial equipment, and we want Germany to help supply them. But we will not send your exports to China, we will send ours and keep yours; we would not like the Chinese to see that you do better work than we.

And German Foreign Minister Heinrich von Brentano, likewise a member of Adenauer's delegation, explained to me that what Khrushchev said to the Chancellor and what Kaganovich said to Carlo Schmid was "bait," part of a campaign to win West Germany as a partner in the development of China and Asia generally.

Adenauer did not "bite." He saw China as a supreme Russian preoccupation, he saw in that preoccupation a hope for Europe. Some observers, citing Lenin, envisage Russia moving into Paris via Peking. In fact, however, Russia may need peace with Paris, Bonn, London, and Washington in order to cope with the rising Chinese giant. (This, incidentally, inspired Adenauer's splendid optimism on the ultimate reunification of Germany.)

Late in the summer of 1956, Jack Raymond of the *New York Times* reported from Outer Mongolia the presence of ten thousand Chinese technicians who, by agreement, could opt for Outer Mongolian citizenship after the expiration of their contractual term of service. Other western observers saw Chinese soldiers engaged in the laying of a railroad from China to Ulan Bator, the Mongolian capital. Except for the interval of Soviet weakness from 1918 to 1924, Outer Mongolia has been a Russian satellite since 1911, when the Manchu dynasty fell, and under Soviet domination all foreigners, Chinese included, were barred from Outer Mongolia. Now Red China has, in effect, reasserted her claim to that former Chinese province.

In North Korea, Manchuria, and Sinkiang (Chinese Turkestan) too, the Soviets were forced to withdraw before Chinese Communist pressure. The Russian bear and the Chinese dragon have embraced, but not in pure love. They are two nations behaving, as they must, like nations, nations having similar and dissimilar aims simultaneously. Detestation of democracy and opposition to the presence of the West in Asia brings them together; suspicion and rival power interests put them on their guard.

In these circumstances, Russia is afraid to refuse any Chinese request for military and industrial equipment. Russia is being drained by China. The Chinese, in exchange, pay with political support of Russia where that suits their purpose. Thus China approved of Russia's fiery suppression in Hungary; and when, on January 17, 1957, Premier Bulganin, speaking at a Moscow function, thanked Premier Chou Enlai, Chou expressed his government's gratitude for Soviet economic aid. That is the quid pro quo. The rivalry remains. In Asia, China has the advantage of population, industrial potential, and geographic position.

Power alignments in Asia are by no means congealed. At present Russia wants to oust the West from Asia (and America from Europe), the better to dominate, or at least influence, the weak, retarded nations of the Bandung world. That they are slow to realize this is one of the wonders of modern psychology. It seems obvious. Or do the Asians and Africans believe that idealistic, peace-loving Russia is completely unselfish? Soviet acts in Asia and Africa are in fact part of Moscow's cold war against the West and China.

Cold war does not exclude hot-war measures. The Kremlin, obviously, was not contributing to a relaxation of Middle East tensions when it supplied jet bombers and big tanks to Colonel Nasser. It was adding fuel to a fire. It was making a friend at the risk—or in the hope—of an explosion which would rock the West and enhance Russian power.

Tsarist Russia too pursued expansionist aims in the Arab and African world as part of her rivalry with Britain and because she could not solve her social problems at home. In this respect, as in others, Soviet Russia walks in the footsteps of her monarchist predecessors. In 1945 and 1946, Stalin publicly tried to take over Turkey. Backed by the United States, the Turks became hard and indigestible. Stalin then asked for a United Nations trusteeship over Tripolitania (Libya) which would give Russia her place in the African sun. This move also failed.

It was inevitable after Britain abandoned her military base at Suez in 1954 that somebody would have to fill the power vacuum. The United States might have seen this simple truth and made an arrangement to replace Britain as it did in Greece and Turkey in 1947. But the idea, apparently, did not occur to the right people. Stalin's heirs waited wisely till the Arab-Israel situation grew to crisis proportions and then shipped heavy arms to one side. That finally gave the Soviets their coveted foothold near the Suez Canal, the throat of Eurasia. To deepen their influence they must keep the region in turmoil. They will exploit and exacerbate the implacable Arab animosity toward Israel. They will fan the ancient rivalry between Egypt and Iraq, which goes back to Biblical times when Iraq was Babylon, and support anti-West Egypt against pro-West Iraq while simultaneously endeavoring to wean Iraq from the West. They will use Syria as a pawn against Iraq and Turkey. In another area they will keep Germany divided and West Germany painfully nostalgic for her eastern third.

In 1946, Stalin could have had peace with the West. But when he saw Germany in ruins, Italy and France politically immobilized by giant Communist parties, England exhausted and the American armed forces going home, he was unable to resist the temptation to bid for the hegemony of all Europe. That precipitated the cold war.

Again at the summit conference in Geneva in the summer of 1955 the Kremlin could have had peace with the West. Indeed peace actually broke out. But the skies darkened when Middle East opportunities knocked at Moscow's gate.

Soviet arms were actually going to Egypt during the Geneva summit conference. Faced with the possibility of expansion and mischief Russia succumbed.

This is the power-politics reality behind Communism's "peace" and "coexistence" propaganda barrage.

Asia and Africa are witnesses and possible victims of a grandiose power contest between Russia and America. One might understand their taking advantage of it or hiding from it, but not being befuddled by it. For clarity's sake they need to recognize the existence and true nature of Soviet imperialism.

Some of the most brilliant Asian and African intellectuals are as naïve as my young Communist friend in Moscow whom I shocked by mentioning Soviet imperialism. Their logic is: all imperialisms we have known were capitalistic; Russia is not capitalistic; therefore Russia is not imperialistic. Perhaps the savagery in Hungary and the brutal Soviet pressures on Poland and the other Muscovite colonies will at last clear away the sophistry and cobwebs. That foreign policy is blind which does not reckon with Soviet imperialism.

Imperialism or power motives actuate Europe and America too. But most western governments are subject to the checks inherent in freedom; witness the decisive effect which the opposition of the Labour party, the press, the church, student groups, and individual citizens had on Prime Minister Eden's Suez policy. For this and other reasons western imperialism is recessive, sclerotic, and apologetic, whereas Soviet imperialism is new and brutal, yet self-righteous, and whoever challenges it is a "Fascist" and "warmonger." Even in its virile middle age, British rule in India, for instance, became its own gravedigger by allowing certain circumscribed civil rights. The Soviet empire must, of necessity, aim to destroy remnants of freedom within, and threaten freedom beyond, its borders.

Whether the order of the day is smiles or frowns, talks

or threats, disarmament or rearmament, the East-West conflict, which is really a Soviet empire-West struggle, will be with us for a long time. It can best be resolved by the growth of democracy in Russia's satellites and the consequent Soviet withdrawal to pre-1939 boundaries. That would belatedly spread freedom inside Russia. The process can of course be accelerated by the further recession of western imperialism and the further reinforcement of civil liberties in the democracies.

Whatever befalls, Russia will not be inclined to seek success through a third world war. Wars have been fateful, and fatal, in Russia's history. They lead to political change or at least to considerable political ferment. The Russo-Japanese war of 1904–5 is an example. The First World War led to the overthrow of tsarism. During the Second World War, as Stalin revealed in a speech on May 24, 1945, "there were moments of desperation" when he was afraid of being ousted. Stalin's heirs know this history. Unless they can be sure of winning a war quickly they will not start it. And how can one be sure in the hydrogen-atomic age?

With a major war most unlikely, and with even small wars ending in stalemate (witness the Korean, Indo-Chinese, and Israeli-Egyptian wars), the world is faced with a new situation. It must find a substitute for war. This is now the essence of international politics. Throughout modern history, the balance of power has usually been readjusted by periodic wars. Today governments are seeking means of adjusting it without wars. Already certain factors have commenced to operate in producing a realignment of world forces. Among these factors one might list: foreign aid; propaganda; pacts and blocs; voting in the United Nations; the trend toward regional unification—in Europe, for instance; the economic decline of some nations and the industrial growth of others; and popular movements against imperial domination.

PART II

TROUBLE IN THE SATELLITES

CHAPTER 11

High Explosive

Stalin used to say that support of the Soviet Union was the only internationalism. The foreign Communist met this requirement by being a Soviet nationalist; his motto was: Russia right or wrong, my country.

But when this foreign Communist became a ruler a conflict arose: was he to be loyal to Russia or to his own native Yugoslavia or Czechoslovakia or Poland or Rumania? Theoretically he could do both, bow to Moscow-Mecca and plow the home field. In practice the Soviets demanded his full allegiance at the expense if need be—and it usually was—of his fatherland. "Russia is your only fatherland," the Kremlin preached, and out of habit and gratitude (for it was the Red army that had raised the satellite bosses to power) the foreign Communist served the Soviet Union.

Marshal Tito was the first to demur. Having fought the enemy during World War II and built up an army and an administrative apparatus in the process, he had the strength, pride, temerity, and sagacity to ask some measure of self-determination. The foolish Red pope, calling this an unforgivable heresy, hurled verbal thunderbolts at the Yugoslavs —they were "Fascists," "Turkish assassins," "Bukharinites," and "butchers"—and, in June, 1948, placed Tito under a ban. Tito survived the anathema and lived to father a cult of his own, the cult of Titoism. It is a high explosive which will crack the Soviet empire.

Moscow always champions the nationalisms which hurt other empires. In its own there must be no nationalism but Soviet nationalism. Titoism is national Communism, a blend of Yugoslav—or Hungarian, Polish, Czechoslovak, Bulgarian, Rumanian, Albanian—nationalism with Communism. Stalin foresaw the damage it could cause his empire.

Like his progenitors Marx, Lenin, and Ivan the Terrible, Stalin was intolerant and monopolistic. His viceroys in Warsaw, Prague, Budapest, Bucharest, Belgrade, and Tirana had to obey worshipfully. Tito, however, intended to reign as well as rule, and when he rebelled with impunity and prospered after the Kremlin had pushed him beyond the pale in June, 1948, he spawned friends in the satellites.

Stalin chastised them with Stalinist ruthlessness. (Any other adjective would be an understatement.) Yet Titoism outlived Stalin, and his heirs quickly realized that it was an indestructible force which they must woo and destroy. To this end Bulganin and Khrushchev flew to Belgrade in May, 1955, in what, in retrospect, has proved to be a far-seeing attempt to save the empire by aborting other Titos.

In the first moment at the airport, Khrushchev, with characteristically planned impetuosity, tried to lure Tito back into the Soviet fold. Rebuffed, the Kremlin pair agreed, in a final communiqué, that there could be two roads to socialism. This constituted a paper recognition by the mother church of a schismatic congregation with missionary ambitions.

Tito's plans included the resurrection (rehabilitation) of executed Titoists, the banishment from the satellites of ruling Stalinists, and the conversion of all Communists to Titoism. On the surface this looked like Everestian vanity, the little Yugoslav tail (sixteen million inhabitants) was trying to wag the great Russian bear. Actually Tito's strength lay in the contagion of an idea which he incorporated: the idea of national independence and relief from imperialist exploitation. Patriotism lay dormant in the subconscious of the foreign Communist while he lived as an exile in the Soviet Union or worked in the illegal underground abroad. It burgeoned and began to pinch when he felt the heavy Russian hand on the satellites and noticed that Tito had eluded it.

Tito's freedom had numerous alluring advantages: Yugoslavia received large quantities of food, raw materials, industrial equipment, and arms (including American jet planes) from the West, and after the 1955 reconciliation Russia too sent aid. Independence made Yugoslavia the object of East-West suitors bringing gifts.

Release from Moscow's vise, moreover, enabled Tito to depart from petrified Stalinist policies at home. After a period of experimentation and hope, the Yugoslav government disbanded the compulsory farm collectives in March, 1953, and permitted the peasantry to revert to private farming on privately owned land. The Titoists, to be sure, retain the ingrained Marxist prejudice against capitalistic agriculture and arouse the peasant suspicion by occasional sighs for village socialism. But they content themselves with fostering cooperative retail shops, cooperative marketing, and cooperative use of machinery, and favoring the few remaining voluntary collectives as examples. Despite the heavy taxation of prosperous peasants and the technological backwardness of farm methods which have prevented Yugoslavia to this day from achieving food self-sufficiency, the situation is a vast improvement for the peasant over collectivization. For the government it means relief from the back-breaking, resentment-breeding task of directing and supervising every minute act in the peasant's daily work cycle. The abolition of imposed collectives has an explosive attraction for Russia's satellites and would have for Russia if the peasants knew about it.

In industry too the Titoists introduced an innovation

which excites interest and admiration in the satellites, notably Poland. Next to collectivized farming, the worst economic abomination in Russia is its twin brother, centralized state management of all industry and trade. At the twentieth party congress in February, 1956, decentralization was briefly discussed as a palliative, and a few quick steps have since been made in that direction. But the opposite of centralization is not decentralization; an office in Kiev or Tiflis can be just as submerged in bureaucratic red tape as one in Moscow. The antidote to centralization is democracy or control from below. This is the goal of the Titoist system of workers' councils which, replacing state-capitalist bureaucracy, manage all Yugoslavia's industrial and commercial enterprises. The goal is still unattained and the system is far from perfect. But as a form of guild socialism or economic democracy the councils have a potential that might even burst the iron ring of Yugoslav Communism itself and permit freedom to enter.

A further Yugoslav departure from Soviet Stalinism inheres in the evolution of the Communist party, which no longer rules. Its rank-and-file members, and its intellectuals, no longer pretend to be the masters of the country. Power resides in the Tito-Rankovich-Kardelj triumvirate, dominated by the towering, leader-type figure of the confident Marshal, and in a number of regional and district party personalities—all enjoying the support of the army and of the vigilant secret police. From being a one-party state, Yugoslavia has become a no-party state. The party as an instrument of power withered away because the state in effect withdrew from direct management of the national economy. In the village the peasant replaced it; in the cities, the workers' councils.

The relationship between Yugoslav people and leadership might be described as musical. Both sides play politics by ear. The people, taught practical wisdom by the rich experience of their history-packed country, listen carefully for indications of government policy and usually conform to it, either out of helplessness or expediency or self-interest. The leaders, aware of their limited popularity and eager not to tread too heavily on the toes of the tough fighting races they rule, have their ears to the ground for grumbles and know when to retreat. That is what happened when the farm collectives were dissolved.

This live-and-let-live truce is a far cry from the total interference of Stalinism and will find an increasing number of imitators in the satellites.

Stalin's heirs understood the pull of Tito: he represented a rejection of Stalinist rigors and rigidity; he stood for nationalism; eastern Europeans admired him as the only courageous Communist who had defied Stalin and survived and actually extracted an apology from the Kremlin. Some Soviet leaders hated him for it all; others sought his friendly cooperation on the assumption that if he accepted Moscow's embrace, the dissidents in the satellites would not seek a divorce.

Khrushchev, accordingly, acceded to Tito's demands.

Were Stalin not visible under a glass in the Red Square mausoleum it might be said that he turned in his grave as one after the other of his national Communist victims throughout eastern Europe was restored to honor while his favorites were dethroned at Tito's prompting.

Here a vehement debate erupted among western experts on where Tito stood. Had he been taken into camp by the Russian? Was he supporting Khrushchev against Kremlin Stalinists? Did he secretly dream of drawing the satellites into a Titoist bloc? In any case, why was Moscow conceding so much to him?

Tito was not returning to the Soviet orbit. Why exchange his independent eminence for the miserable insecure status of a dangling Moscow puppet? Moreover, the Yugoslavs are patriots and would make trouble for him if he voluntarily and foolishly put his and their necks into the Muscovite noose again.

It is equally beyond dispute that Tito lacked the power to force any policy on the Soviet leaders. They would take his advice only if it made sense. What he must have been saying was: national Communism is rife in the satellites and should be conciliated by expelling the Stalinists and adopting a policy of moderation.

The Kremlin's seismograph apparently was registering advance rumblings of the earthquake soon to shake Poland and Hungary, and Moscow therefore granted the Titoist concessions to placate dissatisfied elements.

Presently fire and smoke burst forth. In April, May, and June, 1956, Prague witnessed protests by students and writers. The city of Poznan rose in revolt on June 28 and 29. Elsewhere in Poland, and in Hungary, coming events were casting black shadows before.

At this point the Soviets changed their line toward Tito, either because of a shift of power in the Kremlin leadership or because the same leaders who had flirted with Tito in order to avert trouble now decided that softness to satellite Titoism had actually precipitated trouble.

The new line was laid down in a secret letter dispatched early in August, 1956, by Moscow to the capitals of the "people's democracies" admonishing them to avoid Titoism. In Prague on October 17, 1956, I asked Vaclav David, the Czechoslovak Foreign Minister, about the letter. He said he had never heard of it. The next day I asked Viliam Siroky, the Czechoslovak Prime Minister. He said no such letter existed. "Then perhaps telegraphic instructions or an oral communication," I suggested. "No," he replied, "but there are always consultations."

In Belgrade, during the second half of that month, high Yugoslav officials told me that the letter as printed in the *Washington Post* of October 17 was substantially if not textually accurate. The key passage reads, ". . . Socialism can only be built under the banner of internationalism, in close liaison with the socialist countries, and not under the banner of nationalism, without liaison with socialist countries."

"The banner of internationalism" is Kremlinese for Russia; "the banner of nationalism" is Kremlinese for Yugoslavia. Tito, the letter declared in effect, could not establish socialism. That could only be done by nations intimately associated with the Soviet Union. In other words, do not copy Tito, rally 'round Russia.

In Belgrade the secret letter caused consternation, then anger. On September 19, Khrushchev flew to Yugoslavia and conferred with Tito at Brioni. On September 27, Tito flew with Khrushchev to Yalta. It was Tito's first airplane trip and everybody reasoned that the mission must be very important. He returned home on October 5. The world buzzed with curiosity.

Sometimes the student of politics can extract information which solves a mystery, at other times he is merely allowed to see the logic of a situation. In Belgrade, during the second fortnight of October, the Yugoslavs were revealing no secrets about the Brioni-Yalta talks. But they did accuse Moscow of "insincerity"; its entire policy since the Belgrade visit of Bulganin and Khrushchev in May, 1955, had been "insincere," I was told. Yugoslav Communists who were pro-Soviet when I argued with them in the autumn of 1955 compounded my criticism of Russia with strictures of their own in the autumn of 1956. Most significant, they were contemptuous of the Russian leaders' intelligence. Politburo member Moshe Piyade spoke of "the dumb Russians." Nevertheless, the Yugoslav bond with the Soviets resisted this subjective corrosion. Publicly the Yugoslav government expressed no indignation at Russia's murder-by-tank in Hungary.

The objective logic of the situation is the similarity of Communist interests. To Moscow, Tito's national Communism is repugnant and subversive because anti-imperialist. But the Marshal cautioned the Kremlin that unless it accepted national Communism it might get something much worse: a multiparty democracy which neither he nor it wanted. The Brioni-Yalta talks could only have projected a mutually beneficial bargain by which Moscow would tolerate Tito's influence in the satellites if he undertook to help prevent Titoism from evolving toward democracy as it was destined to do in the first week of November, 1956, in Hungary.

The Moscow "hards" frowned on this marshmallow solution, and, in a manner which would have won the approbation of Papa Stalin, put their reliance in steel—the steel of the tanks that fired shells into the soft flesh of living men, women, and youths in Budapest.

Tito reacted to Moscow's new line with bitterness tempered by comprehension. Bitterness impelled him to lift the curtain on the Brioni-Yalta conversations and to shed light on the factional fight in the Kremlin. He did this in a remarkable speech at the Adriatic port of Pula on November 11, 1956.

Anti-Stalin to his marrow, Tito declared that "the new Soviet leaders saw that thanks to Stalin's madness the Soviet Union was in a very difficult position" at home, abroad, and in the satellites. But in de-Stalinizing they "wrongly dealt with the whole matter as a question of the cult of personality and not as a question of the system . . . They have not launched an attack against that system . . . it was . . . the system which made the creation of the cult of personality possible." In Russia and the satellites, Tito asserted, some Communists are working to bring this Stalin system "back to life and power. Here are the roots which must be corrected."

Yugoslavia, he continued, had improved her relations with Moscow. In Belgrade in 1955 and in Moscow in 1956, the Yugoslav and Soviet leaders signed declarations about differing roads to socialism—this implied recognition of Titoism as a permissible path for the satellites. "Unfortunately," Tito added, the Soviet leaders "did not understand it this way. They thought, 'Well, since the Yugoslavs are so stubborn, we will respect and implement these declarations, but not as they affect the others, for there the situation is different . . .' But this is wrong, because the same elements which provoked the resistance of Yugoslavia in 1948 also live in these eastern countries, in Poland, Hungary, and the others, in some more, in some less." In Moscow, Tito said, he warned the Kremlin that anti-Stalinists in other eastern countries might resist as Yugoslavia had "and this would be much harder to rectify."

Later came Brioni and Yalta: "We saw that things would go in a rather difficult manner as far as other countries were concerned because the Soviet leaders had different attitudes toward these countries—toward Poland, Hungary, and others. We did not, however, consider this attitude tragic since we perceived that this was not the attitude of the entire Soviet leadership but only of a part which had, to a certain degree, forced its attitude upon the other part."

Despite this triumph of the Stalinist elements in the Soviet leadership which Tito noticed at Yalta in October, 1956, he still, "judging by certain signs and conversations," optimistically and mistakenly trusted the anti-Stalinist faction to regain the upper hand.

However, Tito admitted, even the anti-Stalin forces in the Kremlin showed "insufficient confidence in the socialist forces" of the satellites. "When the Poznan affair occurred . . . the Soviet men suddenly changed their attitude toward us. They grew colder. They thought we Yugoslavs were responsible. Yes, we were responsible," Tito proudly agreed, ". . . because we made Yugoslavia what she is and the influence of this Yugoslavia extends beyond our borders."

Moscow notwithstanding, the developments in Poland proved favorable, the new Gomulka regime was steering a course toward "democratization and complete independence and also good relations with the Soviet Union," Tito said. The Polish anti-Communist reactionaries consequently lost their chance.

Some satellite bosses did not welcome the Polish changes. One of these was Enver Hoxha, the puny Stalin of little Albania, "a scoundrel," Tito called him, "a so-called Marxist . . . who can only pronounce the words Leninism and Marxism and nothing else." Diplomatically he refrained from castigating the Czechoslovak and other Stalinist leaders.

During this June, 1956, visit to Moscow, Tito revealed in the same Pula speech, he cautioned the Kremlin on Hungary: "We said that Rakosi's regime and Rakosi himself had no qualifications to lead the Hungarian state or to establish internal unity. Unfortunately the Soviet leaders did not believe this and they all said Rakosi was an old revolutionary and that he was honest, et cetera. As far as I know him, especially after the Rajk trial and after all other things, I cannot assert that he is honest. For me, such people are the most dishonest in the world . . . On my journey to Moscow some were surprised that I did not travel through Hungary. But I did not travel through Hungary because of Rakosi. I said I would not go through Hungary even if it cut the travel time to a third."

When Moscow finally did oust Rakosi, Tito continued, it replaced him with Ernoe Geroe, "who in no way differed from Rakosi." But it was clear that "the Hungarian people absolutely opposed the Stalinist elements who were still in power." Moscow's mistake of retaining Rakosi too long and putting Geroe in his place provoked the Hungarian revolution.

These anti-Kremlin recriminations mirror one side of the true Tito; he vilified Moscow for obstructing the introduction of Titoism and took the occasion to taunt Russia with having thereby sown the wind and reaped the Hungarian whirlwind.

Next Tito showed his other face. Although the Soviets

erred in interfering with tanks on October 23, 1956, at the
first outburst of popular frenzy against the Geroe regime, the
second armed intervention a few days later, Tito affirmed,
was justified, for "the Soviet government could not tolerate
any interference from the West and the return to power of
the Horthyites and of the old reactionary forces." Why did he
arbitrarily brand them as reactionaries when all the evidence
shows that they were workers, students, peasants, soldiers,
and intellectuals inflamed by the horrors of prolonged Stalinism? Because, Tito said, "they gave orders against the use of
the word 'comrade' and removed the red stars." Communists
and secret policemen were hanged. "It was a general massacre. In Sopron twenty Communists were hanged . . . This
was done by the ferocious Fascist and counterrevolutionary
mob. The Nagy government . . . instead of fighting these
developments . . . issued a declaration denouncing the Warsaw pact which tied Hungary to a military alliance with
Russia and the other satellites and announcing her independence, as though that was the most important thing in this
difficult situation, as though Hungarian departure from the
Warsaw pact was of any significance." (To the Hungarians
liberation from Soviet tutelage was of utmost significance,
indeed it is their essential aim, for while Russian arms rule
Hungary no freedom is possible.)

If the Soviet's second intervention with tanks "had to rescue socialism in Hungary then, comrades," Tito declared, "we
can say that we consider the Soviet intervention necessary
although," he continued in disregard of the discrepancy, "we
are against interference in the domestic affairs of other countries."

He repeated for emphasis: the second Soviet armed intervention which began November 4 "was a bad thing, but if it
carried out the rescue of socialism in Hungary in order to
permit the further development of socialism . . . then this
whole affair would be a positive one—but on condition that

the Soviet troops withdraw the moment the situation in Hungary becomes settled and peaceful."

Tito is an artist; all great politicians are. In this speech he helpfully painted his self-portrait. The most prominent color is red. He is a Communist. If blue stands for independence, there are large blotches of it in the painting. But the white of democracy is missing. Titoism's ideal would be a system of sovereign Communist nations, not dominated by but linked to Moscow (and to Yugoslavia), each evolving economic and social forms that suit its national personality but none abandoning government by an oligarchy which speaks in the name of the dictatorship of the proletariat.

One evening in Belgrade late in October, 1956, I received an unexpected phone call from Milovan Djilas, once a member of the Yugoslav Communist party's Politburo and fourth man in the Belgrade hierarchy, but ousted in 1954 from the leadership and party membership and now a private citizen. He asked me to come to his home or to meet him in town, which meant in a café. (Obviously, I thought, Belgrade is not Moscow.)

Djilas, formerly a passionate Titoist, and close friend of Tito, had sinned by publishing a series of articles in a Yugoslav Communist daily advocating greater personal liberty for all citizens and free elections. That these writings could appear in a Communist state was proof of considerable liberalism, but the subsequent punitive expulsion showed that even national Communism reacts against democracy.

At the party hearing where Djilas was criticized and ostracized, Tito discerningly traced his heresy to western influences that were dangerous to a one-party dictatorship. And, in fact, Djilas later moved to a more advanced position—which he could only outline in the foreign press; he urged a multiparty democracy for Yugoslavia.

When I arrived at Djilas's home in October, 1956, he told me he had no political ambitions—strange statement for one who had been so near the power summit, yet believable because he is essentially an intellectual interested in ideas. Be that as it may, his faith in a western-type social democracy had grown more fervent. He even outlined an article in a future Yugoslav charter of freedom which would stipulate that none of the political parties could represent a religion, or a national minority, or the idea of monarchist restoration.

In a way Djilas's personal history parallels the progress of Hungary from Stalinism to Titoism to the democracy which the tanks temporarily flattened. Djilasism is something Tito fears in his own country and in the satellites and Russia. He wants the evolution away from Stalinism to stop at Titoism.

However, the inventor rarely controls his invention, any more than the mother can tie her offspring to her apron strings. Titoism is a greased inclined plane, or a halfway house for a weekend of history. Whether it lasts a year or ten, it is no more than a phase which, by the laws of dialectics, will pass.

From their own point of view, therefore, the unregenerate Stalinists are right. "Keep off the inclined plane," is their policy. Titoism, they suspect, willy-nilly carries in its bloodstream the germs that will ultimately kill Communist dictatorship and Russian imperialism. Kremlin Stalinists prefer the permanent deep freeze and must view with alarm the portentous results of the Titoist thaw in Poland and Hungary. At the least, they hope to keep it from spreading to the other satellites. If possible they would recapture the two prodigals, and Yugoslavia, and return them to the bosoms of Mother Russia and Father Stalin.

Now came the perfect curtain scene of the play. Moscow launched a furious attack on Tito, whose national Communism is a mortal menace to the Soviet empire, and Tito arrested Djilas, whose social democracy is a mortal menace to Yugoslav Communism.

Both performers acted in character. Quite humorlessly, after Russia had interfered with tanks in the affairs of Communist Hungary and had tried to interfere in the Communist party elections in Poland, *Pravda* (November 19, 1956) charged that Tito's speech at Pula reflected "a tendency to interfere in the affairs of other Communist parties." A fine example of Hottentot double-standard morality! Moreover, Tito's attempt in that address "to divide Communist parties into 'Stalinists' and 'non-Stalinists' can, objectively, only cause harm to the Communist movement." Continuing, *Pravda* compared Tito's statement that "the cult of personality" was not the sin of a man but of the system with similar inventions of "reactionary propaganda in its battle against Marxism-Leninism." In general, *Pravda* stated, "the speech contains a number of declarations which, both in form and substance, contradict the principles of proletarian internationalism and the international solidarity of the toilers." These are wicked words.

The Kremlin, however, may have found consolation in Tito's arrest of Djilas which followed immediately on the *Pravda* attack. The position of Djilas had been anomalous since his banishment from the leadership in 1954, for though he was a lone-wolf democratic opponent of the Tito regime, it requited his frank hostility with magnanimous tolerance. But Djilas's article in the New York weekly *New Leader* of November 19 must have struck Tito at an irritable moment and in a sensitive spot. "The experience of Yugoslavia," wrote Djilas, "appears to testify that national Communism is incapable of transcending the boundaries of Communism as such, that is, to institute the kind of reforms that would gradually transform and lead Communism to freedom." Tito could not enjoy this stab in the face. Djilas made it much worse by saying that Yugoslavia's role as a catalyst of national Communism in eastern Europe was no longer crucial. National Communism in Poland and Hungary now had a momentum of its own and did not depend on Tito. Finally, and unforgivably, Djilas accused the Yugoslav government of abandoning its principles by not voting in the United Nations Security Council against Russian military intervention in Hungary. It did this, he said, to defend "its narrow ideological and bureaucratic class interests," that is, to protect its dictatorship against the democracy which threatened from Hungary.

For this article, which was far less critical of the Yugoslav government than hundreds of articles in the Polish press that condemn the Polish government, Marxism, Communism, and Russia, Djilas received a sentence of three years' imprisonment.

Tito can arrest Djilas but he cannot arrest the course of freedom in Yugoslavia or in other Communist lands. Moscow may reprimand Tito but it cannot bid the tide of nationalist liberation which engulfs all empires to stand still before the Soviet empire. History does not stop even on dictators' orders.

The dilemma of Yugoslavia, which is the dilemma of all national Communists, was well put at the Bombay Asian Socialist Conference in November, 1956, by Sutan Sjharir of Indonesia. Turning to the Yugoslav fraternal delegates, he said, "Can you really work for the increase of freedom while you practice totalitarianism?" You can up to a point, but the point is quickly reached, and then the Titos must arrest their Djilases and retreat, or go on and give up totalitarianism. This is the problem that now faces Yugoslavia and Poland and will ultimately face all the satellites. Their nemesis is the human being's innate desire to be free. Even a person born in prison wants liberty.

Soviet imperialism is fully aware of the satellites' dilemma and consequently opposes national Communism with the same animosity it brings to individual liberty. Therefore, and despite all the coming and going and conferring between Tito and Khrushchev and Co., the new, post-1955 Yugoslav-Soviet friendship died aborning. It was buried by *Pravda* attacks and Belgrade replies, and finally by Koca Popovic, Yugoslav Foreign Minister, in a speech to the Federal Assembly on February 26, 1957, in which he stated that his country had no intention of joining the Soviet camp. He charged, moreover, that "Stalinism . . . brought incomparably more evil to the cause of socialism in the period following World War II than all imperialistic conspiracies combined." Moscow retaliated by cutting aid and trade to Yugoslavia.

Thus Tito has arrived at the dark end of a blind alley. Communism obstructs his relations with the West; nationalism blocks his friendship with Russia. In domestic policy too he has reached an impasse where his political support is as limited as his economic progress.

The Yugoslav situation cries out for a revolutionary release from the strait jacket of dictatorship. Tito needs Djilas. Nationalism plus democracy would bring Tito more strength than national Communism.

CHAPTER 12

The Four Laggards

Mr. Viliam Siroky, the Prime Minister of Czechoslovakia, said, "over 90 per cent of the population" supported his government. Incredulous, I asked the opinion of a taxi driver. "Maximum 10 per cent," he replied. That makes at least 100 per cent.

In the Soviet Union one usually had to extract opposition views; in Czechoslovakia they gushed forth spontaneously. The day before the end of my second 1956 stay in Prague, I went into the State Bank to convert surplus crowns into dollars. The teller put a blank with carbon copy into his typewriter and filled in numerous particulars. Then he typed out a second questionnaire with carbon copy. He signed both and passed them to a superior at his elbow for countersigning. "What a waste of time and energy," I observed. "In any other country I would have handed in the crowns and received the dollars twenty seconds later."

"Not in any other country," the superior official corrected, "in any western country." He was showing where his sympathies lay.

I sat down beside a taxi driver and gave him my destination. "Speak German?" I asked.

"No," he replied.

"English?"

"Sorry, no."

"Russian?"

"No, no, no," he shouted and pumped his thumbs downward violently. He was venting his resentment of Russia.

Standing before a painting at an exhibit of modern art in a Prague museum, I said to an unknown man beside me, "Doesn't look like socialist realism, does it?"

"And a good thing it isn't," he said.

He was a young sculptor. I asked about his work. "The creative person is not honored," he whispered. I inquired about general conditions. He looked around; there were other visitors within earshot. He put his fingers in front of his lips; then he crossed his wrists and pressed them together.

This pantomime of silence and slavery I saw many times during my sojourn in Prague. Nevertheless, people did talk even with strangers. Walking one day down a broad corridor of the Foreign Office, I asked a man for directions. He proved to be the head of a geographical division who had worked in the department before the war under the late Foreign Minister Jan Masaryk. "Wonderful figure," I volunteered.

"A patriot and gentleman," he commented.

We were standing near a window and both of us looked down into the courtyard on whose stones, on March 10, 1948, Masaryk died. Whether he was pushed out or he jumped out because the Communists left him no other choice, it was murder. The man shook his head sadly. . . .

"And how are things now?" I asked after a pause.

"We miss our freedom," he said.

I could report forty similar conversations.

Under a dictatorship, however, opposition may exist for years without exploding unless ignited by a spark or match. Stalin's death in March, 1953, encouraged hopes of liberation or at least relaxation in Czechoslovakia. When, instead, the Prague government announced a monetary reform for June 1, 1953, which amounted to confiscation of savings and wages, workingmen in Pilsen, supported by trade-union leaders and even Communists who tore up their party cards, went on strike, and masses of people congregated in silence at a spot where American soldiers fell in combat with Nazis. General Patton, commanding U.S. tanks, liberated Pilsen in May, 1945; citizens demonstrated for their American wartime liberators as a protest against their peacetime Russian oppressors. None of them required a historian's equipment to realize that had Patton captured Prague—only three hours by road from Pilsen—rather than idle and let the Soviets take it, Czechoslovakia would have remained free. (The whole face of Europe would be different today if Anglo-American armed forces had been permitted by their governments to precede the Russians into Berlin and Vienna.)

Pilsen was a flash in the dark. It is too early to assess its significance or to say that it had none.

The next Czechoslovak flare-up occurred in April, May, and June, 1956, and was clearly the result of the Moscow twentieth party congress and its repercussions in Poland and Hungary. In those two countries students, journalists, and writers were laying down the verbal barrage for the revolutions soon to follow. In Czechoslovakia students and writers likewise came to life. Poets took the lead. At the writers' congress which opened in Prague on April 22, 1956, and lasted a long week, Jaroslav Seifert, a Czech poet, used both indirect rhetorical questions, whose import was clear, and direct accusations. "Again and again," he said, "we hear at this congress from not unimportant personalities that it is necessary for writers to tell the truth. This must mean that during recent years the writers did not tell the truth. Now, did they or did they not? Voluntarily or involuntarily? Willingly or unwillingly? Without enthusiasm or in hearty agreement? . . . I ask you, where were all of us in 1948, when Czech literature was 'presided over' by a man without the knowledge even of the Czech language . . . Where were we when this man dispatched groups of twenty-year-old boys and girls who, with

the energy of youth, ordered the plates of Czech books
smashed and destroyed? . . . Where were we when many a
librarian, out of caution, cowardice, anger, or improper enthusiasm, laid his hands on our libraries to destroy them and
to build . . . new libraries consisting of books published only
after February, 1948," the date of the Communist seizure of
power?

Quoting John Stuart Mill and Voltaire, he exclaimed,
"Think of the writers in jail; let us think of their human fate.
We have no right to judge their guilt or innocence. But as a
Czech poet I have a right to express my opinion that they
have suffered enough for their political guilt and errors."

This brave assault was not an isolated performance. "It was
unhealthy and humiliating for Czech literature," said Frantisek Hrubin, another poet, "that during the past years its
problems could not be discussed frankly. Poets were compelled to write festive tirades, but a corrected proverb would
say that love enforced is not really love." He complained that
Jiri Kolar, who "would shed blood rather than adapt himself
and lick boots," was "forced into isolation and his existence
eventually destroyed. This is inhuman and uncultured . . .
If many of us are not ashamed today our children will be
ashamed tomorrow." At the time of the funeral of a well-
known Czech poet, Hrubin declared, "I wrote some verses
but cannot find them because at that time it was not very safe
to carry such things in one's pocket."

Ladislav Nmacko, a Slovak writer, addressing the same
congress, called out, "They arrested my friend whom I re-
spected and liked. They upset my thoughts . . . my conscience was alarmed."

These and many similar outbursts so disconcerted the
party management of Czechoslovakia that its biggest piece
of artillery, Antonin Zapotocky, President of the Republic,
the most influential Communist in the land, was rolled into
action. He admitted, citing the Moscow twentieth party con-

gress, that the cult of personality had hurt Czechoslovak literature. That congress, he said, "established an unusually favorable atmosphere for all creative forces in art." But—the cannon began to resemble a corkscrew—"it is necessary, in particular, to wage a hard and consistent struggle against the remnants of the old world, against bourgeois ideas, theories, and opinions which remain in the minds of people." Nevertheless, "the writer must be completely free and fix his own artistic task." However, the party "of course considers and will consider as its political aim the open and honest winning of all writers to its side for the cause of socialism and communism."

President Zapotocky's broad assurances and veiled admonitions must be read in the light of subsequent events. Some authors were released from prison, but frank speaking and the official publication of such outcries as those of the poets stopped abruptly. When I mentioned this in October, 1956, to Minister of Culture Frantisek Kahuda, Foreign Minister Vaclav David, and Prime Minister Viliam Siroky and said the writers had been frightened into submission, all three answered in almost the exact words: "No, the writers expressed their opinions and we as Communists expressed ours. After all, we have the same right to free speech." But the voice of the government is terrifying thunder.

Parallel with but probably independently of the writers, the students vented their anger. Both groups were reacting to the Soviet twentieth party congress in February, 1956. In April, students at Prague, Bratislava, and other universities began drafting resolutions which they displayed on bulletin boards and circulated by airmail and motorcycle couriers to schools throughout the country. These were compressed into a composite resolution submitted to Minister of Culture Kahuda on May 12. Its contents, reported by Sidney Gruson in the *New York Times* of May 28, and confirmed, at least in part—but even that is startling—by Czechoslovak govern-

ment sources, were truly remarkable if one considers that it
was drawn up by youths, in their early twenties at the oldest,
whose brains had been baking in the Marxist-Leninist fur-
nace for eight years. The resolution demanded that the people have the right to control members of Parliament and
recall them; that more than one political party be permitted
to function; that the radio and press report news honestly
and immediately; that the jamming of foreign radio stations
stop; that western literature and films be made available; that
citizens enjoy freedom to travel; that political prisoners be
amnestied, investigators responsible for extortion of confessions be punished, and court records be published; that the
Soviet flag be displayed only on Soviet holidays and not, as
customary, whenever the Czechoslovak flag appeared; and
that the Soviet national anthem be heard less frequently.
"*One* country, *one* flag, *one* anthem," the students of Prague's
Charles University chanted. In addition, the students wanted
better housing, fewer courses in Marxism-Leninism, and no
compulsory study of the Russian language.

These demands were not granted. On the contrary, the
students were gagged. In language which neither they nor
the writers could fail to understand, party and government
publications ordered criticism stopped. *Zivot Strany* declared, "The Communist party of Czechoslovakia has stated
and will continue to state that it will not grant 'freedom' of
expression to hostile viewpoints . . . We understand freedom
in the class sense as freedom for workers, not for exploiters
and their agents." *Mlada Fronta* said, "Our Communist party
has called attention to alien, unsocialistic tendencies which
have recently been manifested by some writers and a small
part of the university student body. We have to wage a battle
against all such influences."

In a summary of his tour of Czechoslovakia and other satellites, John Freeman, editor of the London *New Statesman
and Nation,* wrote in the July 21, 1956, issue of his paper,

". . . Jiri Hendrich, the Central Secretary (Ideology) of the Czech Communist Party, when asked to discuss in theoretical terms what 'democratization' really means, answered me with concrete instances of the decentralization of industrial and economic planning . . . When I asked Jiri Hendrich in Prague to define the political changes as defined by the Czech party, he surprised me by beginning his answer with these words: 'Basically nothing has changed here.'"

I too concluded after visiting Prague that the Czechoslovak leadership was 100 per cent Stalinist and deeply convinced of the necessity of remaining so. It refused to step out onto the slippery slope of de-Stalinization for fear that popular and intellectual discontents would quickly drag it down to the "hell" of democracy. Instead it stood firmly planted on the flat rock of unyielding totalitarianism. "If you give the people a finger you get troubles like Poznan and the cold revolution in Poland and the hot one of Hungary . . . If you muzzle the malcontents early you don't have to summon the tanks later." These rules seem to guide the Czechoslovak Communist hierarchy. I found it difficult to argue the point with Prague officials; by their standards—and for the present—they are right. Even a little appeasement is dangerous when opposition is so widespread. I merely could not accept their proposition that this was "socialism" and "freedom." Moreover, they cannot sit on the lid forever.

The chief reason why the Czechoslovak government was able for so long to pursue a stern Stalinist course is, in the opinion of most experts, the country's relatively favorable economic condition. Arriving in Prague from Moscow, I found the higher standards of the former particularly impressive. The people seemed better dressed, gayer, and healthier than in Russia. The shops had more and finer goods and smaller crowds—because of high prices. The regime did not appear to waste large sums on "Stalinallees" or other façades. Prague as a city, in fact, though beautiful as ever, looked rather down at the heel; its buildings, buses, and trams were mostly pre-war. The Soviet Union, apparently, planned to make Czecho-slovakia a source of machine tools for other satellites and for Asian and western nations, and therefore supplied considera-ble quantities of raw materials to the Czechs who, being good workingmen and experienced organizers, put them to excel-lent use. Finally, since Czechoslovakia is 80 per cent indus-trial, the results of collectivization, while debilitating, were less disastrous than in the other, more rural "people's de-mocracies."

The second reason for Czechoslovakia's relatively smooth course since Stalin's demise is that whereas Poland, Hungary, and Bulgaria had purged their national Communists and thereby kept Titoist sentiment alive, Czechoslovakia purged her arch- and much-hated, Moscow-trained Stalinist, Rudolf Slansky, secretary-general of the Communist party, who was tried in November, 1952, together with thirteen others and executed. Though Slansky's successors were no less Stalinist and equally subservient to Moscow's wishes they seemed a relief by contrast with him. None among them was a Titoist. Poland had a national Communist alternative to Stalinism in Wladyslav Gomulka, as Hungary did in Imre Nagy. This was not the case in Czechoslovakia. No one of the post-Slansky Communist masters could make an appeal for mass support on the ground that he had been victimized by Moscow. They were all Moscow-appointed. Knowing how infinitesimal was their popularity (it is roughly in inverse ratio to the vote: 86 per cent of the total electorate voted Communist on May 30, 1948; 97.9 per cent on November 28, 1954), the leader-ship pursued the astute policy of leaning ostentatiously on the Soviet Union. On every possible occasion, including the most incongruous, the Czechoslovak Communist system stresses its intimacy and eternal identification with the Krem-lin as if to say to the people, "We know you don't love us, but our Big Brother does and he is very strong." *Rude Pravo* wrote on September 7, 1956, "The attitude toward the Soviet Union is no subject for discussion." Obviously not, for without the Soviet Union the present regime would be defunct. But though Russia guarantees the survival of the present Czechoslovak government by the threat of sanctions and interventions, no Soviet troops are stationed in the country. Czechoslovakia has consequently avoided the irritation caused by the presence of Russian soldiers in Hungary and Poland.

For the rest, Czechoslovakia has adapted some of the skillful administrative tactics of the old Austro-Hungarian empire, of which she once formed a part, to the harsh Communist regime. Concessions are made to reduce tension but they are not announced lest they provoke demands for more or recall the government's past errors. (Thus, in addition to writers, two Roman Catholic bishops, several of Slansky's co-defendants, and Maria Svermova, Slansky's deputy as party secretary, were quietly released from jail.) Alexej Cepicka, Minister of National Defense and Deputy Premier, lost those offices in a split second of de-Stalinization—he was cordially disliked—but received an important position as balm. Citizens are not usually persecuted when overheard expressing their hostility to the government in private, but are sternly penalized for public statements which might warrant the conclusion that the authorities had gone soft. If discontent mounts owing to a foreign crisis or an internal circumstance, the government has enough economic margin to raise wages here, reduce prices there, broaden the flow of commodities to a particularly disaffected area, and occasionally open the door of collectives to let uncooperative peasants out and regenerate "kulaks" in. Sometimes, as in the Slansky trial, the government uses anti-Semitism in an effort to win public backing; more often it stresses the danger of reborn German militarism. (Communists go on the assumption that since it is difficult to hate two enemies they can deflect hostility away from

Russia by keeping anti-German feeling alive.) And the Communist system never lets its subjects forget that it can wield a big stick. The reminder often takes the form of loud unproven assertions about a new plague of imperialist agents and spies who will be exterminated ruthlessly. By now the public recognizes this as a warning from the secret police to behave and beware.

Czechoslovakia (population fourteen million) is culturally and technologically the most advanced country in eastern Europe but also the leading laggard among the satellites. The other three are Rumania, Bulgaria, and Albania. In the struggle for national independence and personal freedom, the people of Poland and Hungary have left these four far behind.

Like Czechoslovakia, Rumania cuddles close by Russia's side. The official Bucharest daily, *Scanteia,* said on September 2, 1956, "The great experience of the Soviet Union and its Communist party is and will remain for us the principal source of teaching and inspiration, which will spare us many errors and fumblings." This is at once a rejection of Titoism and an espousal of the Kremlin. Yet the Kremlin caused the Rumanian puppet leadership some sleepless months when it de-Stalinized. For whereas de-Stalinization in Russia repaired broken political fences and entailed only a safe dose of liberalization as a by-product, in Rumania it would mean opening the floodgates to a wave of criticism and freedom which might sweep the regime into the discard. When Dr. Sarvapalli Radhakrishnan, the Vice President of India, addressed a special session of the Rumanian Grand National Assembly on June 27, 1956, and said, "The individual should not be a unit lost in an anonymous crowd, for the highest value on earth is a human individual. Truth is revealed to the individual," the startled puppet-parliamentarians sat on their hands. When he told them that "It is therefore essential, according to our view, to allow full scope for expression to minority and opposition parties," their faces grew a yard long. "Across

the centuries of despotism and dogma, we have had warnings
given us of the poison cup, the cross, the stake, the torture
chamber, and the concentration camp . . . Parliament, in our
view," he continued, "is to express, not suppress discontent."
Fortunately he was an honored foreign guest, speaking by
invitation, else he would have been transported to a concentration camp. His speech was not published.

That same month a Rumanian novelist and essayist named
Alexander Jar spoke in a similar vein at a writers' congress
in Bucharest and has not been heard of since. Mr. Jar declared that the Communists educated their members in a
"spirit of cowardice." Writers, he said, "lead a double life."
Literary criticism had fallen to a low ebb and the Communist
party was using police repression against a number of authors.
Jar tried to break the ice and produce a thaw; he broke his
neck. He was denounced as "anarchical, bourgeois, and in-
dividualistic," and, inevitably therefore, expelled from the
party.

Communist Party Secretary Gheorghiu-Dej himself addressed that writers' congress and froze their incipient revolt
by some well-chosen chilling words about the duty of art and
literature to serve party and state.

("Where does freedom of artistic creation attain real
breadth?" asked the October, 1956, Moscow *Kommunist.* "In
socialist countries," it replied. Notably Rumania, Czechoslovakia, and, of course, the Soviet Union.)

Mr. Khrushchev himself is our witness that there is discontent among Rumanian students too. In a speech to the Moscow Komsomol published in *Izvestia* on November 10, 1956,
he said, "Having noticed some unhealthy moods among the
student youth in one of the universities, the Rumanian comrades decided to speak frankly with the students and with a
number of their parents. In the interview they put such
questions:

" 'You are studying in the institute and receiving a stipend?'

" 'Yes,' the representatives of the students replied.

" 'You have a dormitory and good professors?'

" 'We have,' the students agreed.

" 'Do you want to study?' they were asked.

" 'We do,' they replied.

" 'Then study better, and look more deeply at life. If some of you don't wish to study go to work and then you will certainly better understand the life of the working people.' "

The Rumanian students no doubt took the hint—and it would not be lost on the Muscovites either.

By hints, sticks, and carrots a nation is reduced to a pulp of uniform consistency. The Special Correspondent of the London *Times*, writing in that paper on August 15, 1956, noted "the turgid dullness of the Rumanian press, the general slowness of the 'de-Stalinization' of the regime—if, indeed, that process can really be said to have begun at all." The correspondent "looked in vain for signs of change." The same pattern as in Czechoslovakia (and for the same reasons), only worse because the country is poorer; therefore the repression and corruption are greater. The new rulers use the palaces of the dethroned kings; a new upper class lives like the expelled aristocrats; bread—except in Bucharest—is rationed in this once rich agrarian land; the peasants are pushed into collectives, expensive industries rise, and real income falls. This is Rumanian Communism.

Rumanians have a proverb: "The water passes; the stone remains." They are optimists. Another proverb says, "The bowed head avoids the saber." A third: "Fraternize with the devil until you are over the bridge." Hans Ulrich Kempski (Munich *Sueddeutsche Zeitung* of September 18, 1956) quotes a Rumanian who said to him in Bucharest, "Our government tells us that the sea contains the sweetest water we could possibly drink. So all of us lap it up—and secretly we spit it out again." The same journalist reports that "despite the material distress I met no one who poured out his wrath or even hate on the politicians of the country. They are regarded as straw men . . . Not Eisenhower but Tito is the symbol of freedom for the average Rumanian." One person only, he found, estimated the Communists' popular support at 10 per cent; others put it at 3 to 5 per cent. But in a "people's democracy" that does not matter. When election time comes the Communists poll over 97 per cent of the ballots, and in "Parliament" everything is approved by unanimity. Popular consent is absent, but excellent Soviet divisions and an effective secret police fill the political vacuum.

Bulgaria, the third laggard, offers a little variety, with murder in the courtroom thrown in.

Traicho Kostov was born in Sofia on June 17, 1897. A journalist by profession, he joined the Bulgarian Communist party and in due course became its secretary-general and the Deputy Prime Minister of Bulgaria. In June, 1949, the police arrested him. His trial lasted from December 7 to 12, 1949. On December 16, 1949, he was executed. Not an unusual biography for a Communist east of the iron curtain. Death resulted from Titoism.

Episode Number 2: "The Twentieth Soviet Communist Party Congress and the Lessons to Be Derived from It by the Bulgarian Communist Party." That was the title of the address delivered in Sofia on April 11, 1956, by Todor Zhivkov who occupied the post, once held by Traicho Kostov, of the Bulgarian Communist party's secretary-general. The new man stated in his speech that "innocent comrades were accused and unjustly sentenced." Kostov, he affirmed, was one of them.

So Kostov received absolution in the grave. But living Titoists receive short shrift in Bulgaria.

It was natural that Kostov should have been murdered, because, to Stalin, a Bulgarian Titoist was worse than a Titoist anywhere else. For with Titoism as a bridge, Bulgaria might unite with neighboring Yugoslavia and form a South-Slav

Federation which, Stalin suspected, would declare its independence of the Soviet empire.

Georgi Dimitrov, the first leader of Communist Bulgaria, a leonine man who had defied the Nazis at the famous burning-of-the-Reichstag trial in Leipzig, was a friend of Tito, and quite innocently, for he was also a simple man, he advocated a federation to include not only Yugoslavia and Bulgaria but also Czechoslovakia, Poland, Rumania, Hungary, Albania, and Greece—not Russia. This therefore sounded like secession. *Pravda* of January 29, 1948, fiercely denounced Dimitrov. On February 12 six Soviet leaders—Stalin, Molotov, Malenkov, Zhdanov, Suslov, and Zorin—met three Yugoslav leaders, and three Bulgarians—Dimitrov, Vassil Kolarov, and Traicho Kostov—in Moscow. "Stalin was glowering and ceaselessly doodling in his notebook," one of the Yugoslavs reported later.

"You wanted to shine with words," Stalin shouted at Dimitrov. ". . . Such a federation is impossible."

In 1949 Dimitrov fell ill and was brought from Bulgaria to Russia for treatment. Among other troubles he suffered from diabetes, and one hears that he received excellent treatment but was given no insulin. In any case he died on July 2, 1949. This was just a few days after his comrade, Traicho Kostov, who attended the Stalin meeting with him, was arrested in Sofia.

Obviously Stalin would tolerate no federation of independent national-Communist states. They had to remain satellites. Moscow since Stalin holds Bulgaria in the same tight embrace lest she forge a link with Yugoslavia and leave the empire. As long as possible Russia will suppress all deviations, discontent, and dissidence in Bulgaria.

The fourth laggard is impoverished little Albania on the Adriatic (population: 1,300,000). How it can be Communist nobody understands. It is an isolated, backward, bandit-ridden, bandit-ruled country supervised by pistol-toting Soviet emissaries. But the coastline offers many hide-outs and bases from which Soviet submarines could go marauding in the Mediterranean. In the circumstances Albania has no will of its own and gives every promise of remaining a pale carbon copy of Moscow until somebody snatches it or the Russian empire crashes. The Yugoslavs, who are contemptuous of the Tirana regime, easily could smash their neighbors but are afraid to upset the Balkan applecart and invite a Soviet invasion. So Albanian Communism will stand till the avalanche sweeps it away. Meanwhile it continues to execute "Titoist" critics and opponents and to initiate quarrels with Belgrade.

All four laggards are coping with the resentments of dissatisfied populations who would free themselves if they could, and will when they can. These regimes were imposed by Moscow between 1944 and 1948 and have failed to rub off their birthmark or win popular approval.

CHAPTER 13

The Eternal Triangle

When Stalin died on March 5, 1953, and the
Malenkov-Beria-Molotov trio temporarily took over, an electric impulse went through the empire: the monster had
perished; deliverance seemed near. This proved illusory. His
spirit marched on and no liberation was in sight. But in the
Russian zone of Germany the hand that held the rudder
seemed suddenly to have lost its cunning and confidence. To
make matters worse, orders from the Kremlin confused the
Moscow marionettes, for they were told to favor the middle
class and peasants, in the hope of getting them to produce,
and to cut workers' wages. Walter Ulbricht, Otto Grotewohl,
and Wilhelm Pieck, the three Soviet satraps in East Germany,
must have felt that Moscow had stood them on their heads;
kicking the workers and courting the capitalists was not exactly according to the Communist Bible.

The workers took the same view and rebelled.

At first the Soviet press and its satellite echoes naturally
said the revolt of June 16 and 17, 1953, was the work of Fascists and rowdies. But the data published subsequently in
East Germany proved beyond dispute that a zone-wide proletarian revolution took place against the "proletarian" dictatorship imposed by Moscow. The workers, moreover, enjoyed
the backing of nonworkers.

The East German uprising in June, 1953, swept away the

Ulbricht-Grotewohl-Pieck government. Then the Russian tanks came, recaptured the streets and the factories, and restored the puppets to their thrones.

Since June, 1953, the managers for Moscow give no indication of having regained faith in themselves. On the contrary, after the secret Khrushchev speech of February 24, 1956, which all adults have heard in foreign broadcasts (many also read it on visits to West Berlin), the German authorities in the zone appear to be afflicted with incurable uncertainty.

In Russia the tilting of the Stalin idol leaves some belief that the despot served Russia's interest. In the satellites, and especially in East Germany, his fall pulled Communism down with it. Shorn of their ideology, the East German rulers stand exposed as naked quislings who cannot expect the seventeen million inhabitants of the zone to respect them. Some probably do not respect themselves.

The extent of demoralization in the East German Communist party can be judged from a statement made by its Politburo member Karl Schirdewan to the Central Committee Plenum and published in the official *Neues Deutschland* on November 28, 1956. It is necessary, he said, "to oppose with firmness and strength the symptoms of depression among party members and the upsurge of hostile discussions." Developments in Hungary and Poland, he added, had confused many Communists and created a "situation where even the Politburo was not in a position to give out information about everything at once." The clear implication from the context is that Moscow had to be consulted first. He also spoke of the necessity of combating "symptoms of confusion, uncertainty, and deep concern about peaceful developments." The party, Schirdewan promised, would defend itself "politically," that is, by argument, and "with security measures," that is, by arrests. The speech in fact was followed by arrests of students and professors and by a campaign of intimidation. Leon Davicho, East Berlin correspondent of the Belgrade *Politika*, reported to his paper of December 2 that "some unpleasant incidents" had occurred in Leipzig and other places "involving students . . . Workers are talking more and more about striking. Must we wait," Davicho wonders, "for student demonstrations before it can be decided that Russian will not be an obligatory language for students in all departments of the universities?" The quarrel is not with Russian as a language; the quarrel is with Russia.

East Germany is a perfect case of divorce between power and people. The government does not govern the country any more than terrorists govern a city. In fact the citizenry is deaf to appeals and propaganda. To the limited extent that being left alone is freedom, the zone won its freedom in the June, 1953, uprising. The authorities bother the people as little as possible in the hope that the people will not bother them. This freedom, however, does not extend to thought, public speech, publications, political activity, or scientific research. The students and intellectuals—except the rich writers—are therefore as disaffected in East Germany as everywhere in eastern Europe.

A special circumstance exacerbates East German sentiment against the regime: other satellites are riled by Russian domination and Communism. In the eastern zone these, to boot, divide Germany in two.

Reunification has become the major issue in West German politics, but life takes its tolerable course. To the eastern zoner, however, the partition of his country is a perpetual vexation. It hurts his patriotism and pocket, and as long as he remains in the East he is tormented by the question whether or not to escape to the West. On the one hand he wants to get away from his exhausting job, the pervading grayness, the bureaucratic chicaneries, the lying press and radio, and the physical hardships; most food is still rationed, housing conditions are abominable, and clothing has a Soviet quality. On the other hand, his children may be studying in universities on free scholarships, he may own a piece of property to which he is attached, he would have to sell his furniture, linenware, and kitchen utensils at a ridiculously low price, and there may be old folks in the family who would be a hindrance across the line.

Between 1949 and September 20, 1956, two million East Germans resolved this dilemma by going West. A million of these escaped via Berlin, to which access is relatively easy, and of the million, half were men of military age who refused to be recruited into a Red army.

This is not only a crushing vote of nonconfidence in the zonal regime. Two million out of a total remaining population of seventeen million represents a sickening drain of manpower. Goods shipped to the Soviet Union at below world market prices and the high maintenance cost of a huge Russian army of occupation are a further drain. Reunification, consequently, becomes an East German obsession, and the feeling communicates itself, albeit in diluted form, to the brethren in the West, the more so since travel between the two segments of Germany was facilitated in 1956 by barrier lifting in both.

Moscow, however, has a veto on reunification. Though the eastern zone economic squeeze is yielding the Kremlin diminishing returns, military and political considerations argue against a Russian withdrawal.

East Germany is the most western Soviet strategic position in Europe. Europeans fear Russia more because her armies are in the zone. That is an advantage for Moscow. Germany reunified would acquire a common frontier with Poland. That would be a disadvantage for Moscow.

Germany, Poland, and Russia are an eternal triangle, but love is alien to it. Today strong Soviet armed forces are quartered on Poland for two reasons: first, all Russian lines of land communication with East Germany run through Poland, and since Moscow has an army in East Germany it

must have another in Poland. This excuse would lose its validity if Russia withdrew from East Germany. Second, Russia
presented Poland with substantial German territories after
the Second World War. These territories, east of the line
formed by the Oder and Neisse Rivers, are still claimed by
West Germany. Russian troops in Poland ostensibly safe-
guard the Oder-Neisse border against West German irre-
dentism.

That the Soviets should pose as Poland's protector is an
ugly irony. Three times in history tsarist Russia helped to
partition Poland. In 1939, Soviet Russia did likewise with a
cynicism that would be admirable had it not been the preliminary to the outbreak of World War II. The damaging
evidence has been made available in a recent book, *Der
Ausbruch des Krieges, 1939*, by Michael Freund (Verlag
Herder-Alber, 1956), consisting of documents from the secret
archives of the Hitler government. On August 18, 1939, Nazi
Foreign Minister Ribbentrop sent telegraphic instructions to
his ambassador in Moscow to seek "an immediate interview
with Mr. Molotov" and to tell him that "The Fuehrer deems
it necessary, in the efforts to clarify German-Russian relations,
not to permit surprise over the outbreak of a German-Polish
war. He regards advance clarification necessary if only to be
able to consider Russian interests in connection with this war
. . . You must, in this connection [the last sentence reads],
keep in mind the decisive circumstance that an early outbreak of a German-Polish war is probable and that we are
therefore greatly interested in my immediate visit to Moscow."

What could be more simple? Hitler had decided to make
war on Poland and wanted to divide the spoils with Stalin in
order to keep Russia neutral.

Another document dispels all doubts. It is a secret protocol
signed by Ribbentrop and Molotov in Moscow on August 23,
1939, and provides for the partition of Poland between Ger-

many and Russia at the Narev, Vistula, and San Rivers. Whether any kind of Polish state was to exist in the future would be determined by Moscow and Berlin in "a friendly agreement."

When Nazi Germany was defeated, the Soviet government erected a Polish state ruled by the Moscow-appointed Lublin Committee. To make certain that that state would always gratefully submit to occupation by a Russian army, Moscow graciously gave it the German territories east of the Oder-Neisse line.

Now in exchange for reunification, Germany might renounce the Oder-Neisse territories. This is a delicate domestic-political matter, for of West Germany's fifty million inhabitants eleven million come from areas annexed by Poland and Russia, and an unpatriotic willingness to write them off would hurt the politician or party that proclaimed it. However, the German yearning for reunification has grown so intensely painful that the moment reunification became a practical possibility—but not earlier—West Germans might find it more difficult to forego the opportunity than to surrender the Oder-Neisse territories. Indeed, a few far-seeing West Germans are already advocating—in private—the immediate unilateral renunciation of the Oder-Neisse lands as a friendly gesture to Poland.

By all means, therefore, Moscow must prevent (1) the loss of East Germany, (2) the reunification of Germany, (3) Polish-German friendship. They are all bound up together and they would result in Russia's military withdrawal from Germany and Poland, and in the withering of the empire.

The Kremlin's chief propaganda weapon against this development is West German rearmament, which it painted as a bogy before even one West German had donned a uniform. But if West Germany were disarmed and neutral, Russia would be in a worse position, for the Poles, fearing Germany less, would be more inclined to improve relations with Germany.

So whether West Germany is rearmed or not, or neutral or not, Moscow will hold East Germany as long as it can in order to keep Germans and Poles apart and have a hand in Polish internal affairs.

If Germany were reunited, Poland would be free. If Poland were free, Germany could be reunited. The question is whether Poland can liberate herself from within by her own efforts. East Germany would thereby be cut off geographically from Russia and have to merge with West Germany.

Thus the eternal triangle is the key to the future of Germany and of the Soviet empire. It makes Poland the keystone of the imperial Russian edifice.

CHAPTER 14

Poznan

And King Belshazzar summoned a thousand nobles to a feast; and as they ate and drank, fingers appeared on the wall and wrote four mysterious words which none of Babylon's wise men could decipher. Then Daniel, the refugee from Judea, was summoned. "Mene, Mene, Tekel, Upharsin," he read. Mene: God hath numbered thy kingdom, and finished it. Tekel: Thou art weighed in the balances, and art found wanting. Upharsin: Thy kingdom is divided, and given to the Medes and Persians.

Written on the wall of the Kremlin are the Soviets' Mene, Mene: "Tito, June, 1948." "East Germany, June, 1953." "Poznan, June, 1956." The fingers move on and write: "Poland." "Hungary." The commissars have been weighed in the balances and found wanting. The days of their empire are numbered and it shall be divided among those whom it enslaved. The Belshazzars know it but know not what to do.

In all the events that foreshadow the end of Muscovy's foreign domination, nothing is so heartening as the intuitive wisdom and faith of the captive peoples and the folly of Russia. Poznan illustrates beautifully the instinctive mass knowledge of where; why; and when to stop.

Poznan was Poland's postwar revolutionary Genesis. There is always something before the beginning. But Poles who recount the story of their country's climb toward freedom commence with Poznan. For the events of Black Thursday, June 28, and Black Friday, June 29, 1956, in Poznan, a city of 330,000 inhabitants, cut open the body politic of Poland and revealed diseased organs. Poznan warned the leaders in Warsaw that if they did heal it their system would die.

As in East Berlin on June 16, 1953, so in Poznan the original grievance was a wage complaint in one enterprise. It should have been handled and settled by the trade unions long before it came to a head. But the trade unions were government controlled, the government was exploiting the workers, and the workers did not trust the trade unions or the government. Since all wage earners labored under the same unredressed grievances, the trouble soon enveloped the whole city. Within hours the strike grew violent and in that violence the people displayed their abhorrence of the Communist regime.

It began at ZISPO. The "Z" in ZISPO is for factory; "I" is for in the name of; "S" for Stalin; "PO" for Poznan. ZISPO is an old locomotive works employing over fifteen thousand persons. The discontent which had been mounting for some time became so serious that on Friday, June 22, according to a Warsaw Radio broadcast at 9:50 P.M. on July 6, Assistant Minister of Machine Industry Demidov, and the chairman and secretary of the national trade union of metallurgical workers, made a special trip from Warsaw to ZISPO, listened to protests about low wages and high taxes, and promised to deal with them on their return to the capital. But the very next day, the same official broadcast stated, "a large number of employees gathered in the main reading room and demanded the sending of a delegation to Warsaw."

Monday, June 25, a delegation of twenty-seven men was elected. They arrived in Warsaw at nine Tuesday morning, reached the Ministry of Machine Industry which manages ZISPO at 11:45 A.M., and remained there until 7 P.M. in consultation with the Minister, Roman Fidelski, his assistant Demidov, and others.

The Ministry must have felt that the ZISPO situation was very explosive, for despite these prolonged negotiations in Warsaw on Tuesday, Fidelski and Demidov agreed to go to Poznan (175 miles west of Warsaw) on Wednesday and face the ZISPO workers.

The Polish Communist version declared that Fidelski had met the workers' demands during the Warsaw talks. But in that case why should he have had to argue the matter with the ZISPO force on Wednesday? The fact is that the ZISPO meeting addressed by Fidelski was a stormy affair. An article entitled "In ZISPO I Speak with the Workers," by J. Baron, in the Polish daily *Glos Szczecinski* (The Voice of Szczecin or Stettin) of July 3, quotes Taszer, chairman of the ZISPO delegation to Warsaw, as saying that when he reported to the Wednesday meeting on the conversations with Fidelski "the workers were not satisfied." Thereupon, Taszer told Baron, Fidelski took the floor and tried to explain the agreement. But, according to Taszer, the workers "couldn't understand and couldn't translate all this in terms of money."

Fidelski's Waterloo was the question of norms. The norm is a Communist managerial device, practiced in Russia and the satellites, for the sweating of labor under the piecework system. It is a unit of production for a unit of pay, say, ten bolts for ten zloty. But as soon as the employees of a plant achieve the prescribed unit of production the norm is raised —from ten bolts to twelve, for instance—but the pay remains stationary, and any worker who does not produce the twelve bolts suffers a cut in income. Fidelski promised, according to Taszer, that when the present norm was reached it would no longer be raised. The workers, however, apparently, did not trust him, "did not understand." Describing Fidelski's troubles at the ZISPO meeting, Warsaw Radio said on July 6, "Men were saying clearly that these were promises, and that we will gain nothing through promises. Yes, this was quite a heated moment during which one from the Ministry answered questions."

Disappointed, ZISPO went on strike the next morning. The force reported to work at 7 A.M. and a few minutes later left the plant and began the four-mile march to Red Army Street in the center of town. Simultaneously the workers of almost all other Poznan factories, and of stores, government offices, the railroad and urban transportation facilities, bakeries and hotels quit and joined the procession. It was a planned, organized walkout.

Some time between 8:30 and 9 A.M. a foreign businessman took a photograph of the demonstration from the window of his hotel on Red Army Street. The street, eighty to a hundred yards wide, was filling with many thousands of citizens. In the left center of the picture, outside a government building, foreign flags are flying in honor of the annual Poznan International Fair.

The strike and the fair were related. Through the visitors to the fair the discontented workers were telling the world. And they assumed that with innumerable foreign businessmen and attendant foreign journalists on the scene, the government would hesitate to shoot the strikers down. The procession was moving toward the fairgrounds.

Another photograph reveals four men sharply silhouetted against the sky as they stand on the roof of a high cylindrical tower. They had just lowered the red flag and hoisted the Polish national banner—white horizontal bar above a red bar. The two visible clocks in the neighboring rectangular tower give the time as 9:37 A.M. So early in the day the strike had taken on a political coloration. It was anti-Red.

The Poznan daily *Gazeta Poznanska* of July 20, 1956, stated that the strikers "took possession of a radio car." Mr. G., a British machinery exporter who, with his partner, was walking to the fair when they were picked up by the demonstration and carried along like logs on a high tide, noted the slogans that boomed forth from the radio van: "This is a peaceful strike"; "We want bread"; "Poland must be free"; "Nothing can keep us down"; "We want to live like the West." Gesticulating men on the roof of the van shouted further demands: "Free elections and better working conditions"; "Lower prices"; "Disband the secret police"; "Release political prisoners."

After a short interval the demonstration advanced on the walled jail. A rumor had spread among the strikers that several members of the ZISPO delegation to Warsaw were under arrest. This was apparently untrue. But some people in the crowd believed it, and others probably wanted to liberate incarcerated victims of the regime.

The prison authorities surrendered without resisting. They displayed a white flag from a window and replaced the red flag on the roof with the Polish national banner. While a large number of prisoners walked out through the wide-open gates to the jubilant cries of the multitude, young people rushed into the prison and seized the wardens' weapons.

"Now," Mr. G., the British businessman, relates, "the radio van opened up again and summoned the procession to Communist party headquarters." Several foreign eyewitnesses have described the scene in European journals: children slid down the bannisters; workers roamed from one floor to the other of this citadel of power testing the thickness of the carpet with their shoes and, in one case, deliberately defiling it. Women derisively draped toilet paper around the marble columns. Portraits of Polish and Soviet leaders were taken from their frames and torn to bits. "In a passage," writes one foreign observer, "an angry group cornered a suspected party man. His face was gray with fear."

A photograph taken by a foreigner shows two crudely made signs in top-story windows of the party building. One read, "Freedom"; the second, "Bread." A banner on the roof bore the inscription, "We want bread." A person with a sense of humor scrawled another: "Building for Rent."

From party headquarters the crowd moved on the U.B. building. U.B. are the initials of Urzad Bezpieczenstwa, or Administration of Security; in simpler terms, the secret police. At the U.B., for the first time that day, shooting occurred and blood flowed. A number of U.B. men were killed; one of their tommy gunners was lynched, another trampled to death. Children, women, and civilian men died in the fight. Here too the Polish army came on the scene. Tanks appeared. Dramatically and politically the sanguinary events in front of the U.B. fortress were the highlight of the Poznan story.

The battle for the U.B. lasted several hours. It was the kind of battle which, though lost, makes history and spells ultimate success.

The multitude marched on the U.B. in search of ZISPO delegates who had not been found in the jail. But once the procession stood face to face with the U.B., agency and symbol of Communist oppression, the uncoded law governing the conduct of crowds came into operation. The missing delegates were forgotten. The building acted on the enraged mass like a red flag on an untethered bull.

A month after the Poznan events I sat in a quiet room in the ancient precincts of Oxford University talking with one of its teachers. From twelve noon to one o'clock on Thursday, June 28, the Oxford economist, member of a visiting delegation of British economists who chanced to be in Poznan that day, stood at the corner of Dombrovski and Mickiewicz Streets, at the station which jammed foreign broadcasts. Strikers and youths had gone into the station and hurled its expensive electronic equipment through the windows. Walking amid the debris, where he picked up a bracelet-like piece of chromium-plated metal which he showed me, the Oxford don heard a Polish workingman say, "They had four million zloty to spend for this but I didn't get enough bread."

Across the street from the ruined jammer, strikers transformed into rebels during a brief morning were attacking the U.B. building with stones and gasoline-filled bottles (Molotov cocktails). Apparently they expected tanks, for where Dombrovski joins Kochanovski—the street on which the U.B. house is located—they built a barricade consisting of felled trees and overturned trams. Near by they parked trolleys and pushed others over on their sides to impede military vehicles.

Presently the U.B. replied to the stones and Molotov cocktails with bursts from their burp guns. "Among the first victims," the economist reported, "were two women and two children."

"At twelve-thirty," he continued, "two lorries filled with infantry, but wearing no steel helmets, and two Russian-made T 34 Stalin tanks, rolled into Dombrovski. The people cheered the troops and seemed confident that they would side with the rebels."

The soldiers dismounted from the trucks but did not take their rifles and machine guns with them. Immediately strikers climbed into the trucks, grabbed the arms, jumped over the barricade, and joined those who were fighting the U.B. An anonymous eyewitness report in the London *New Statesman and Nation* of July 14 confirms this account. "The people were swarming all over the lorry and I saw rifles and ammunition being passed from hand to hand. The officer, white-faced and still wearing his revolver, was being dragged away by a group of men. A tank clattered toward the U.B. building, its commander standing in the open turret. There were some derisive shouts from some people in the crowd. As soon as the tank stopped, people swarmed over it and again I couldn't see exactly what happened. I edged my way towards it. After talking to some people, my interpreter said gleefully: 'We have the tank.' A second tank was taken in the same way."

The behavior of the troops, and especially of the tanks, has special significance for the light it throws on the mood and loyalty of Russia's satellite armies. In Munich I studied a large collection of photographs of the Poznan insurrection. One showed a tank, with the Polish eagle and the number 264 painted on its flank, against a background of homes and trees. Thickly massed around it were workers, junior office employees, and young men and women looking like university students. Two men who had been lifted up on the far side of the tank's superstructure are seen arguing with the uniformed crewman in the turret. On the near side of the tank's huge steel body a woman stands next to a crewman who is bending over and talking to somebody down in the machine. This was clearly a parley for the surrender of the tank.

Another amateur but excellent photographer, Mr. Robert Davies, Secretary of the Department of Applied Economics at Cambridge University, England, showed me his Poznan pictures when I visited him at his home. One depicted that same tank, Number 264, firing point-blank at the U.B. building. Black smudges on the U.B. wall, puffs of smoke, and falling plaster indicate where the tank's shots hit their target. The tank had been surrendered.

Mr. Davies says the tank used only its machine guns, not the cannon. He heard no bursting of cannon shells. In fact soon the machine firing ceased. He believes the mixed civilian-military crews were unable to reload the machine guns or fire the cannon. Mr. Davies' Oxford colleague says the tanks —at least two and possibly three—had purely civilian crews who could not move them about or use their armaments.

Obviously, though the city-wide strike was prearranged, the rebels' military action was unexpected and poorly executed. Three tanks maneuvering expertly around the sides and back of the U.B. headquarters and supported, as they would have been, by eager civilians on foot armed with equipment taken from willing soldiers, could easily have captured that U.B. building. But before long the tanks were stationary and silent.

At one o'clock the army on Dombrovski Street threw some weak tear gas into the crowd. "I can only presume," the Oxford economist commented, "that this army unit was now divided into two factions. They did not fight one another, but one threw the tear gas and the other was either neutral or anti-U.B." The crowd, however, did not disperse; instead the soldiers withdrew after doing the least they could do in the performance of their military duty. Mr. Davies picked up a tear-gas container. The people told him it was Soviet. It was not. They also said that the U.B. defenders were Russians. That too is doubtful. But the statements reflect Polish sentiments.

Now the Oxford teacher shifted to the corner of Mickiewicz and Krasinski. A white-collar office employee said to him, "The East Germans and Chinese eat our butter, the Russians take our coal and don't pay. Nothing is left for us." At one-thirty several tanks rumbled down Mickiewicz toward him. But they stopped for the dense multitude. Shouts of "Are you Poles?" rose from the people. A smiling crewman in one of the turrets clasped both his hands above his head and shook them back and forth to express sympathy. The tanks did not fire.

Meanwhile the desperate assault on the U.B. continued. Casualties were being carried back from Kochanovski to Dombrovski. Ambulances raced through the city. Trucks and automobiles brought in nurses from outside Poznan. On Dombrovski a soldier, bandaged around his head, who had been fighting with the rebels against the U.B., shook his fist angrily and cried, "Bread," as he was lifted into an ambulance.

At two o'clock the Oxford economist left the scene. Approximately half an hour later a lynching took place and Mr. G. saw the entire horrifying spectacle. It appears that some time after two a U.B. unit made a sortie from the building. An officer ordered a U.B. soldier to fire but he refused, and the

officer shot him down. Other U.B. men did fire and a civilian
was wounded. As people stooped to pick him up, the U.B.
aimed their tommy guns at them, and Mr. G. counted four
casualties. Now the crowd, infuriated by this as well as by the
act of the officer, rushed the U.B. gunmen. They surrounded
one and lynched him.

"I hate to ask you to do this," I said to Mr. G., "but exactly
what happened?"

"I saw them rip off his ear first," he replied. "I did not see
his arm torn off, but as they pushed him about I saw him arm-
less and blood gushing from his side. Then they threw him to
the ground and jumped on him. His body was a pulp." The
U.B. temporarily held its fire, either because it was afraid to
engage in a wholesale massacre or did not think it wise to
enrage the rebels any further. The fighting, however, continued. Rebels fired on the U.B. from the street, from the roof of
the five-story jamming station, and from other vantage points.

Thursday afternoon tanks, estimated at between seventy
and two hundred, all T 34 giants, were brought into the city
of Poznan from the region of the Polish-East German frontier.
But a Polish-speaking Rumanian, whom I interviewed in Munich, said he saw some of these tanks on Friday abandoned
and crewless in streets far from the district where the U.B.
battle raged. He, and others, watched unarmed soldiers
Thursday afternoon and all day Friday loitering at street cor-
ners either singly or in pairs or surrounded by civilians and
chatting amiably with them.

Thursday evening, between eight and nine, Mr. Davies
went to the railway station near the fairgrounds. Steady
streams of tracer bullets raced over the terminal while over-
head circled two jets and an old biplane dropping flares.

At the jamming station the rebels held out against the government forces until Friday afternoon. Friday, at 4 P.M., the
Polish-speaking Rumanian was at the railway station when
he heard that "the rebels are retreating." Outside he actually

observed troops pursuing civilians; but the soldiers, he said, looked completely disinterested and simply fired short bursts now and then from their machine guns without taking aim, as though they were playing a friendly game.

In the two Poznan days, according to Prosecutor-General Marian Rybnicki's announcement on July 17, fifty-three persons, including nine U.B. men, were killed, and three hundred wounded.

Fighting subsided on Saturday, but anti-aircraft artillery, tanks, and infantry were posted throughout the city. Everywhere, Poznanites fraternized with the military.

The Polish army was an unreliable instrument against the people. The U.B., despised before the Poznan insurrection, now drove the populace to fury. The workers had been paying for the regime's mismanagement and bad planning and were disaffected. All these grave symptoms of a collapsing system were compounded by the demoralization of youth. Even in the West the notion had taken root that though Communist countries might not enjoy the approval of their adult inhabitants they certainly commanded the zealous support of the youth. Poznan disproved it.

On July 11, 1956, the Communist daily *Gazeta Poznanska* published an article entitled "The Young Workers of WFUM" (WFUM is a machine-tool plant in Poznan) which said that on June 28 and 29, "Bogdan Obst, former chairman of the factory's Young Communist League and now one of its members, participated in provocational acts . . ." That means he participated in the uprising.

The Poznan daily *Glos Wielkopolski* of July 10 carried an article by Piotr Zycki called "Quo Vadis" in which he described an attack on a Poznan suburban police station at 6 P.M. on June 28 by some thirty "fourteen-, sixteen-, eighteen-year olds, clutching guns, grenades, revolvers, automatic guns." Three girls in jeans were among them. They searched the station for arms. "The role of leader was played by Joseph

R., an inhabitant of P., an ardent activist and president of the local Young Communist League group, still wearing—oh irony!—the conspicuous Communist Youth badge." Similar attacks took place elsewhere, the article asserts.

Why, Mr. Zycki asks, did so many adolescents assault public buildings in Poznan? "The reasons for the spontaneous, I would say reckless, part of youth in the incidents," he replies, "should probably be sought above all in the mistakes we made."

He explains: "What have we given our youth? Not very much, it must be said, especially taking into account a somewhat complicated political situation where ideas put to the youth in school are often fought at home. The young people, torn by opposing currents, sprinkled with the dust of falling statues [Stalin], fall into the clutches of cynicism. From this there is only a step to a complete lack of idealism." Translated, that means complete anti-Communism.

Sztandar Mlodvch, a Polish youth magazine dated July 4, 1956, calls for changes in the Young Communist League. "If we do not do that," the paper warns, "if we continue to isolate ourselves from the needs, dreams, and everyday work of the youth, it will be threatened with final, irrevocable ossification."

Shooting from the top windows of their building, U.B. gunners killed a boy of sixteen. Demonstrators dipped a Polish flag in his blood and carried it to the fairgrounds for foreigners to see. The scene was amply photographed. The bloodstains on the upper white bar of the national banner stand out with blood-chilling distinctness. Around and behind the flag marches a dense procession of youths, some eight to ten years old, most of them older. In the front rank strides a middle-aged woman of serious mien. Everybody looks sad, bewildered, determined.

Wiktor Woroszhilski, a well-known Polish Communist poet, returned in July from a year's stay in Russia, and on

July 29, 1956, the chief Warsaw literary weekly *Nowa Kultura* published a diary-like article from his pen. "What can be more amazing," he writes, "than to see one's own son whom one has not seen for a year. How he's grown! But even before we have had time to accustom ourselves to these physical changes, little Felek begins to tell his story with some emotion: '. . . they dipped the banner in his blood and swore vengeance . . .' I did not suppose that a seven-year-old would know anything about blood and death or that politics would have reached him in the isolation of his Lodz playground."

If seven-year-old Felek knew what happened in far-off Poznan then his contemporary Stefans and Vaneks and Josefs know, and the teen-agers of Poland know, and their elders of course. The Poles are a romantic nation with long memories. "They swore vengeance," little Felek said.

CHAPTER 15

Secrets of the Secret Police

Moscow is always true to itself. It was on Poznan. The day the insurrection occurred, the Soviet press and, echoing it, all the newspapers and radio stations of the Communist world, Yugoslavia included, knew, without any investigation or evidence, that it was the work of "foreign imperialist agents," "American spies," and "Polish counterrevolutionaries." In the fat lexicon of Kremlinese these words mean "the people we don't like." They may be workingmen, Young Communists, or Communist leaders, they may be writing truthfully about what they know and think, but if it does not suit the Moscow book they are "reactionaries."

The Yugoslavs soon recovered and withdrew the drivel about spies in Poznan. The Polish Communists, realizing that their existence was at stake, were in no mood for nonsense. The daily *Zycie Warsawy* of July 24 admitted that the "first communiqué was prepared in a hurry when the situation was extremely tense and shooting still continued in the streets of Poznan." Now, it apologized, "it would be wrong to concentrate attention merely on provocateurs and imperialist agents." The Warsaw official *Trybuna Ludu* of July 6 said Poznan was "a particularly serious warning, a particularly bitter lesson to our party and . . . above all to the trade unions . . . The workers had a basis for dissatisfaction . . . The strike . . . was in no small degree precipitated by the bureaucratic warpings of the proletarian state . . . The principal conclusion which we should draw from the Poznan events is the necessity to turn from words to deeds in our economy. Otherwise, conflicts can arise of which Poznan was the extreme example."

Moscow was in a different mood. The Kremlin which never, God forbid, interferes in the affairs of other countries, rushed Prime Minister Bulganin and Defense Minister Marshal Zhukov to Poland. Zhukov naturally wished to know whether the Polish army still had any value for Russia after Poznan. Bulganin went on a city-to-city lecture tour in which he told the Poles what to do. In Warsaw, on July 21, he explained that of course "we Marxist-Leninists" believe in "socialist democratism." But "we cannot overlook attempts to weaken the international ties of the socialist camp under the guise of so-called 'national peculiarities.'" No Titoism. He also derided attempts to undermine the strength of the "people's democracies" under the guise of a false "extension of democracy." No freedom. Specifically the press must adopt "a correct, Marxist attitude." No free speech. The Polish press had been critical of Russia and of the Polish Communist leadership.

Mr. Bulganin also instructed the Polish government not to abandon the economic policies which had led the country to Poznan, privations, and the brink of disaster. When the people grumble, Bulganin was saying, tighten the screws, use the knout, gag the mouths.

Poland, however, was disinclined to adopt Russian methods which could only produce more Poznans and make Warsaw completely dependent on Moscow for tanks to suppress revolt and for economic aid with political strings.

The Polish people had shed so much blood since Hitler invaded their soil on September 1, 1939, that they would rather not shed any more. Poznan did not spread, as East Berlin's strike on June 16, 1953, spread to the entire zone, because the nation hoped one Poznan was warning enough. And since additional Poznans were present in embryo the Polish Communist leadership could not accept Bulganin's costly advice. Forced to choose, the Polish Communists rejected rigorous repression, which would make them supine vassals of Russia, and chose freedom—but only to the extent that conditions and their own Marxist background permitted.

Moscow had already made a considerable contribution to the ruin of Poland's economy by taking enormous shipments of coal, the country's chief export, and paying pennies instead of dollars for it; by egging Warsaw on to expand the armaments industry ("In the space of two and a half years," Edward Ochab, Communist party secretary, said at Poznan's ZISPO in August, 1956, "we created an important artillery production industry, produced planes and tanks, and equipped our army with modern weapons"); and by ordering huge Polish investments in heavy industries which yielded nothing the people could eat, wear, or otherwise consume. Despite their Marxist boasts, Communists cannot foresee, much less prevent, the normal operation of universal economic and social laws. The results of Warsaw's policies included: inflation; the peasant's refusal to supply the city with food in exchange for devalued zlotys which he could not spend; declining productivity in factories and mines; widespread alcoholism among men and women; urban overcrowding; hooliganism and profligacy among the youth; low morale in the party; and two days in Poznan.

Now Bulganin counseled more of the same. Instead of turning the other cheek, Warsaw wanted to turn its back. In practice this was and is difficult. For a Polish Communist government must serve two antagonistic masters, Moscow and the Polish people; its best means of escaping from this dilemma would be to subject itself to the control of the people and tell the Kremlin that the people do not allow it to serve Russia.

In 1948 it was the Yugoslav government that broke away

from the Soviet embrace, and it could do so without introducing democracy. There Titoism or national Communism sufficed. But Poland must give the people freedom in order to be free from Soviet domination. (Will a free Poland wish to be Communist?) This makes Warsaw's task much more complicated than Belgrade's.

By some political divining rod, many Polish intellectuals as well as Communists and ordinary citizens discovered that their national liberation lay imbedded in personal liberty. To reach it they had to drill through and dig away the intervening obstacle: the secret police, or U.B. The best instrument for the purpose was free speech.

This is the essence of the zigzagging events in Poland since the middle of 1953.

The death of Stalin brought no perceptible change in Poland. The death of Beria did. For it was the Soviet secret police that governed the satellites. As soon as the Russian army invaded an East European country in 1944 and 1945, a local Communist was installed as Minister of Interior. In Hungary and Czechoslovakia this happened before the Communists won complete control of the government. The Ministry of Interior is in charge of the secret police, and in each instance a little-known Soviet officer was in charge of the Ministry of Interior. Through it he ruled the nation. Given the power to arrest and prosecute, and with agents strategically placed in all departments to gather politically compromising and personally embarrassing information, this is not as difficult as it seems.

There was general knowledge that this system existed. But by one of those history-making accidents which, however, is more than a coincidence, for it flows from the nature of a totalitarian police state, the world now has a detailed description of the inner workings of a Soviet satellite. The accident was the escape to the West of Lieutenant Colonel Joseph Swiatlo, deputy director of the Tenth Department of the Pol-

ish Ministry of Public Security. The Tenth Department kept
personal files about the topmost Communist leaders of Poland. Swiatlo came to it in 1948, after secret-police duty in the
provinces. Referring to his activities in the "Bezpieka," common name for the Polish secret police, Swiatlo said, "In the
course of my services in the Bezpieka I arrested nearly all of
the prominent party and regime officials who were imprisoned during that period," including Gomulka.

A man with a long record in the upper echelons of an organization which falsifies, spies, tortures, and kills would not
normally be accepted as the best source of pristine truth. But
the revelations made by Swiatlo have been proved correct by
events in Poland. In fact they demonstrably upset the Polish
government and reshaped its policy.

Swiatlo, a Communist for twenty years, had, on personal
instructions from Boleslaw Bierut, the Polish Communist
party secretary, and other members of the Politburo, carried
out numerous delicate, discrete assignments. In December,
1953, his immediate superior, Colonel Faygin, the head of the
Tenth Department, took him to East Berlin to consult the
East German chief of security. (The satellite police systems of
course interlock.) From there he crossed over to West Berlin
and presented himself to American officials. In September,
1954, in Washington, he was interviewed by the press, and
subsequently he broadcast his long story into Poland. It was
repeated without cease by the Voice of America, Radio Free
Europe, and other media, and also distributed in pamphlet
form by balloons.

The highest Polish leaders were Bierut, Jacob Berman, and
Hilary Minc. "On orders from Bierut," Swiatlo said, "I gath-
ered incriminating evidence against comrade Jacob Berman
and kept a personal file on him. On the other hand, Jacob
Berman instructed me to establish a personal file on Wanda
Gorska, Bierut's mistress. It is obvious that strict observation

of Gorska enabled me to keep an eye on Bierut and that is just what Berman wanted."

But before Bierut rose to eminence, he was in the pay of the Soviet NKVD. At that time—1946—the Polish Communist party was led by its secretary, Wladyslaw Gomulka, a zealot who had spent years in prison in prewar capitalist Poland. That saved his life, for the leading Polish Communists who lived in Russia were executed on Stalin's orders in 1938, and their party was thereupon disbanded. This could not increase Gomulka's affection for Moscow. Nor did he remain ignorant of the NKVD's penetration into the Polish Communist government.

Early in 1947, Gomulka startled Poland and the Communist world by uttering a forbidden heresy. In *Nowe Drogi* (New Ways), the party monthly, he stated that whereas in the Soviet Union legislative and executive functions were exercised by one body, in Poland "the dictatorship of the working class and in greater measure the dictatorship of a single party is neither essential, nor would it serve any purpose . . . Poland can proceed and is proceeding along her own road."

This proclamation of two roads to socialism was premature Titoism. Gomulka compounded his sin by declaring that "there will be no collectivization in Poland." Such divergence from the rocky Soviet path would make him popular with the Polish peasantry, thereby reinforce his government, and reduce its dependence on Moscow.

Gomulka, obviously, was a marked man. In June, 1946, Bierut attacked him publicly for "conscious and willful revision of Lenin's evaluation . . ."

"Preparations for the physical liquidation of Gomulka began in 1948," Swiatlo testified. "At that time Gomulka was still the all-powerful secretary-general of the party and had around him men absolutely devoted to him, such as Spychalski and others . . . Bierut decided that first the solidarity of the group had to be broken. Somebody had to be designated

who would break away and himself strike Gomulka and his
collaborators. The choice fell on General Marian Spychalski," member of the Politburo and Deputy Minister of Defense.

While the secret police manufactured the case against
Gomulka he was expelled from his government and party
posts in January, 1949, and from party membership in November, 1949. Bierut succeeded him. That facilitated the
softening up of Spychalski.

During the war, Spychalski had been the chief of intelligence in the Polish Communist underground People's Army.
He had a brother named Josef who was at the same time an
officer in the anti-Nazi non-Communist underground Home
Army loyal to the Polish government-in-exile in London.
(The two armies were at daggers drawn, for if the People's
Army won, Poland would be pro-Russian, if the Home Army
won, Poland would be pro-West.) Brother Marian maintained contact with non-Communist Josef and took advantage
of it to send a pair of his intelligence agents, Lechowicz and
Jaroszewicz, into the Home Army as Communist spies.

When the war was over, General Marian Spychalski, with
the knowledge of Bierut, rewarded the two agents. Lechowicz
became Minister for Food, and Jaroszewicz his deputy. However, in October, 1948, Lechowicz and Jaroszewicz were arrested and accused of having entered the People's Army as
anti-Communist agents employed by the Nazi Gestapo. Other
persons around Politburo member Spychalski were arrested
on similar trumped-up charges.

Swiatlo says none of those innocents confessed. But Bierut
and his colleagues told Spychalski that they had incriminated
him. Whether or not Spychalski believed this he saw what lay
in store for him if he did not comply and, accordingly, made
a speech against Gomulka at a plenary session of the party's
Central Committee.

Needless to say, Spychalski was attacked by the very next

plenum of the Central Committee for having concealed his past connections with agents of the Gestapo, and in 1951 Swiatlo personally arrested him.

Spychalski's attack on his close friend Gomulka, his subsequent arrest, the arrest of his cronies, and the expulsion of Gomulka must have puzzled many party and nonparty Poles. Swiatlo's exposures, in his own voice, supplied plausible explanations and the connecting tissue.

Prisoner Spychalski, however, refused to bear false witness against Gomulka. Other prominent Communists were arrested, but they too yielded no evidence. Swiatlo traveled to Czechoslovakia several times before and during the Slansky trial, and to Hungary in connection with the Rajk trial, hoping to find data which, when published, would blacken Gomulka's big reputation and justify his arrest in the eyes of the party and population. These endeavors proved vain. Nevertheless, Swiatlo states, "In July, 1951, it was decided to arrest Gomulka."

Polish Secret Police Chief Stanislaw "Radkiewicz called me into his office," Swiatlo said in his broadcast. "There I found all the Security deputy ministers, including Romkowski, Lietowski, Swietlik, and the Soviet advisor at their head. Radkiewicz gave me orders to go to Krynica, arrest Gomulka, and bring him back to Warsaw. He said that this was on Bierut's order . . . The task was not easy. I knew Gomulka had a gun with him. Therefore I had to prepare everything so that, on seeing me, he would not shoot either himself or me . . .

"It was 7 A.M. when I arrived in Krynica and entered Gomulka's room in the New Resort Hotel. His wife, Zofia, was not home. She had gone into town for a short while. Gomulka knew me very well. Therefore I entered, said, 'Good morning,' and added that I had come on orders from the party to take him with me to Warsaw. At first Gomulka refused . . . In the meantime his wife returned and made some fuss." They talked till 10 A.M. Swiatlo says he kept trying to persuade

Gomulka to go voluntarily. Gomulka's bodyguard was under Swiatlo's orders. Perhaps this too became clear to Gomulka. Finally he consented to accompany Swiatlo. He was driven to a private villa near Warsaw. "I placed Gomulka's wife, Zofia, separately in a neighboring house. I was personally responsible for these buildings . . ." Swiatlo declared.

Bierut wished to stage a Gomulka trial after the patterns of the Slansky, Rajk, and Kostov trials. Gomulka refused to cooperate in his own death by confessing. Bierut personally interviewed an old Communist named Alexander Kowalski and suggested to him the lies he might affirm in court to the detriment of Gomulka. The man, a former metal worker, declined the role.

"Consequently," Swiatlo declared, "other methods were resorted to. However, even the most skillfully used provocations could not extract anything . . . eventually Romkowski and Faygin started to give him the works together. They interrogated him uninterruptedly for seven days and with such intensity that Kowalski lost his mind. He was taken to a lunatic asylum at Tworki and died there . . ."

Time passed. The Kremlin pressed. "Now and then the Soviet advisors asked Radkiewicz: 'What are you going to do about Gomulka?'" But "Gomulka did not admit anything and others did not incriminate him. . . . Moreover, his followers still represent a certain strength inside the party. They remember that Gomulka was the creator of the party . . ."

Gomulka was never tried.

Knowledge is power everywhere, but especially when the pervading secrecy of a dictatorship makes it so rare. The knowledge which Swiatlo hurled into the Polish air lifted the roof off the life of the leaders and they squirmed visibly. Addressing Bierut by his party name, "Comrade Tomasz," Swiatlo said, "you falsified the referendum and the elections of 1947 and 1952. You remember that I was a member of the special commission formed in the Security organization which prepared the minutes of all regional electoral commissions for you in 1952. All you did was to insert the necessary figures. You, Comrade Tomasz, liquidated the legal opposition and the real political parties, using, among other methods, a special liquidation group of murderers attached to the Central Committee. . . .

"If you speak so loudly today," Swiatlo continued, "about your link with the masses and about socialist morality, perhaps you will also describe how you yourself live." Knowing Bierut would not, Swiatlo did: ". . . you have at your disposal not less than ten luxurious little palaces . . ." and he named them with exact locations. "All these palaces and villas are furnished with fabulous splendor." He depicted it in minute detail, the furniture, the luscious banquets. In Bierut's villas "Comrade Wanda Gorska does not even try to pass as a secretary. She has at her disposal numerous furs, underwear of the thinnest French and Chinese silk, dozens of pairs of shoes, and dozens of hats. . . . All this is in brutal contrast with the gray and harsh manner of the Polish worker's life."

In his revelations Swiatlo devoted special attention to Stanislaw Radkiewicz, the chief of the secret police and member of the Polish Politburo: "Radkiewicz knew, for example, that during the interrogations in the Ministry by Captain Kedzia, a subordinate of Colonel Rozanski, director of the Investigating Department, Lieutenant Colonel Dobrzynski, head of a section in the Fourth Department, was killed . . . He was arrested in connection with the Spychalski case. The Bezpieka did not disclose Dobrzynski's death. Nor did it disclose the death of Cesanis, murdered by the same Kedzia . . . Radkiewicz also knew about the report of Morczarski . . . In this report he mentioned more than thirty ways of extorting confessions which had been applied to him by Colonel Rozanski." Others reported "how Rozanski beat them during interrogation, knocked out their teeth, abused them with insulting words, spat on them, and kicked them . . . All these details were known to Radkiewicz but he failed to take action . . . The Ministry of Security is headed formally by Radkiewicz, but in practice the chief is Radkiewicz's so-called advisor, Soviet General Lalin." The Personnel Department of the U.B., Swiatlo asserted, is composed almost entirely of Russians and headed by Colonel Nikolai Orechwo. Orechwo's wife, Russian, "is Comrade Bierut's typist, so that Bierut is well watched from all sides." The director of the Financial Department of the U.B. is also a Russian, Colonel Kisilev, Swiatlo stated.

Swiatlo's revelations rattled the regime. Though Polish publications called him a traitor and liar they never attempted to refute his specific allegations. Too many highly placed Communists in Poland and Russia knew his evidence was grounded in incontrovertible fact. Indeed the acts of the Polish government confirmed Swiatlo. Colonel Anatol Faygin, Swiatlo's immediate superior, was arrested, and the Tenth Department officially abolished. Deputy Minister of Security Roman Romkowski was arrested. Rozanski, head of the Investigating Department, accused by Swiatlo of sadistic cruelties, was likewise arrested, and when he later received a sentence of five years' imprisonment the Warsaw weekly *Po Prostu* (In Simple Terms) complained in April, 1956, that the punishment was too mild. "Who is Rozanski?" the paper asked. "Everybody in Poland knows this. . . . To put it plainly, he simply tortured innocent people."

On December 7, 1954, only a few weeks after Swiatlo began broadcasting, Radkiewicz was dismissed as chief of the U.B. and appointed, instead, Minister for State Farms. (Later he went to prison.) The U.B. itself was split in two and both sections were completely reorganized. Explaining this reform over Radio Warsaw on June 17, 1956, Edmund Pszczolkowski, new chairman of the Committee for Public Security, said, "It is a year and a half since the third plenum of the Polish Communist party Central Committee adopted resolutions with regard to security. . . . One of the basic organizational changes is the liquidation of the former Ministry of Public Security and its replacement by the Committee for Public Security. This is not merely a change of name . . . [these changes] brought serious and positive reforms in the interrogation procedures of the Security apparatus . . . Many employees of various grades were expelled . . . the personnel was reduced by over 22 per cent . . . many of those guilty of distortion were expelled. Those who applied improper interrogation methods were prosecuted." The U.B., he affirmed, has ceased interfering in party affairs by arrests and trials. The problems of political life, he declared, "can be the exclusive subject of political solutions, and administrative methods [secret-police methods] are inadmissible."

In December, 1954, not long after Radkiewicz was dismissed, Gomulka and his wife were released from prison. Later the government liberated General Marian Spychalski.

Nowe Drogi, the Communist party's ideological monthly, reacted quickly to Swiatlo's September, 1954, revelations. In the magazine for December, 1954, an article said, "Among individual functionaries of the Security Service a peculiar view has arisen that they have the right to put themselves above the employees of other government departments, above other members of the party, above the mass of the working people, that they have the right to disregard the laws of the people's government and the constitutional rights of citizens . . . Hitherto the party's control over the Security apparatus was insufficient."

Any secret police is hated by the people. After Swiatlo's exposures it was reviled and condemned, and deprived of defenders. The Polish press complained that officials dismissed from the U.B. could find no other work; they had become repugnant. Moscow needed no resort to inventions about foreign spies to explain the attack on the U.B. building in Poznan on June 28. The U.B. was the object of universal hatred. It began, after Swiatlo's 1954 broadcasts, to lose its self-confidence, inviolability, and authority. Fearing it less, Polish tongues were loosened and writers and journalists hit out more freely against the abuses of the Communist regime. The Polish revolution had been born.

CHAPTER 16

The Pen Is Mightier Than Moscow

The ferment began privately in 1953. Polish writers, editors, journalists, students, and professors were irked by the strait jacket of dogma. The wagging of Moscow's cautionary finger only increased the yearning to shed the shackles.

The public pen-protest movement began mildly in 1955, and reached a crescendo in the middle of 1956, when, together with Poznan and a deteriorating economic situation, it changed the government and the government's policy and produced open defiance of Russia. The pens plowed and planted the field; the politicians and people brought in the crop.

In January, 1955, a journal warned officials against misreading the signs of the times in the Polish villages; the peasants were not taking to collectivization. In December of the same year *Zycie Warsawy* showed by concrete examples that Polish scientists had spent much time and money on great research projects only to discover from a European or American journal which accidentally fell into their hands that their problems were already solved. Why did the ministries waste millions by saving a few hundred zloty on subscriptions to foreign magazines?

These two truths established the range of the matter-of-fact criticism with which the Polish thaw began. Suddenly,

however, the curtain was raised on an unprecedented kind
of barbed comment against general conditions. The curtain
raiser was "A Poem for Adults" by Adam Wazyk, a much dec-
orated Communist and editor-in-chief of the official organ
of the Polish Writers Union. Soon after *Nowa Kultura,* the
foremost literary weekly, printed it on August 21, 1955, it became a national sensation. The poem expressed Wazyk's revulsion against the ugliness, the grimness, the crassness of life,
the lies of the official liturgy, the fakery of Marxist incanta-
tions:

> I refuse to believe, my friend, in casting of spells,
> Nor will I have faith in brains kept under glass.
> I believe that a table has only four legs.
> I believe that a fifth is a chimera.
> And when chimeras flock together, my friend,
> Man dies of a sick heart.
>
> Here it is, the truth,
> When the din of boredom's copper coin
> Blots out the goal of enlightenment,
> When vultures of abstraction feast upon our brains,
> When students are jailed within windowless textbooks,
> When the lamp of imagination goes out,
> When good men, out of the blue,
> Deny us the right to good taste,
> Then it is true,
> Ignorance knocks at our door.
>
> They swallow sea water and shout,
> "Lemonade,"
> Later they sneak back home
> To retch,
> To retch.
>
> A-running they came and a-crying,
> "Under Conditions of Socialism
> A Wounded Finger Will Not Hurt You."
> They cut their fingers,

They felt the pain.
They doubted.

They changed men into wet nurses.
I heard a scholarly lecture:
"Without Economic Incentives Suitably Arrayed
We Cannot Achieve Technological Progress."
There you have the words of a Marxist!
Here is a knowledge of real laws for you
And an end of Utopia.

Adam Wazyk's "Poem for Adults" was read by grownups
and recited by youths. The party bosses were shocked and
alarmed. They attempted to turn off the faucet of criticism.
Valiantly the intellectuals stood their ground. *Nowa Kultura*
inaugurated 1956 with an article in its January 1 issue which
heralded "the revival of criticism" as "positively helpful." It
had already eliminated much "varnishing, that is, falsifying
of reality . . . Catchwords and slogans have bored the listeners for a long time and finally they are beginning to bore
their very authors." The writer condemned "that discordant
optimism, that satisfaction with life unsupported by deeper
thought, that affirmation of the new without any knowledge
of it." Bad dramatic criticism was "one of the causes of our
chronic crisis in playwriting." Of course, the outside enemy
would quote these denigrations but "there is only one method
of extracting the foe's most poisonous tooth: take away his
monopoly of criticism" by criticizing.

An author in the Lodz *Kronika* of January, 1956, fired a
shot at Communist propaganda: through Free Europe Press
balloons "copies of Milocz's *Captive Mind* and Orwell's *1984*
have reached us. Facts which were true but unfavorable to
us and which were ignored by our propaganda have been
seized by the enemy . . . Our propaganda remained silent
when a fire broke out in a mine or when hooliganism became
a universal calamity." Here one sees the critic still trying to
justify his attitude, trying to win freedom.

Now the twentieth party congress in Moscow came and went. "A few years ago I was a dogmatist," wrote Kat in *Nowa Kultura* of March 25, 1956. "I answered questions simply, 'Yes' or 'No' . . . When I was asked about a war I answered that capitalism brings wars, just as a cloud brings rain . . . I was happy as a dogmatist. Today I am a dogmatist no more."

Presently *Trybuna Ludu,* the Communist party's official Warsaw daily, dared to touch a subject which was taboo in Soviet publications. On March 29, 1956, it quoted a letter from a Polish reader who had been studying the Moscow twentieth party congress and was puzzled. "So," comments the newspaper, "the man simply asked this: in what and in whom is one to believe? What is true and what is false? There is nothing strange in his question. Many a person pursues the following train of thought: if I could believe in lies and take them for the truth, who is going to guarantee that what I think is the truth today will not turn out to be a lie?" The very posing of this question had a salutary effect.

Only three days later, *Trybuna Ludu* aired a startling proposal. Why, it asked, was the Polish Sejm or Parliament such a dull affair devoted to rubber-stamping government decrees? "Do not such motions require discussions, a clash of opinion?" it demanded. "Then why does unanimity always prevail . . . There is too little debate in our Sejm."

When the nineteenth session of the Polish Council of Culture and Art opened in April the lessons of the Moscow party congress and the secret Khrushchev speech were well assimilated. *Przeglad Kulturalny* of April 5–11, 1956, published excerpts from Jan Kott's comments before the Council: "The wedding gown of liberalism fell off and the most repulsive despotism appeared in all its nakedness . . . It is a truth that compels us, at the least, to realize the emptiness of our patriotism . . . We have granted our confidence to everybody. We thought everything that happened in our camp advanced the cause of mankind . . We have tried to explain reality and not to learn the truth. To explain and justify. At any price! Even at the price of truth." In the first years of the Russian revolution, Soviet literature served a useful purpose. But "in the early 1930's literature and art ceased to speak the truth . . . Art was used not to justify the political system but a political organization . . . Literature which was not allowed to speak about crimes, literature which had to keep silent about trials shocked the conscience . . . Literature with its mouth sealed had to wander further and deeper into lies . . . The Marxist analysis of the development of literature and art stopped at the threshold of the twentieth century. Everything after that was subordinate to the false and generalized theory about the mechanical growth of art in socialist society and the equally mechanical decay of art, culture, and literature in bourgeois societies."

Poland, said the speaker, was sucked into this Soviet maelstrom of decadence. "There began a slow, merciless process of dying conscience, a spreading moral—and not only moral—blindness . . . The writer, scientist, and artist was treated with increasing frequency as a pupil who is being checked as to whether he has done his homework." In the last two years, to be sure, Poland had stirred, Mr. Kott stated. More than anywhere else in the socialist camp, "the attempt to wash the lies and impotence out of literature and art has overcome the obstacles . . . [Nevertheless] we have received neither help nor encouragement from the party leadership."

The great Soviet glacier was beginning to recede from Poland. The thaw had become a freshet. Polish intellectuals were aiming shafts not only at the Kremlin but at the lesser Kremlin in Warsaw. No secret police touched them. The population acclaimed them. Occasionally an editor got into trouble. Now and then an article was proscribed by the censor. Usually the knuckle-rapping did not hurt. Editors and writers had their patrons in the highest party circles. In fact

it was the factional split in the party and the curbing of the
U.B. that made the thaw-freshet possible.

Revolt, *Trybuna Ludu* of April 5, 1956, revealed, was now
gripping the Communist ranks. Wherever the proceedings of
the Moscow twentieth party congress were discussed, Polish
Communists demanded "open party life." Members insisted
on knowing what happens in secret sessions.

And always the intellectuals harked back to their period of
enslavement to Moscow. "Was there a period in my life,"
asked Witold Wirpsza in *Przeglad Kulturalny* for the latter
half of April, 1956, "when I was really convinced that the
defendants in the Moscow Trials were traitors and Fascist
agents? No. I have always had a doubt, or, to put more pre-
cisely, I felt uneasy."

If only the Moscow *Literary Gazette* could publish such a
statement or reprint one from its Polish contemporary!

The same issue of *Przeglad Kulturalny* carried another
significant article. The Bezpieka (U.B.), Ludwik Maj wrote,
no longer gave them orders. Fine. But was that all? No, there
was also the opium. "This is our guilt. We have grown ac-
customed to lead a comfortable life in which someone thinks
for us and talks for us and we carry out everything like man-
nequins." Mr. Maj was in torment. He had believed in Stalin.
There were dangers in de-Stalinization. Would it bring back
capitalist kulak farmers? "Go and ask my mother whose life
was broken because of a kulak . . . Should we forget the class
struggle altogether?" He was struggling with the past and
himself, struggling and thinking in public—a new, and
healthy, development.

A contributor to *Glos Robotniczy* of April 26, 1956, likewise
felt perturbed: "When a storm falls on dry land it brings not
only life-giving moisture. There is also damage, streams of
dirty water break the grain and carry away the soil." The
Moscow twentieth party congress, he said, had stimulated
enemy efforts in the villages to disrupt the collectives. "Those

third-rate prophets say now, after the twentieth congress, it's
the end of producers' cooperatives . . . the troublemakers
have another argument in their pockets: 'Have you heard
about Gomulka? . . . He was probably right when he refused
to countenance collectives.'"

Gomulka sat in his prison cell, but the country was talking
about him. Freedom protected a prisoner.

Poland had entered a period of political effervescence. *Trybuna Ludu* of May 3, 1956, reported "a dozen or so" party
meetings in one industrial enterprise in Silesia. Topic: the
twentieth party congress. "Perhaps for the first time, party
members at their meetings criticized the work of the Sejm and
of individual deputies . . . What is more valuable after the
twentieth congress is probably the fact that more and more
people express their thoughts boldly. But these are only the
first shoots . . . Many workers are still afraid." They wonder
whether "the fashion of criticism will pass and then who
knows how one may be punished for this."

Debates ensued. One writer stated that after Khrushchev's
revelations every Communist had "soiled hands." Another replied, "I do not think so." One was accused of being a sup-
porter of Mahatma Gandhi and advocating "clean hands." He
denied it. References abounded to Swiatlo's story though his
name was not mentioned.

"We cannot ignore the opinions of opponents or even of
enemies," S. Kozicki wrote on April 15, 1956, in *Po Prostu*.
It is wrong, he contended, "to put an equals sign between the
concepts of 'enemy' and 'political opponent.'" These were
new and brave words, yet a little safety catch was added: "of
course that does not mean . . . freedom of speech for all kinds
of political riffraff." On the other hand, "let us admit—after a
break of many years—that our enemies were and perhaps will
again frequently be right in their analyses of certain phenomena of our political and social life." The remedy is truth.

"Truth strikes the propaganda trumps from the enemy's hand."

Meanwhile readers commenced to react. They were writing letters to the editors. "It is a good thing," *Zycie Warsawy* declared on April 30, 1956, that "each copy brings sharp and sincere criticism of past distortions and errors, and of the surviving rigidity and old habits . . ." Why didn't you tell us earlier? citizens were saying.

On May 20 the same newspaper condemned the jamming of foreign stations. If everybody heard them without interference their statements could not be distorted and exaggerated by "unintelligent or simply spiteful listeners."

Djis I Jutro (Today and Tomorrow) of May 13 complained that Poland had been cut off from the West. "All non-progressive publications stopped arriving at the beginning of 1950 . . . We must . . . compete boldly with the art of the West . . . One cannot create art of one's own without knowing the art of other nations . . . It is time to end the custom by which only an artist who is a member of the Communist party or a sympathizer can receive a 'cultural visa'" to travel abroad.

Glos in June, 1956, ventured into a field where cowards feared to tread: Polish foreign relations. The author of the article was not quite satisfied with the fact that "in the past eleven years the current of Polish foreign policies flowed in the same river bed with Soviet policies." He understood the reasons for this situation, but it did not preclude some Polish initiative. "At one time, we permitted ourselves to be overwhelmed by emotions and to loosen our ties with France with whom we have so many common interests." Relations with Scandinavian countries had been neglected too. "All good foreign policies must be elastic . . ." He went as far as he could at the moment.

Literary magazines forsook their special field and undertook deep expeditions into human and philosophical aspects

of life. "Can we continue not to perceive the indifference, the
fatigue, and depression in the attitude and consciousness of
the masses?" asked *Zycie Literackie* of June 3. ". . . the point
is not only higher wages. The employee and the employer.
That is where capitalism began. That is also where socialism
began . . . It really seems that the worker is indifferent as to
whether his employer is a capitalist or the socialist state . . .
Can we wonder about the quite understandable wish of the
factory director to keep his privileges to the end of his life?"

The author of this article, Miroslav Fligier, moved on to
another sensitive problem in industry: "Assuming that piecework pay is based, with no miracles, on quantity only, the
simple consequence would be the use of all means to speed
up production regardless of costs. Quantity at any price." As
one solution, Mr. Fligier suggests that "the employees receive
logical and direct share in the profits of the enterprise." In
Russia all this would sound like treason.

Many Polish Communists were vexed and alarmed by such
probings into the basic assumption of their creed. They answered back in whispers against intellectuals; and, since some
intellectuals were Jews, they indulged in anti-Semitic whispers as well. Edda Werfel answered back in *Po Prostu* of
June 17. These two cross currents remained in evidence until,
at the climax, they clashed.

Nowhere in the Communist world has there been such sober
thinking and plain speaking on the profound problems of the
system; and since the system is, with minimum variations,
similar throughout the Red orbit, the Poles have performed
an important service of enlightenment on the functioning of
Communism. The Poznan insurrection was approaching. Nobody of course anticipated it, but economic issues were moving into the center of attention. *Po Prostu,* the bravest of the
journals, struck at many unmentionable evils. An article in its
issue of June 10 dealt with the growing unemployment: "Now
we have depopulated villages, neglected farming, and excess

labor in towns." Half a million persons were temporarily unemployed. Two weeks later the magazine published a broader
treatment of the economic crisis under the intriguing title "Is
This the Twilight of Marxism?" by Wlodzimierz Godek and
Ryszard Turski. They began with the proposition that there
are inner contradictions under socialism. For instance, "our
small industries and artisans not only failed to develop and
grow in the last ten years but, on the contrary, actually retro-
gressed . . . there are hundreds of thousands of acres of fal-
low land . . . our agriculture has been at a standstill for ten
years . . . we take only minimum advantage of the produc-
tive possibilities inherent in our agricultural economy, especially in individual farming . . . Isn't there a contradiction
here?"

Moreover, "Enormous wastage of materials and of the
means of production in the socialist system can be as harmful
and destructive as depressions in the capitalist system. Isn't
there a contradiction here too?

". . . A week ago, the conference of economists came to
an end. The agenda included reports on the outcome of the
six-year plan and on the prospects of the next five-year plan.
Unfortunately members of the government who were scheduled to deliver reports refused at the last moment. Why?

"Why has the five-year plan not yet been officially ratified
although its first six months have already elapsed?

". . . In our system, which is based on scientific planning,
everything seems to prove that the reverse is the case." Industry and agriculture are out of step and there is "chaos in
the farm-collective movement." Another socialist contradiction.

The two authors interviewed a minister of the government.
He told them that further mechanization and automation
could vastly increase production and reduce the number of
workers needed. Then why was it not introduced? "He is prevented from doing it by the threat of unemployment in the

country. The question of where dismissed workers are to seek work has ceased to be a rhetorical question . . ." In addition to half a million unemployed the writers estimated "on the order of two million" redundant workers. Socialist feather-bedding. Technical progress is thereby delayed and a premium put on inefficiency.

The authors dig even deeper: "Overtime? For many workers in this country overtime represents a second wage . . . The work which he takes thirteen hours to complete could often be done well in seven hours. . . . The worker works very hard because he must live. He must secure for himself and for his family at least the most elementary means of subsistence. He must therefore, given the present system of material incentives, stretch out a seven-hour job into a period twice as long." This "points not only to the absurdity of our way of doing things but also to certain anti-humanitarian elements inherent in our system . . ."

They emphasized additional contradictions: shortages of goods yet concealed unemployment. (They might have mentioned another: more beverages and less to drink. Philippe Ben, Warsaw correspondent of the Paris *Le Monde*, gave the details in his paper of August 3, 1956. More beer and mineral water had indeed been produced that summer. But forty million metal stoppers were needed whereas the plan provided for only twenty-five million. Worse, only 56 per cent of the plan was fulfilled. So the bottles remained unfilled.)

Delving to the fundamental source of this economic disease, Messrs. Godek and Turski arrived at a single conclusion: It is the fault of the bureaucracy which directs the national economy. The political manager has ousted the expert. The inexpert, impersonal manager was draining away the people's vitality. The job of director has become a profession. Example: "There is a certain director in a certain district town of the Cracow region. At first he was in charge of culture. He ruined the newly established and hopeful municipal theater, for which they transferred him to a better-paid position as director of an industrial plant. After a few months' directorship he was put in jail—for money lacking in the cash till. Following an investigation he was released and again nominated director, this time in another district institution. And the same story repeated itself: missing funds, investigation, court sentence, and a few months in jail. When the director left prison he was rehabilitated and given a new directorial post. And the same story was repeated five or six times . . .

"The position of director of the District State Farm Board in a certain region was held by representatives of the following professions: a carpenter, a man without a profession . . . next an electrical engineer (they say he was the best), then the former chief of the district Security police, etc."

This "crystallization of the profession of managers," the two authors declare in their final paragraph, is the "serious danger" threatening the Polish socialist economy.

Godek and Turski never answer the question posed in their title. We are not told whether this is the twilight of Marxism. Four days after the article appeared Poznan burst into a fierce protest against the mismanagment of the state's big business by aloof, incompetent directors, and against the misconduct of the secret police toward human beings. It was the twilight of the Polish Communist leadership. Russia tried to prevent the eclipse and to check the flow of free speech. But the thaw which had become a freshet and then a torrent was now a flood. It swept Gomulka in and Khrushchev, Molotov, Mikoyan, and Kaganovich back to Moscow. The poet's verses and the scribblers' pens started it all. Critical magazines were sold and resold at black-market prices until their print was illegible. Their ideas were taken up by a spate of newly founded, independent discussion clubs, hundreds of them, each of which attracted vast audiences. People wanted to talk. They wanted to listen to the truth. The U.B. arsenal contained no weapon against this. Moscow was no match for it.

CHAPTER 17

The Bloodless Revolution

A Polish journalist recounts the following episode: when Boleslaw Bierut, Poland's Number One Communist, who died in Moscow in March, 1956, lay in state in Warsaw, the journalist's maid asked for time off to see the body. "But you're mad," the journalist scolded. "You are seventy and have varicose veins. The temperature outside is below zero and you will have to queue six hours before you get to see the corpse. Besides, I know you are anti-Communist. Why then this sudden interest in Comrade Bierut?"

"I want," she explained, "to see the man the Russians killed."

There is no proof that Bierut died an unnatural death. But the rumor of Russian foul play made him a Polish hero.

Poland's national mind retains a vivid memory of four Russian partitions, plus invasions, suppressed revolutions, and repressive rule. This black record weighs on Communists and non-Communists alike. To all of them Russia is the synonym of tyranny, and never more so than now. For Poles, Russia is the uncouth East. Judging by their writings and speeches, Polish party members feel that the Soviet Union has been the kiss of disease to Communism in Poland. This awareness is not made less painful by the realization that but for Russia there would be no Polish Communist regime at all. Overwhelmingly Roman Catholic and largely peasant, Poland is not admirably suited for a voluntary Communist experiment. Soviet power is therefore Communism's strongest protector in Poland. The indebtedness is galling, the umbilical cord a noose, yet the relationship must remain so long as Polish Communism cannot stand on its own achievements and while Russia needs Poland as a buffer against western democracy. They depend on and hate one another.

Russia's reputation for culture and finesse has not been exactly enhanced in Poland by the irascible, bull-in-the-Kremlin manner of Nikita Khrushchev. Poles call him "the muzhik," by which they do not mean gentleman. He brought Bierut's body to Warsaw for burial. The obsequies over, he turned to the real business of the trip: the election of a successor. Polish Communism is not blessed with a plethora of talent. In 1938, Stalin butchered the leaders of the party who had fled to the socialist fatherland for safety from their capitalist compatriots. The war, Hitler's concentration camps, and the U.B. took a further toll. Now, with Bierut gone, Berman very unpopular for his association with the U.B. and close identification with Moscow, and Hilary Minc *hors du combat* as a result of leukemia, the task of selecting Poland's Number One Communist was not easy. At the meeting of the Central Committee convened to cast the ballots, the majority clearly wanted Roman Zambrowski. Khrushchev rejected him. "There are too many Abramoviches here already," he advised the assembly; in other words, too many Jews. A storm broke. "You're an anti-Semite," shouted Madame Romama Granas, a deputy member of the Central Committee. He fumed and threatened to leave the hall. "I saved the Jews of the Soviet Union," he exclaimed, and told how, at the time of the Doctors' "Plot" in January, 1953, Stalin planned to have all Soviet Jews deported to Siberia. Only thanks to his resistance and that of several other Politburo members, Khrushchev stated, was the measure canceled.

(In Moscow, in 1956, my Jewish friends informed me that

the final preparations for their banishment to the Arctic had already been made and they hourly expected the order to depart. When Beria, in April, 1953, announced that the physicians had been falsely accused and were being released and rehabilitated, even Jews who never thought of themselves as Jews were jubilant, and that day telephones in Jewish apartments never stopped ringing; they congratulated one another and received congratulations from Christians.)

He opposed the choice of Zambrowski, Khrushchev explained to the Polish Central Committee, not from any dislike of Jews, but because the elevation of a Jew to the post of first secretary of the party would turn more Poles against Communism. In deference to Khrushchev's veto, Zambrowski's name was withdrawn. Khrushchev proposed Edward Ochab for the job. The prospect did not please Ochab. He was a freak "Hamlet" among Communists, too irresolute and too honest to qualify for the office. At Khrushchev's urging, however, he accepted.

A fierce struggle for supremacy now developed within the leadership. It made Poland a newspaperman's paradise, for each rival group had its journalistic pen bearers and editorial shields, and, especially in the watershed Moscow-versus-Gomulka crisis when Russian military intervention impended, there was little that a good Polish reporter or even an active western colleague could not ascertain straight from "the horse's mouth" by frequenting the right café or cultivating the right connections with the contending factions.

The party had split into two segments: the hards and the progressives. The hards were the Natolin group, so called because their outstanding figure, Marshal Konstantin Rokossovski, resided in the Warsaw suburb of Natolin. Rokossovski, a Soviet citizen of Polish descent, became a marshal in the Russian army in the 1930's, but Stalin later sent him to a Siberian concentration camp. Released to fight Hitler, he distinguished himself as a talented strategist in many campaigns.

After the war, Stalin decreed that Rokossovski was a Pole and appointed him chief of the Polish armed forces and of the Soviet army of occupation in Poland. The Marshal himself had no flair for politics but let his glory shine on the Natolinites who did.

Arrayed against these hards stood the liberals led by Prime Minister Josef Cyrankiewicz, a former social democrat, a former inmate of a Nazi concentration camp, a westerner, and an intellectual. Ochab often sided with him; more frequently he tried to be the swaying balance in the center.

As soon as Ochab was elected first secretary in March, 1956, the Natolins took the offensive. General Kazimierz Witaszewski, Rokossovski's deputy in the Ministry of Defense and Chief Army Political Commissar, delivered a ringing address in Lodz excoriating the thaw intellectuals and aiming several unmistakably poisoned arrows at the Jews' among them. (Witaszewski had purged Jews from the Polish army when Stalin "uncovered" the Soviet Doctors' "Plot" in January, 1953.)

Witaszewski was the Natolin group's candidate for the Politburo. They expected the July plenary session of the Central Committee to confer the same honor on Wiktor Klosiewicz, president of the Polish trade unions, a hated puppet directing a puppet organization.

While these intrigues evolved, and before Ochab could properly survey the complicated political scene, the bomb of Poznan burst under his secretarial chair. In the acrid smoke-filled atmosphere the leadership groped for a policy. Brain-splitting questions confronted them. Was Poznan the result of the criticism-flood and the relaxation? Or did it spring from incomplete de-Stalinization? Should the party get tough and revert to repression or grant more reforms? Clamp down or let up?

In this vacillation, the Poznan trials were postponed again and again. Warsaw floundered. When the trials did take place, none of the strikers or strike ringleaders stood in the dock; the regime dared not arouse the ire of the working class. Of the hundreds of persons arrested many went free. Only twelve young men under or a little over twenty were prosecuted, nine for firing on the U.B., three for the brutal lynching of a U.B. corporal; and the sentences, interspersed with a few acquittals, were so mild, the trials so unsensational (and fair) that their educational effect was negligible and their psychological impact nil or minus. It was clear that the population would not submit to harsh treatment.

Immediately after Poznan, Prime Minister Cyrankiewicz announced the government's intention to continue the liberal course; and when the July plenary session convened, Witaszewski and Klosiewicz failed of election to the Politburo. On the other hand, Rokossovski raised Witaszewski's army rank, and the Natolins were strong enough to oust Jerzy Morawski, leading figure of the thaw-freshet-flood, from his post as editor of *Trybuna Ludu*.

Meanwhile the economic situation steadily deteriorated, and political paralysis threatened. The machine of state was skidding, spinning on the brink of an abyss. The liberals realized that unless a firm Polish hand took the wheel Moscow would. The Natolins saw a rising tide of anti-Soviet sentiment. Victory in the factional fight would be worthless if disaster intervened.

All eyes turned to Wladyslaw Gomulka. For more than a year and a half since his release from prison at the end of 1954, he had been living in retirement. On August 5, 1956, the party restored him to rank-and-file membership. Then the government offered him a position which he rejected. Conscious of the crisis, conscious of the bargaining advantages it gave him, he held out for all or nothing. His minimum was maximum: first secretary of the party. The source of his strength was simple to explain: a national Communist, he had resisted Russian control; a man of common sense, he had opposed involuntary collectivization.

Government and party emissaries beat a path to Gomulka's private dwelling. As the emergency deepened, the queue of courtiers lengthened. Everybody considered his authority the now indispensable prop of the system. The Politburo officially briefed him on its proliferating problems. The Natolin hards and the liberals competed for his favor. The Natolins were reconciled to Gomulka's entry into the Politburo but not as first secretary. They hoped to capture his influence and prevent him from using it. He, on the other hand, insisted that the Russian hand be weakened, and to this end made common cause with Cyrankiewicz and with Ochab who was only too glad to terminate the "terrible experience"—his words—as first secretary.

Gomulka laid down conditions: those responsible for secret-police cruelties were to be punished; General Marian Spychalski and other innocent victims of the Bierut-Berman-Minc U.B. regime must be rehabilitated; Hilary Minc, economic dictator, father of collectivization and of the crushing overinvestment in heavy industry, must resign from the Politburo; Gomulka proposed the same kind of eclipse for Franciszek Mazur, commonly considered by Poles a Soviet agent, and for Zenon Novak, a principal Natolinite in the Politburo. Most difficult, Gomulka insisted that Rokossovski quit the Politburo; this constituted an undisguised challenge to the Kremlin and could only be interpreted as a threat to its power in Poland.

Minc and Berman resigned from the Politburo. Mazur disappeared into Russia. Zenon Novak resigned. The alarmed Natolins sent signals to Moscow.

In this tense atmosphere the party Central Committee convened at 10 A.M., Friday, October 19. Ochab called the members to order but hastened to inform them that the meeting would have to adjourn immediately so that they could rush to meet Khrushchev, Mikoyan, Molotov, and Kaganovich whose plane from Moscow had just put down at the Okenicie Airport near Warsaw. The Russians had not been invited. Ochab received the news only a few hours before their arrival.

The Polish Politburo and other top Communists, together with Gomulka—still only a rank-and-file party member—drove to Okenicie Airport. There they discovered that the four Soviet leaders had brought with them fourteen Russian generals. Rokossovski met them. So did Marshal Koniev, Soviet commander of all the Warsaw Pact armed forces.

This descent from Moscow was at once sensational and sinister. The quartet of Soviet leaders were the political point of a Soviet military spear. In the night before their arrival, the Soviet divisions stationed on Polish soil, reinforced by one division brought in from East Germany and another from Russia, converged on Warsaw. Units of the Soviet fleet appeared demonstratively before Gdansk (Danzig) and Stettin. Needless to say, Moscow never interferes in the affairs of foreign countries; Khrushchev, Molotov, Mikoyan, and Kaganovich simply wanted their words in Warsaw to carry more conviction.

There was a little man at Okenicie Airport named Komar. General Vaclav Komar. He had commanded the Balkan Division of the International Brigade in the Spanish Civil War; when World War II began he enlisted in the Polish army in France. Recently the government had appointed him Commander-in-Chief of Poland's Internal Security Police (KBW), a large, well-armed and armored unit. As soon as the Russian troops moved on Warsaw, Komar maneuvered his KBW men into a circle around the city. At the airport Komar casually told Rokossovski that if the Soviet army hoped to get into the capital it would have to fight its way through. His corps had manned the bridges and roads leading to Warsaw.

During the night, chosen workingmen had been summoned to Warsaw's factories, given weapons, and instructed to stay in readiness on the premises in case the Russians invaded.

It is probably safe to assume that Rokossovski whispered this information to the four men from the Kremlin, who must have realized, as their cars entered Warsaw, that instead of having the Russian army to back up their arguments they were actually surrounded by hostile Polish armed forces.

Once in Warsaw, the Polish Communists left the Russians and returned to the hall where the members of the Central Committee were anxiously waiting. Ochab reconvened the session which quickly elected Gomulka and three of his supporters to the Central Committee. Then the deliberations were again suspended; the Polish leaders, Gomulka too, would now confer with the Russians in the Belvedere Palace in Warsaw.

These talks lasted until 3 A.M., and at 6:40 that morning the four Russians flew away to Moscow. The confrontation ended in a Polish victory, and Polish pride being what it is, and Gomulka having been, next to Komar, the hero of the encounter, it is not surprising that details leaked out.

Khrushchev placed the issue squarely before the conference in a ninety-minute peppery opening speech. Moscow would welcome Gomulka in the Polish Politburo. Several of his close co-workers might enter with him. But the Kremlin had no intention of relinquishing control; Gomulka must not be first secretary, and Rokossovski must remain in the Politburo.

The deliberations swirled around this central problem. Now and then the Poles conferred in the room among themselves. They speculated on the composition of the Soviet delegation. Could not Khrushchev alone have spoken for Moscow? Why the four? To impress? Were Molotov and Kaganovich the "Stalinists," as Tito called them, and Khrushchev and Mikoyan the "progressives"? But they were echoing one another, they all wanted the same thing—to keep the reins of power in Poland. No Polish ear caught any discord in the Soviet quartet.

The Russian four also held little whispering confabs, usually with Soviet Ambassador Ponomarenko who was present. Embassy attachés brought reports about events outside the Belvedere Palace: in most cities the workers' militia had been alerted. Factories were heavily guarded by Polish armed shock troops. Soviet commanders in Polish army units were expressing doubt as to whether Polish officers and soldiers would obey orders to march on Warsaw.

Nevertheless, Khrushchev played the trump card: if his terms were not accepted Russia would use force. At this Gomulka stood up and quietly announced that he wished to reply. But he could not do it at this conference. He was going to the Warsaw radio station and broadcast to the Polish people. He would tell them what had transpired in the Palace.

The Russians' position crumbled under their feet. They smiled, they explained, they swore eternal friendship to Poland. There was much to discuss. Poland needed economic aid to lift her out of the crisis. They hoped to see Gomulka soon in Moscow . . . Friendly handshakes and a dash through sleeping Warsaw to Okenicie Airport.

The plenum of the Central Committee reconvened later that day and heard a long address by Gomulka. The next day, October 21, its seventy-five members proceeded to elect a new Politburo of nine. Ochab received 75 votes; he voted for himself. Gomulka received 74; he didn't. Cyrankiewicz 73. Zambrowski and Morawski were tied for eighth and ninth place with 56 votes. Rokossovski received only 23 votes and therefore failed to keep his seat in the Politburo. The same session elected Gomulka first secretary of the party, top political leader of Poland.

Gomulka and Poland had won a decisive battle. In a limited sense, October 21, 1956, was Poland's independence day.

But in the continuing war with Russia Gomulka faced many difficulties, not the least of which was the turbulent temper of the people. It expressed itself emphatically in various ways —in an exchange, for instance, between speaker and audience at a meeting in Gdansk two days after the plenum. The speaker, Wladyslaw Matwin, one of the secretaries of the Central Committee, told the huge crowd that "in our party . . . there are progressive and reactionary forces . . . forces that would like to go back or stand still."

"Who are they?" the listeners demanded.

"You know, comrades," Matwin replied, "who has and who has not been elected to the Politburo."

"Out with it," the audience shouted. "Courage." "Be frank."

"Dear comrades," Matwin pleaded. "These are matters of little importance. The important thing is the further development of our country."

"What about Rokossovski?" the audience prompted. Matwin tried to avoid an answer, but the chants persisted. "My opinion of Comrade Rokossovski," he finally complied, "is this: I regard him as a good military man. But I do not share his political views."

Next, Matwin was asked about the actions of the Soviet divisions during the critical days. "I understand," he commented, "that you are concerned with the movements of the army. This matter was discussed the day before yesterday at the Central Committee plenum. The orders were issued by the Minister of National Defense [Rokossovski]. The Minister explained that the movements of the army were connected with routine military exercises."

This statement, according to the Gdansk *Kontrasty* of October 25, was greeted with loud laughter. "The Central Committee," Matwin went on, "pointed out that the fall exercises are conducted at shooting ranges and do not require the presence of tanks on the highways."

"What about the Soviet warships?" the audience yelled. The Russian men o' war had been seen from Gdansk.

The Central Committee, Matwin declared, had asked Rokossovski to explain the presence of those ships riding at anchor in the port.

The Poles were tough and vocal. The press kept them informed. Gomulka had to ride two balky horses, the Polish people and the Russian government. Poland was in a revolutionary mood. Workingmen were expelling managers and directors from factories, in some cases bodily. Peasants were breaking out of the collectives, disbanding the machine tractor stations, and purchasing their equipment, and—unheard of under satellite Communism—buying and selling land. Army units were voting to dismiss their commanders. Officers insisted that Rokossovski quit as Minister of Defense and go back to the Soviet Union. Protests rained on Gomulka against the further use of Russian civilian experts. Listeners demanded that jamming of foreign radio stations stop.

On October 29, Gomulka made an off-the-record speech to about one hundred prominent Polish journalists. It was a plea for calm. He had had a letter a few days before from Khrushchev asking him to send back any soviet experts he did not need. But Poland's geographical position did not resemble Hungary's. Hungary might take a neutral stance, renounce the Warsaw Pact, and ask the Russian army to withdraw. Not so Poland, which needed Soviet military protection of the Oder-Neisse line against West Germany. The nation had exaggerated the importance of the Russian troop movements in the night of October 19–20. True, the tanks tore up some roads and became involved in several "unfortunate incidents . . . with victims." A bill for the road damage would be sent to Soviet headquarters. But while still in Warsaw the Soviet leaders ordered the Soviet units to return to their barracks. He had made that a condition of the continuation of the talks in Belvedere Palace. The Polish army, Gomulka stressed, cannot be ruled by meetings, officers were not to be elected democratically by privates, nor should the army pass resolutions in favor of further liberalization. Neither must the nation expect bourgeois democracy. He did not intend to legalize a Catholic party, a peasant party, or any second party. Press censorship remained in force. The B.B.C. would not be jammed if it restricted itself, as in the past, to the transmission of objective news. Other stations would earn the same privilege if they behaved similarly.

Gomulka aimed to substitute discipline for the agitated, ebullient Polish mood. The Hungarian revolution, which broke out two days after his election to supreme command, complicated his task. The Poles immediately expressed their sympathy for Hungary by giving blood and money. The Soviet and satellite calumnies about Hungarian "counterrevolutionaries" and "Fascists" found no echo in Poland. Quite the contrary. The Polish attitude toward Hungary was formulated in a remarkable article by Roman Jurys in *Zycie Warsawy* of November 23 entitled "Poznan-Budapest." "The people's revolt," he wrote, "was equally great in Poznan and in Hungary—a revolt of the working class . . . Let us reject the version about agents . . . What was common to Poznan and Hungary was the enormous saturation of hatred for the Stalinist system of terror and the apparatus which carried out that terror . . . in Poznan the employees of the Security organization had to pay with their blood for the sins of those who extracted excessively high taxes and organized farm collectives as well as for those who misplanned the raw material supply of our industries and reduced wages . . . in this regard there is no difference between Poznan and Hungary . . . Another feature common to Poznan and the Hungarian rising is, in my opinion, that . . . the party disappeared quickly from the surface of political life . . . The third feature of the Hungarian rising is the unusual ardor of the struggle for sovereignty." Mr. Jurys saw the same phenomenon in Poland, where, he said, "it is not at all accidental that the struggle for sovereignty coincided with the period of democratization." Through democracy to Polish sovereignty. In Hungary likewise. (This is something Tito did not appreciate.) Russia's "withdrawal from Stalinism," Jurys wrote, "would be much more difficult and dangerous" than in the satellites. It was this lag that bred Moscow's hostility toward Poland and Hungary: "I see the main reason . . . in the unequal development of democratization in our country and the Soviet Union."

In giving warm understanding, as well as blood, to Hungary, Poland stepped out of satellite line and ceased toeing the Moscow line. The foreign Stalinists reacted with fury. When Edgar Faure, speaking in the French Chamber of Deputies, lauded the Poles the entire house applauded—except the Communists. The Rumanian, Czechoslovak, and particularly the East German puppet press and radio disseminated distorted accounts of the Gomulka revolution and scurrilously attacked the new trends in Polish policy. The East Berlin *B.Z. am Abend* of October 22 was confiscated by the East German authorities for publishing excerpts from Gomulka's speech of October 20, but the press of the zone vigorously condemned his words without quoting them. This malevolent satellite chorus, Warsaw surmised, was directed by a Kremlin baton, and the thought disturbed the Polish leaders who were not yet certain about Moscow's plans: would it strike with tanks as it had in Hungary and for the same reason? Poland as well as Hungary was in revolt against Russia; in both, however, the people wanted democracy, whereas the leaders hoped to evolve their own non-Muscovite pattern of Communist rule.

Gomulka, consequently, was walking a tightrope over an abyss. If he allowed the people to push him too hard he would provoke Russian anger and perhaps armed retaliation. If he did not make concessions to the anti-Russian fervor of the population he would lose support and be forced to yield to chaos and Russian quislings as in Hungary.

Bending this way and that way on the tightrope Gomulka quickly demonstrated his skill as an agile statesman. He replaced Rokossovski with General Spychalski as Minister of Defense. (Rokossovski forthwith cynically resumed his Soviet citizenship and was appointed Deputy Minister of Defense under Zhukov.) Spychalski sent home the Russian military advisors in Poland . . . The Writers' Congress was postponed: it would have been the occasion for demonstrations of friendship for Hungary and antagonism to Russia . . . Gomulka released Cardinal Wyszinski from arrest. Huge crowds greeted the Roman Catholic primate when he returned to his palace in Warsaw. He blessed them and called for calm in the interest of Poland. Subsequently Gomulka visited the Cardinal and conferred with him and a group of bishops who had not collaborated with the regime. In his first sermon the primate urged moderation and caution. Church and state, each in its own way, and both because they were aware of the twin menace of Russia and confusion, sought to induce a more temperate, less emotional popular attitude. A grateful Gomulka permitted religious instruction in government schools . . . Still balancing, Gomulka went to Moscow. At the Warsaw station the multitude that saw him off shouted, "Wladyslaw, be firm; Wladyslaw, be firm." He returned with a promise of 1,400,000 tons of Russian grain in 1957; a credit of 700 million roubles in Soviet goods; the cancellation of all Polish debts to the Soviets—this in inadequate compensation for the mountains of coal taken from Poland during the past eleven years at giveaway prices; and, most important, a recognition of Poland's sovereignty and her right from time to time, in accordance with changes in the world situation, to determine jointly with Moscow the locations and numbers of Russian troops stationed on Polish soil. Moscow had thus conceded a paper veto to Warsaw on their military collaboration.

Veto or no, the Soviet divisions remain in Poland, and that means Russian power and Polish irritation. Is the economic aid another chain around Gomulka's neck? In criticizing Tito, *Pravda* stated that his acceptance of help from the "imperialist West" served an anti-Soviet purpose. This attack on Tito constituted a warning to Gomulka. Again the Polish leader did a two-step twist on the tightrope. Stefan Jedrychowski, a member of the Politburo who accompanied Gomulka to Moscow, said, "Our achievements in Moscow have in principle eliminated the necessity of a loan from the West." Lest the deep bow to the east upset Gomulka's equilibrium, he bent in the other direction; this, Jedrychowski continued, "does not exclude the possibility of such a transaction under conditions which are favorable to us." Shortly thereafter the optimistic Poles sent a mission to Washington in search of large U.S. government credits.

Underlying all recent social phenomena in Poland (Poznan, the revolt of the intellectuals, and the Gomulka revolution) is the universal recognition that Communism ruined the country's economy. Gomulka himself made this manifest on October 20, in his astringent, cruelly analytical speech to the Central Committee plenary session. "In 1949," he said, "coal output per working day per worker throughout the industry amounted to 1,328 kilograms. In 1955, it dropped to 1,163 kilograms, that is, by 12.4 per cent . . . In relation to 1938 . . . output per working day per person employed in the mining industry dropped in 1955 by 36 per cent. The economic policy in relation to the mining industry was marked by unpardonable thoughtlessness. The system of work on Sundays was introduced and this could not but ruin the health and strength of the miners and at the same time make it difficult to maintain colliery installations in proper working order. The practice was also introduced of employing soldiers and prisoners in a part of the collieries."

In sum: despite enormous capital investment in mining,

coal output was down as a result of managers' incapacity and workers' disinterest. (If one could only have the same kind of confession from the Soviet government.)

Next, agriculture. "When estimating the value of overall production per hectare of arable land we arrive at the following picture," Gomulka said. "Private farms: 621.1 zlotys; co-operative farms: 517.3 zlotys; and state farms: 393.7 zlotys, at constant prices. Thus the difference between private and cooperative farms amounts to 16.7 per cent, while in comparison with state farms, private farm production was higher [in 1955] by 32.2 per cent." And this, Gomulka added, although the state paid out billions and billions to the collective farms in the form of direct subsidies, reduced taxes, free use of machinery, and so forth. "It is a sad picture," he remarked. "In spite of great outlays they had smaller results and higher costs of production. I do not mention the political aspects of the problem."

With the same crushing frankness he dissected the failure to improve housing.

Finally he addressed himself to Poznan. He rejected the Muscovite propaganda. "The clumsy attempt at the presentation of the painful Poznan tragedy as the work of imperialist agents and provocateurs was very naïve indeed. . . . The causes of the Poznan tragedy and of the profound dissatisfaction of the entire working class are to be found in ourselves, in the leadership of the party, in the government. The inflammable materials were accumulated for years. The six-year plan, advertised in the past with great energy as a new stage of the high growth of living standards, disappointed the hopes of the broad working masses. The juggling with figures which showed a 27 per cent rise in real wages during the six-year plan proved a failure. It only exasperated people even more and it was necessary to withdraw from the position taken by poor statisticians." And poor politicians. (Could this sort of juggling be going on in Moscow?)

It seems fairly obvious that Poland, with or without Gomulka, cannot lift herself out of the pit of the past unless foreign aid is made available. Russian means are too inadequate, Russian methods too communistic to restore her economy. Nor has Moscow the wish to make Poland strong materially and therefore independent politically. Gomulka, consequently, needs ever more western assistance, which even without (or especially without) strings must hurt the imperialist East. Paradoxically support given to Communist Poland weakens Communist Russia and reinforces Polish yearnings for democracy. Warsaw cannot yet allow a second party, but groups in the Sejm will speak for the peasants, the Catholics, the intellectuals, the workers, and the Communists. Gradually the voice of the Communists may lose its disproportionate volume.

Poland's road to greater freedom is, however, blocked by Russia. Anti-Russian feeling, therefore, is sure to grow. A minor brawl in Szczecin (Stettin), on December 10, 1956, for instance, ended in the smashing of the Soviet consulate's windows. But usually, Polish patriotism inhibits the free expression of Polish hatred of Russia. It was to this sense of discipline that Gomulka appealed during the parliamentary elections of January, 1957, when he said, "If you cross out the names of Communist candidates you will cross out Poland from the list of European nations." Nobody could have stated it more clearly: the defeat of the Communist party, Gomulka was saying, will bring in the Russian tanks and the erasure of Poland as a separate state; vote Communist or be annexed by Russia. (Yet some Asians persist in regarding the satellites as independent nations.)

Gomulka used the threat of Russian armed intervention to win the elections overwhelmingly. Anti-Communist Poles voted Communist to avoid a Hungarian blood bath in Poland. But this only stores up trouble for the Polish Communist regime and for Russia. The Polish people will be dreaming of liberation from both.

Moscow has swallowed Gomulka but not digested him. It would destroy him at the first opportunity. When Chinese Prime Minister Chou En-lai visited Warsaw from January 11 to 16, 1957, he advised Gomulka to "do as you please but don't talk about it." This is the Chinese Communist principle; the Kremlin dislikes advertised defiance. But sealed lips are only the beginning of subservience. Already Gomulka has felt the need of paying lip service to Moscow by proclaiming, in March, 1957, that the Hungarian revolution was a counter-revolution. Deeds follow words. Zenon Novak, an outstanding Polish Stalinist-Natolinite, is Vice-Premier in the new Polish government formed after the recent parliamentary elections. No doubt Gomulka included him either in response to Soviet pressure or as a sign that he was ready to behave. The anti-Gomulka Stalinists are raising their heads again in Poland and receiving encouragement from Russia. They are using anti-Semitism, the traditional weapon of Polish reactionaries, to win popularity and hurt Gomulka. Polish Jews—the eighty thousand (out of a prewar Jewish population of three million) who survived Hitler's gas chambers—are fleeing the country. *Trybuna Ludu*, the official Communist party organ in Warsaw, commenting on this sad development, said on February 20, 1957, "The fact that application for emigration and the desire to emigrate have recently reached mass proportions among the Polish Jews is proof of how painfully the Jews have felt the increasing anti-Semitic feeling." The newspaper then proceeded to reassure the Jews and to promise that "those who commit anti-Semitic excesses are being and will be punished, and racial theories will be opposed . . ." It is in Gomulka's interest to fulfill these promises. But anti-Semitism runs deep in Poland, and Moscow will not scruple to employ it as an added means of enslaving the Polish people. Poland is far from free and Russia is far from reconciled to the loss of power she has suffered in Warsaw. Gomulka's balancing act between Moscow's insistence on obedience and Poland's urge to freedom is a perpetual hazard.

How Poland can achieve national independence is unpredictable. Politics cannot be blueprinted. Presumably a day must come when the satellites will become more of a hazard to Russia than an asset. Presumably some future ruler of Russia will realize that the colonial empire is all burden and no blessing, all outgo at the expense of the Soviet population's living standard and no income. Satellite freedom depends on the freedom of Russians to demand a better life.

Meanwhile the West should remember that although Communism was imposed on the satellites by armed power, it did originally have an intrinsic appeal which consisted in the rejection of the past and the promise of a bright future. After twelve years of misrule, misrepresentation, and misery nobody now gives a fig for that promise. Nevertheless there can be no harking back to the past. For eastern Europe the world of pre-1939 is dead beyond recall. The peoples of the satellites are still hoping for something new.

No compulsion rests upon the free world to offer Poland or any captive state a substitute program or an ideal. That would be an offense to their culture and an infringement of their independence. The ideal offer is unconditional friendship and a recognition of the right of each nation to create a social system in its own image.

CHAPTER 18

1848, Not 1984

The Hungarian revolution of October–November, 1956, justifies a new faith in human beings and in the simple, homely virtues of heroism, honesty, decency, and love of freedom. Eleven years of Communist rule in Hungary left men's souls untouched; the Kremlin failed to reach them. The heart is deaf to Russia's vocabulary. Moscow is bankrupt; it has tanks and jails, but no ideas or ideals. Brute power is powerless.

Some had believed Communism would conquer the world. How is that possible when it can only kill and not convince? By killing Hungarians Russia killed Communism. Death resulted from exposure—exposure of its true nature.

The pessimists, the Cassandras, George Orwell in *1984* said man would be robotized by the dictators; the race would survive as slaves. It is not true. Hungary proves that Communism is not the future. This is not the age of totalitarianism. It is the era of liberty and liberation from imperialism. Hungary has paid a high price in lives and suffering to bring this message to mankind. But it has earned the deathless gratitude of modern civilization.

More than 2 per cent of the Hungarian population has been forced to take refuge abroad. Many thousands were killed by tanks and guns. More thousands are in prison. Unknown numbers have been transported to Siberia. It is a national tragedy.

Yet it is the most radiant tragedy of our time. It reasserts the indestructibility of the human spirit.

There were those who contended that Communism represents progress and that its defeat would mean the triumph of reaction. In Hungary morality, truth, and democracy triumphed. Hungarians have seen too much deceit and ruthlessness; their accent is on purity.

Who rebelled in Hungary? Everybody. All contra Moscow. The all includes even Communists. Moscow successfully united Hungary against foreign domination and domestic repression.

Condemning Stalin, Khrushchev said in his speech to the twentieth party congress, "Stalin acted not through persuasion, explanation, and patient cooperation with people, but by imposing his concepts and demanding absolute submission to his opinions." How is Khrushchev different from Stalin?

"Beat, beat, and once more beat," Khrushchev quoted Stalin as ordering. Shoot, shoot, and once more shoot, is what Khrushchev did. But what alternative has he? The Kremlin has no other weapons. It wanted to use them in Poland. It used them in Hungary.

Mass uprisings against tyranny are contagious. A spark from the Polish revolution flew over to Hungary. This follows the pattern of 1848. The revolution of 1848 against monarchy and feudalism, for liberty and independence, spread from France to Germany to Italy to Austria to Hungary. In April, 1849, the Austrian government appealed to Tsar Nicholas I of Russia for military aid. The despot obliged. Lenin wrote in 1900, "The tsarist government holds not only our own nation in slavery, it sends it to subdue other nations which rise against their own slavery, as happened in 1849, when Russian troops suppressed the revolution in Hungary." (V. I. Lenin, *Collected Works.* Fourth Russian Edition, Vol. 4.)

Everything has changed, but Russia still holds its own peo-

ple in slavery and sends Russian soldiers to suppress revolution in Hungary. Who are the counterrevolutionaries?

The hero of Hungary's 1956 revolution is Sandor Petoefi,
who died in 1849 by a Russian saber. In 1849, Petoefi was
twenty-six years old, yet the Hungarian nation knew him. He
was its revolutionary bard. When the uprising came he wrote
"There Is a Thought Within Me."

> There is a thought within me
> To die in the comfort of my bed,
> To slowly wither as a flower
> On which a secret worm has fed.
> Don't give this death. Oh God
> Don't give this death to me.
> Would that I were a tree that lightning strikes,
> Torn by the storm, uprooted from the ground;
> Would that I were a rock on the crevasse edge
> Hurled by the wind, chasm bound.
> When men tear off their yoke of captivity
> And raise their heads to the feast of Liberty
> And purple banners in the breeze unfurled
> Proclaim these holy words to all the world,
> *Freedom.*
> And where from East to West
> The trumpet sounds
> And the people conquer the barricades—
> There let me fall, on *this* battlefield
> There let my young blood flow from my heart.

He had his wish. True to his verse Sandor Petoefi volunteered to fight. A Cossack sword cut him down.

By the Danube stands a monument of Petoefi with up-
raised arm and tousled hair. Ever since Soviet tanks have rid-
den the streets of Budapest, women have been placing little
bouquets of flowers at his feet. Like him they would rather
die than live in chains.

Great spirits are immortal. For more than a century Hun-

garian children have recited Petoefi's uplifting lyrics. He is
in their blood. Though a remote monarch's fur-capped mer-
cenary sliced through Sandor Petoefi's brain, he survived to
return the blow. Ask a Hungarian where the 1956 revolution
began and he will reply, "In the Petoefi Club." There poets,
writers, and others rehearsed freedom's song with the people.

But before the voice of opposition can be heard in a one-
party police state the party must become disorganized and
the police demoralized. That happened in Poland prior to the
thaw and Poznan. It also happened in Hungary. Actually
the decomposition of the Hungarian Communist party and
the disintegration of the secret police (AVH) were concur-
rent, for having shared the task of terrorizing, suppressing,
and Stalinizing they also moved in unison toward their decline and fall.

The history of postwar Hungary began as well as might
be expected, for in 1945, in the presence of a Russian army of
occupation, the authorities permitted free national elections
which gave the Communists only 17 per cent of the vote as
against 57 per cent to the Small Holders (peasants) party.
Soon, however, the mask fell; on February 26, 1947, Bela
Kovacs, the general secretary of the Small Holders party, was
arrested and disappeared; later his party was suppressed, and
the Communists, needless to say, won a big majority in the
next elections. All seemed to be going very well for Moscow
and its Hungarian helpers.

Normality, however, is incompatible with Communism,
which, born in the storm, always sows the tempest. When
Russia's troubles with Tito began in 1948, the earth in neighboring Hungary heaved sympathetically. There followed a
made-in-Moscow heresy hunt of national Communists. It
needed big game. One of the scapegoats, held high to intimi-
date the rest, was postwar Hungary's first Minister of Interior
in charge of the secret police: Laszlo Rajk, a member of the
Communist Politburo. Arrested on May 30, 1949, tried in Sep-

tember of the same year, he confessed, and the instructed court sentenced him to death by hanging.

The stage manager of Rajk's trial was General Gabor Peter, chief of the secret police. He also supervised the arrest and ungentle investigation of Cardinal Mindszenty, Archbishop Groesz, American businessman Vogeler, British businessman Sanders, and thousands more. His turn to sit in a prison cell came in January, 19 3. Subjected for fourteen months to the treatment he knew so well, he "confessed" to "crimes against the state and nation," and on March 12, 1953, was sentenced to life imprisonment. Simultaneously the former head of the Ministry of Justice, a department intimately related to the secret police, received nine years in jail, and hundreds of fellow-torturers, investigators, "judges," and policemen were purged and punished. This could not have raised the morale of the secret Security organization. The mounting evidence in Communist states that the hand which wields the "flaming sword of the revolution" (approved synonym for secret police) is sooner or later hacked off, depressed the oppressors and deprived their job of its allure. The fate of Beria, who in 1953 followed his predecessors Yagoda and Yezhov to the Moscow execution dungeon, supplied the crowning proof that a nemesis pursued secret-police bosses.

Dissidents in Hungary—as well as Poland—took courage, especially when Imre Nagy became Prime Minister in Budapest on July 3 1953, in succession to Matyas Rakosi.

Rakosi was a Moscow-trained "hard"; Nagy, born in 1896 into a Calvinist peasant family, had the reputation of "a liberal." The day after he assumed supreme office he announced a "New Course" shifting the emphasis of development and investment from heavy industry to agriculture and light industry.

This program was held against Nagy in the March 9, 1955, official announcement of his dismissal as Prime Minister. Nagy's tenure coincided almost exactly with Giorgi Malenkov's incumbency in the same position in Moscow, and although attempts to establish the exact relationship between Soviet chiefs and satellite chiefs are a dangerous game, it does seem that Nagy in Hungary, echoing Malenkov in Russia, opposed economic extremism and excessive secret-police action. Malenkov, moreover, was the foe and successor of Andrei A. Zhdanov, the heir apparent to Stalin until his mysterious death on August 31, 1948; and Zhdanov demonstrably fathered the 1946–48 era of "socialist realism" repression in Soviet art.

The sentencing of Gabor Peter in March, 1953, and the elevation of Imre Nagy to the Prime Ministry in July, 1953, allowed Hungary's writers some leniency. Nagy was a university professor and a member of the Academy of Science, and therefore rated the distinction of intellectual. Nagy's dismissal in March, 1955, and the substitution of Andras Hegedues, behind whose transparent false-face was descried the grim, Mongol-like bald head of first party secretary Matyas Rakosi, might have heralded another "hard" period. But the secret police had lost its frightening authority, and, as a result of recurrent power shuffles the party had already descended into the political and ideological doldrums. Rakosi's new era of toughness consequently lacked the earlier horror. Nagy, like Malenkov, was not arrested, and with him in the background and perhaps giving them an occasional encouraging nod, the intellectuals began to think and soon to talk thaw and heresy. The trend was strengthened by the flowering of Moscow's flirtation with Tito, which—in May, 1955—brought Khrushchev and Bulganin to Belgrade. This reconciliation proved particularly perplexing to Hungarians. For Laszlo Rajk had been executed as a Titoist, yet now Moscow courted Tito. People needed to re-examine basic assumptions.

The civil war which developed between writers and government was the first battle or in fact the microcosm of the Hungarian revolution. The importance of literature in that revolution can scarcely be exaggerated. Quite correctly the *Manchester Guardian* said in December, 1956, "The Hungarians have been fighting under the sign of the nineteenth-century poet Petoefi." It was the authors' revolt in 1955 which led to the spring, 1956, Petoefi Club phase, and that in turn inspired the historic uprising in October of that year. As in Poland, so in Hungary the pen plowed the field and planted the seeds.

The line-up in the literature-versus-state war and the preliminary verbal salvos make the picture remarkably clear. In ousting Nagy from the Prime Ministry the party declared that "No patience whatsoever can justify . . . the renaissance of idealistic [a Communist curse word] tendencies in science or give free access to decadence, pessimism, and anarchy in art or entitle anyone to slander our people's democratic system under the pretext of 'freedom of criticism' in literature and the press."

To prove that this pronouncement had the force of a ukase, Jozsef Revai, Minister of Culture and Red watchdog of the arts, whom Nagy had discharged, was rehabilitated and awarded the Order of Merit for "outstanding work." The same month, Ivan Boldizsar, a leading thaw man, lost his post as editor-in-chief of *Magyar Nemzet* (Hungarian Nation).

In normal Communist circumstances—that is, if the party and police had not been weakened—these measures might have sufficed to silence the writers. They did not. The ferment continued and manifested itself publicly in an article by Gyula Hay, a very prominent author, in *Irodalmi Ujsag* (Literary Gazette) of September 10, 1955, in which he, a party member since 1919, after pledging allegiance to the regime, deplored the dearth of good drama and the "terrible monotony" of the few new plays produced, and ended with a minor-key yet unmistakable declaration of war. He called for "the death of bureaucracy," that is for the cessation of official interference. "Needless to say," he added, "such a change cannot be brought about without opposition from the advocates of bureaucratic routine. I do not doubt that this fight will end in the victory of progress."

Gyula Hay's article, entitled "Freedom and Responsibility," reflected the political dichotomy of Hungary, for it was Communist in form and anti-Communist in content. "Perhaps the most characteristic feature of our present-day literature," he wrote, "is the common stand taken by the majority of Hungarian writers . . . The direct aim of this unity is an appealing one: freedom in literature." There follows a bow to Communist credo: "Socialist society offers in this respect possibilities that could not even be dreamed of in former social systems. The question, however, is: for what purpose and for whom is this freedom in literature required? . . . There are some, at least for the time being, who need this freedom in order to smuggle unhindered into literature unfruitful, whining jeremiads, the downheartedness of weak souls, a false distorted picture of the world, and remnants of a harmful ideology of the old, dark times." Nevertheless, he would not proscribe such writing; he would merely compete with it. For "the existence or nonexistence of socialist literature depends on whether the common efforts for freedom in literature—which means the removal of bureaucratic-administrative obstacles contrary to [another obeisance] the spirit of party and people's democracy—do or do not meet with success. The development of literature, our principal aim, can only be achieved by abolishing the obstacles to this development. From this it follows that good, progressive literature, the sole antidote to bad, harmful literature, can be victorious only if it can match it unfettered and free from impediments." Mr. Hay was making a plea for the coexistence of non-Communist and Communist art, for plurality and tolerance. He preferred non-Communist art to Communist meddlers, censors, and watchdogs of culture.

The very next issue of *Irodalmi Ujsag* published a poem by

Laszlo Benjamin, a Communist, called "A Writer-Minister" which was a short, sharp attack on Jozsef Darvas, the Minister of Popular Culture. The issue was immediately withdrawn and reprinted without the offending poem which read:

> I expose my soul and I give my soul
> In search of new ideas for my craft.
> Yet nothing helps me to succeed! How can I?
> After a lot of talk I still await a satisfactory
>   explanation
> From a man who aspires to be a writer as well as a
>   Minister,
> And who is *ex officio* Father of the Arts.
> Let me then behold the embodied inspiration,
> Let me see a new work, even a little one . . .
> Don't keep on fooling me, my friend:
> *Hic Rhodus, hic salta!* I'll believe it when I see it.

Communists, writing in the organ of the Hungarian Writers Union, were taking an open stand against the Communist government and its policies. In the impending revolution many nonliterary Communists did likewise.

These literary stabs at the regime won applause and approval in the art world. Emboldened, the Communists in the Writers Union assembled in caucus on November 10, 1955, and drew up a manifesto demanding freedom from the government's "aggressive intervention" in cultural affairs. It listed examples: two managing directors of *Irodalmi Ujsag* dismissed; publication prevented of books and poems which were named; a play banned for political reasons; Communist musicians harassed; the better-known Communist reporters banned from the press and expelled from the party for expressing their opinions. Worst of all, an issue of *Irodalmi Ujsag* was confiscated; "it is certain that the Communist confiscation of a paper edited in the Communist spirit has never before occurred in any of the people's democracies." Other actions were condemned as "despotic, anti-democratic methods of leadership."

This manifesto, when circulated among party members in the Writers Union, collected an imposing number of signatures: sixty-three. Although the manifesto was not published (it appeared in print for the first time on October 10, 1956, on the eve of the revolution), the party leadership scented danger and tried to induce the writers to withdraw their signatures. Only four did.

After this failure, the Central Committee of the Hungarian Communist party drafted a resolution on literature, convened the Communists in the Writers Union, and demanded that they subscribe to the resolution. Most of them refused and ten of the most prominent resigned their offices in the Writers Union. They received a stern party reprimand with a warning that the next offense would mean expulsion from the party.

The resolution thus rejected by the Communist authors was published on December 10. It admonished them for having "lost the socialist perspective . . . their faith in the working class has been shaken and they have fallen prey to pessimism and despair . . . they have become the advocates of the decadent classes and of the most backward strata."

These were not merely literary deviations, the resolution asserted: ". . . behind literary traits of that kind lurks an attack against the people's democracy not of a literary but primarily of a political nature."

Some writers—and the resolution named them—used the Writers Union meeting of November 10 to echo "calumnies spread by the bourgeoisie about the general situation and living standards of the working class and the working peasantry. Under the mask of criticism they adopted a hostile attitude toward leading organizations and functionaries of the party and government. They denied the necessity and right of the party to direct literature." But, said the resolution, "it is the duty of the appropriate party and state organizations—and it will be their duty in the future too—to prevent the publication of pernicious writings."

Thus the party met the writers' revolt with its own declaration of open warfare.

The Rakosi regime might have put a muzzle on the mouths or a boot on the necks of the authors but for the Moscow twentieth party congress in February, 1956, and the secret Khrushchev speech which dissident Hungarians interpreted as their charter of liberty. The Rakosi regime was too Moscow-bound, and too unpopular and despised to contradict this view. Helplessly, in an effort to provide a vent, it organized a Petoefi Club in March, 1956, for orthodox discussions. This was not the first time Communists have borrowed a beloved name to which they had no right. But never did any such abuse boomerang so damagingly into their faces. The short-lived Budapest Petoefi Club became a parliament, a free debating society, a democratic platform. Through it and its provincial children the literary thaw broadened into a people's movement.

Things began tamely with a conference of government economists on May 30. Two evenings later the Institute of Literary History assembled under Petoefi Club auspices to admit past mistakes and to promise amends. June 4 saw a turbulent session of the Hungarian Academy of Science. Ferenc Mucsi complained of the suppression of criticism by the Institute of Communist Party History. Lajos Lukacs said it was time for party historians to do more than merely "explain *ad nauseam* the pronouncements of certain party leaders." Moreover, the Institute of Party History was impeding the correct interpretation of the Moscow twentieth party congress. Arpad Kalmar of the Budapest Lenin Institute declared that the thinking of university students was "on the elementary-school level." The audience applauded. History was being falsified; "I say these strong words whether they please or not." The history of the Second World War had been distorted; "I believe it an exaggeration to maintain that the entry of the Soviet Union into the Far Eastern war was the main factor in the defeat of Japan."

A young writer named Ferenc Santha now mounted the platform and, in effect, made a plea for Titoist national Communism: "In my opinion we can have Communism only if it originates in our own desires, our traditions and blood, and only if it is united with our history." Listeners liked that. "Communism can be established in our country," he continued, "only if that which is alien is eliminated . . ."

Janos Varga, dean of the Department of History of the university, asserted that the Marxist interpretation of history had not won confidence "because it frequently does not tell the truth. I do not mean that it has deliberately lied. I mean that in most cases it dwells on half-truths instead of the whole truth." He condemned "fitting facts to a thesis," one-sided use of sources, and "the improper use of quotations."

Mrs. Erzveset Koves of the Ervin Szabo Library argued, without evoking dissent, that in the teaching of World War II history certain books made it appear as though Great Britain and the United States were the allies not of the Soviet Union but of Nazi Germany. Anti-imperialist forces in America were stronger than imperialist tendencies, she said; Stalinist historical writing ignored these facts. Moscow was already correcting these falsifications, therefore "this problem no longer requires boldness on the part of our historians, they need merely return to the truth. The party's distortion of history had run up against the people's ability to remember." The audience greeted this statement with appreciative laughter. Incidentally, she added, the Social Democratic party had been maligned by the Communists. Yet "we know that the anti-Fascist struggle in Hungary went on not only in the underground but also in Parliament." Though Communists denied this, the public knew better.

Gyorgy Litvan protested that every year teachers had to

reverse themselves and teach the opposite of what they had taught the year before. "All of these contradictions lead to cynicism among youth just when we are constantly preaching against cynicism." Cynicism is also induced by "constantly emphasizing the leading and exemplary role of the Soviet Union." Perpetual attacks on the West, he concluded, merely sowed sympathy for the West.

Gergely Domotor, professor at the Miklos Zrinyi Military School, concentrated on the indifference to facts in the teaching of Hungary's military past. Domokos Kosary made the same point and deplored the necessity of interpreting Hungarian history "in the light of the works of Stalin."

Thus far, none of the speakers had been heckled. Now, however, Madame Erzveset Andics, professor of history at the University of Budapest and chairman of the peace movement, took the floor. Her speech broke up the meeting. More had been done in the past few years to clarify historical truth than in many preceding generations, she averred.

The crowd, consisting chiefly of university students, booed. Professors smiled.

"If anyone," she continued, "tries to prove that Marxist history has committed faults . . ."

Cries of "Don't you think so?" interrupted her.

"And that Marxist historical writing kills our young people's desire for truth . . ."

"It does, it does . . ." the students shouted.

"Let him conjugate the proceedings of the twentieth party congress," she proceeded. "Do not believe him . . ."

"Whom should we believe?" the audience demanded.

"We admit our mistakes," she stated.

"You don't," the listeners argued.

"But criticism does not mean that we must ridicule our accomplishments. That is not the truth, that is not dialectical."

The audience laughed so long she could not finish her address.

Overwhelmed, apparently, by this hostile demonstration, the Petoefi Club officers did not convene another meeting for ten days. The keynote speech at the philosophers' conference on June 14 was delivered by Professor Gyorgy Lukacs, foremost Marxist philosopher and literary critic of Hungary, who expressed regret at the assembly-line production of philosophers who had little culture or knowledge. The next day teachers of the Budapest secondary schools examined their mounting problems. Two days later the instructors at people's colleges who had been discharged during Rakosi's worst period of repression were gathered under the Petoefi Club's roof to air their grievances.

To their dismay the originators of the Petoefi Club now discovered that instead of directing the writers' thaw into a controlled channel they had permitted, or aided, it to overflow into all neighboring fields of culture. In effect, the Petoefi Club had become an open political forum. Petoefi Clubs with the same objective were springing up throughout Hungary. The Communist party looked askance at this development, but it was rocked by inner dissensions, rumors of Rakosi's dismissal ran up and down the land, and nobody yet seemed prepared to lay a rough hand on the Petoefi Clubs.

The Budapest Petoefi Club's activity reached a peak on June 19, 1956. It met, this time, in a theater with a capacity of eight hundred, and that number of invitations was issued for 7 P.M. By 4:30 every seat was occupied. At 6:30 when the proceedings got under way, standees crowded the aisles, window sills, stage, and every other available cubic inch of space. There were at least 1500 persons in the theater, an estimated third of them army officers in uniform. It was a hot, humid evening. By common consent, nobody smoked. Eating and drinking were out of the question. Yet the audience, to a man, remained in the hall until 3:30 in the morning.

Throughout those nine hours, angry waves beat against the dike of dictatorship. There was no plan, no design, only an elemental force fighting the obstacle that restrained it. An unofficial parliament, strange sight in totalitarian Hungary, was in session.

The meeting had been convoked to afford an opportunity for self-expression to Communists who operated in the anti-Nazi wartime underground and to illegal Communists of the Horthy regime who had been purged by the postwar satellite government of Hungary. (Their Communism was probably too idealistic for Rakosi.)

The first scheduled speaker was Marton Horwath, editor of *Szabad Nep,* the party daily. He made a short, nervous, introductory statement: he would indulge in self-criticism; others should follow suit; many mistakes had been committed, they should be re-examined under the aspect of the new line proclaimed by the Moscow twentieth party congress.

Tibor Dery was provoked to reply. Dery, a well-known Communist author, underground Communist fighter under the Horthy dictatorship, had written a novel which the party condemned because it presented an oversympathetic portrait of a bourgeois professor. Much has been heard of late, Dery said, about the evils of censorship. But "let's get down to specifics. Specifically, here is Marton Horwath. He does not speak for himself, yet sometimes it is difficult to know whether he speaks for the party. One day he is on the extreme right, next day on the extreme left, and how can we know what he represents?" (Horwath obviously reflected the aimless gyrations of the Communist party dizzy from the blows inadvertently rained on its head by the twentieth party congress.) Next Dery turned on Jozsef Revai, the former Minister (and hatchet-man) of Culture, "who knows he is telling lies but continues to tell them." As for Jozsef Darvas, the incumbent Minister of Culture, "He's afraid of himself, that is all I need say of *him.*

"What," Dery asked, "is the cause of all our troubles? There is no freedom. I hope there will be no more police terror. I

am an optimist; I hope we will soon be rid of our present
leaders. Let us bear in mind that we are allowed to discuss
these things only with permission from above. They believe
that it is good to let some steam out of the superheated boiler.
We want deeds, and we want the opportunity to make more
speeches. I would not entrust the future of literature to
Marton Horwath. He is responsible, among others, for the distortions in art."

Dery had reached his peroration: "We have been fighting
for so many things," he exclaimed, "but we have forgotten
the chief thing: humanism."

Tibor Merai, the next speaker, a Communist journalist,
assailed Deputy Minister of Culture Mihaly: "How is it he
has been appointed professor of journalism at the university?
He already holds ten jobs." Alexander Fekete, another Communist journalist, back from Moscow that day, reported what
Russian and Yugoslav comrades had told him there: if you
want a cultural revolution in Hungary "you journalists have
got to make it."

A young physicist who gave his name as Janossy, former
research student in atomic science at Trinity College, Dublin,
denounced the regime for jamming western broadcasts. Only
from western stations, he said, had they been able to hear
the secret Khrushchev speech. "Western newspapers should
be allowed to enter Hungary . . . People in prisons must be
rehabilitated. These are tasks for a real democracy."

Gyorgy Nemes, pointing to Horwath who had asked for
criticism, said he would give it to him: of fifty-two journalists
employed by *Szabad Nep* in 1951, only six still held jobs
there. Many of the others were in prison.

A multitude had assembled outside. Thousands blocked the
streets around the theater. An unknown person ordered loud-
speakers erected on the outside wall.

Peter Kuczka, a young poet, now made a frontal attack on
Rakosi, first secretary of the party, boss of Hungary. "A good

journalist," he began, "is characterized by a car, a chauffeur, and a special shop" where he can buy goods not available to the general public. "He must write the truth. However, in our country, the truth must conform to the changing party line. In 1949 Rakosi said Laszlo Rajk was a traitor. In 1955 he said Rajk was a palace provocateur. This year he calls Rajk comrade. The masses have lost confidence not in the party but in its leaders . . . Truth can exist only where freedom exists. We demand a free press . . . What kind of press is it that attacks Imre Nagy in *Szabad Nep* and gives him no space to defend himself . . . It was nationalization that caused the decline and low level of the Hungarian press. We ask the publication of the full text of Khrushchev's speech." This was frank subversion.

Up spoke Madame Laszlo Rajk, widow of the executed man. Greeted with thunderous and prolonged applause, she said she did not wish to be made a heroine because of what happened to her husband. She merely asked that those who murdered him be ejected from office. She too had been in prison for years; Hungarian prisons were a disgrace to a people's democracy. When she finished the audience accorded her a standing ovation.

A young woman who did not state her name, merely that she taught philosophy at the University of Budapest, asked for the floor and called attention to the un-Communist way of life of leading Communists. They lived in five-room villas and forgot that many families had to squeeze into one room; they bought their clothes and food in special closed commissaries while average citizens did not have enough to eat. The party leaders had lost touch with the rank and file and with the common people. "There has to be a change in the party leadership."

"Down with the regime," the audience shouted. "Long live Imre Nagy."

Marton Horwath, editor of *Szabad Nep*, received permission to defend the regime. Boos drowned his voice on three occasions. "Don't insult the party," he urged.

"We're the party," a man in the orchestra replied.

"Let's remove Laszlo Rajk's corpse from the ditch and give him a decent burial," another person cried.

"Why do we call this the Sandor Petoefi Club?" a third member of the audience demanded. "Petoefi fought for press freedom."

"Which we haven't got," a neighbor added.

"That's right," Horwath unexpectedly agreed.

"You're telling us," a listener remarked aloud. The audience burst into laughter; Horwath shrugged his shoulders and resumed his seat.

Word-of-mouth reports of this Petoefi Club meeting spread through Budapest; the event was on everybody's tongue. It became a nation's pride. When a further meeting was called for the afternoon of June 27, 6000 people congregated. It lasted till midnight and its tone, if anything, was more agitated, its speeches more oppositionist, than that of the previous session.

Seven hours after the chairman banged down his gavel and closed the proceedings, Poznan's working class walked out into a general strike. The two events were in no wise connected. But using the June 28–29 Poznan uprising as a pretext, Rakosi shut down all Petoefi Clubs in Hungary on June 30.

However, Rakosi was called to Moscow shortly thereafter, and on July 18 he resigned all his functions in Hungary and went to live in Outer Mongolia with his Mongolian wife.

Ernoe Geroe, Rakosi's successor as first secretary, lacked most of his predecessor's skill and guile but none of his rigidity or ruthlessness. But he operated in different and difficult times which curbed his cruel propensities.

The Petoefi Clubs were again legalized. The writers' revolt flared to new heights. The public murmured against privations and restrictions. The Communists ruled but confusion reigned. All of the summer of 1956, Hungary rocked rudderless in the tempest. The first days of October found Geroe in Yalta seeking to borrow power from Khrushchev and prestige from Tito. Hungarian Communism had obviously lost its grip. Yet nobody preached, and neither the authorities nor the nation expected, an armed revolution. By common assumption, a dictatorship could not be overthrown by force.

The mood of those troubled months before the revolution is perhaps best conveyed by a published poem from the pen of the youthful Communist, Laszlo Benjamin. Tired, completely disillusioned, yet patriotic and dreaming of a freedom seemingly unattainable, he wrote:

> I have no destiny, no religion, nor god.
> The miracle-dreams no longer surround me;
> nor the tactics of self-made gods.
> If—struggling and trouble-stricken—
> I still try to do something and work
> —as well as possible—
> then it is in order that anybody shall be allowed
> to do his work in freedom,
> that he shall not be harmed, or suffer violence,
> nor false charges be brought against him—
> in order that
>   this little Hungary
> shall one day become a real Homeland,
> the country of its nation.

CHAPTER 19

A Macabre Drama

With all Moscow's guidance and their own Marxist direction finders, the Hungarian Communist leaders did not know where they were heading. It is doubtful whether anybody in the government or against it thought the political volcano would blow its top. Yet everything economic and political was clearly out of joint; and in desperation, apparently, the Budapest pigmies grasped at a straw: they ordered the disinterment of Laszlo Rajk's remains and their burial in the tomb of Hungary's national heroes, the Kossuth Mausoleum, so named after Louis Kossuth, father of the 1848 revolution.

October 6, 1956, Budapest factories, offices, and stores closed, and several hundred thousand citizens marched past the metal coffins of Rajk, Andras Szalai, Dr. Tibor Szonyi, and Major General Gyorgy Palffy—Communists executed in 1949 for "Titoism."

Leading members of the Hungarian government and Communist party took turns in the guard of honor. Ferenc Muennich, a former Hungarian ambassador to Moscow, spoke and referred to those responsible for the executions as "sadistic criminals whom, however, we do not want to try on the day of the funeral." One of them, Stalin, was beyond trial. Mr. Bela Szasz, surviving codefendant of Rajk, said, "We want to bury not only the dead but simultaneously the period when violence ruled." Deputy Prime Minister Antal Apro declared that the men they were reburying had been the victims of "false and provocative accusations."

Mrs. Rajk, bareheaded, a raincoat thrown over her shoulders, stood among the spectators. Inside the coat she held a boy of seven close to her. His eyes had a look of nonunderstanding. Next to Mrs. Rajk stood Mrs. Szalai, another woman widowed by that judicial murder. Her hand rested on the shoulder of her little daughter who looked at the ground. Neither child knew its father.

Rajk was forty when they hanged him. He fought in the International Brigade in Spain and was appointed secretary of the illegal Hungarian Communist party during the Second World War. In the postwar Hungarian government he served as Interior Minister and then Foreign Minister.

On May 30, 1949, a police car came and took him and his wife Julia away. That very day they separated her from him, and she never saw him again though they were in the same prison. While they tortured him and tried him she was near but inaccessible. She was near enough to hear him being hanged. "Geza," an officer called the hangman by name, "the execution can be carried out." "These words I heard," she reports, "and also the chair being taken away from under his feet . . . And in the great morning silence I understood that a physician had declared him dead." She was imprisoned in a cell directly over the execution place, and during her incarceration she heard fifty-one other executions.

"It was awful what they did to a man like Laszlo," she exclaimed to a Yugoslav journalist who interviewed her after the official funeral and to whom she recounted these gruesome experiences.

When they arrested Rajk and his wife they also arrested their four-month-old son, Laszlo Junior. Although they had relatives in Budapest the boy was not given to them. His name was changed to Istvan Kovacs and he was brought up

by people who did not know whence he came. Two and a
half years later a secret-police official called on Julia Rajk's
sister and asked whether she would take the boy. But they
would not bring him into her apartment or allow her to come
for him. At the appointed time, at the corner of Vaci Street,
"a curtained car appeared. It stopped, the door was opened,
the child was left in the street, and the next minute the car
disappeared."

During the five years she spent in prison, Julia Rajk received no news of her son. She was tortured, she duly confessed when she could bear it no longer, and then they
sentenced her. In 1954, she was released but not as Julia Rajk
or Mrs. Laszlo Rajk. The authorities gave her a paper saying
she was Mrs. Laszlo Gyorki. She was denied the right to use
her own name; "Rajk" was an unmentionable word in Hungary.

In July, 1956, a big car stopped in front of Julia Rajk's
home on Jozsef Katona Street where she lived with her son
and her mother. Out of it stepped the Prosecutor General of
Hungary. He brought two documents. One annulled her sentence. The other annulled Laszlo Rajk's sentence and declared that all the charges against him were invented. Now
she could again be Mrs. Laszlo Rajk. Her husband had been
rehabilitated. "I think," she told Dr. Zelmanovich, the correspondent of the *Vjesnik* of Zagreb, Yugoslavia, "that now
the whole Hungarian nation should be rehabilitated." She
would work for it.

Laszlo Rajk's reburial, macabre though the scene was,
made amends. But it could not have been inspired by remorse
or a sudden accession of decency. Ernoe Geroe, the new first
secretary, hoped it would bring him some degree of popular
support. It inevitably produced the opposite effect. For now
all Hungarians knew, from the government's mouth, the enor-
mity of the crime and the inhumanity of the regime that
ruled them.

In the presence of death, men brush aside nonessentials and delve to fundamentals. In reviewing the Rajk story, Hungarians discarded the Communist theory about two kinds of truth. "Slowly, with at least half of our mind," one journal wrote at the time, "we came to believe . . . that party truth can be more important than objective truth, and that truth and the momentary political benefits are identical conceptions." Therefore they were expected to believe Rajk guilty in 1949 and innocent in 1956. But "This is a horrible thought . . . If the momentary political benefits are the tests of truth then a lie can be 'true' because it is momentarily useful. A fake political trial may become a true trial . . . this attitude . . . contaminated those who invented the fake trials . . . it poisoned the atmosphere of our public life . . . blurred our sight, paralyzed our critical faculties, and finally made it impossible for us to observe the simple truth." At the funeral they recognized the truth and saw the Communist system in all its naked dishonesty.

Nobody quite knows why or how revolutions erupt. But certainly the lie of the Rajk trial, re-emphasized by the reburial, added fuel to the nation's red-hot wrath. Seventeen days after the funeral Hungary rose in revolt.

CHAPTER 20

Hungarian October

The Russian Bolshevik revolution occurred on November 7, 1917. But according to the old Julian calendar, which the Soviets later abolished, the date was October 25, and therefore the Bolsheviks call their revolution the October revolution or simply: October. The Gomulka revolution took place on October 21, 1956; the Hungarian on October 23. October is the month of revolutions.

Non-Hungarians said, What a pity the Hungarian revolution did not wait until after the American Presidential election on November 6. It would have received more attention in the United States. Others deplored its coincidence with the Suez crisis. The answer is that no one can prescribe to a revolution. It obeys its own mysterious laws. When the people's cup of sorrow has overflowed and their patience is exhausted an irrelevant incident or an irrational move may precipitate the storm. In reality, therefore, only the first act of a revolution is authored by revolutionists, all the preparations are the work of the government in power. The Tsar and the Provisional government made the Bolshevik revolution; Moscow made the Gomulka revolution; the Kremlin and its Hungarian Communist puppets are responsible for the outbreak of the anti-Russian, anti-Communist Hungarian revolution. Moscow charged that foreign agents fomented the Hungarian revolution. No doubt about it. They were Moscow's agents. Their misdeeds, mistakes, and misconceptions gave birth to the Hungarian revolution and their continued misconduct fed it.

Lenin was accused by his enemies of being a German agent. Reactionary counterrevolutionaries, with no sense of history, always find this excuse. How could one agent or ten thousand induce a country to rise unless it was ripe? Can foreign agents or foreign radio broadcasts produce a revolution in Great Britain, or western Germany, or Sweden, or India?

Communists must maintain the fiction of foreign agents—though they can adduce no proof—because to concede the existence of domestic opposition would topple their entire ideological house of cards. If the workers are antagonistic to a Communist regime, where does that leave the "dictatorship of the proletariat"? If peasants mutiny, where is the "workers' and peasants' state"? If intellectuals are disaffected, Communism is a failure. How, moreover, could Communists reconcile opposition against them with a 99.7 per cent vote for them in the last election?

I have often argued with Communists about democracy and the multiparty system. They contend that in the absence of hostile classes and of opposition no second party is necessary; "the country is over 90 per cent behind us," the Prime Minister of Czechoslovakia said. When facts dismiss this fantastic claim there is a single alternative: either permit more than one party or shout "foreign agents."

Another fallacy needs to be examined: it has been alleged that but for the Anglo-French landing at the Suez Canal Russia would not have employed its tank army to suppress the Hungarian revolution. This unproved assertion ignores the dates and the essence. Moscow used tanks in Hungary beginning October 23. The Israelis did not cross into Egyptian territory until October 29; the Anglo-French ultimatum to Egypt was delivered on October 31; western troops landed

in Port Said on November 5. But dates apart, Moscow had
to use tanks else it would have lost Hungary. Moscow used
additional tanks when Hungary threatened to transform itself into a multiparty democracy. To permit democracy in a
country on the Soviet frontier and in close proximity to other
satellites would have been ruinous. Even Tito did not welcome it and therefore condoned Russia's military intervention. A democratic Hungary would be a revolver aimed at
the temple of Communism. Russia had to nip this peril in the
bud, and even a world otherwise totally at peace could not
have deterred her. Suez or no Suez, the Kremlin knew the
western powers would not precipitate a third world war to
rescue Hungary. Suez or no Suez, Russia could not be
coerced by the United Nations or by international public
opinion. Then what did Moscow have to fear? Russian failure
in Hungary may call for a new policy. But when the eruption
came Moscow was bound to fight with every means at its
disposal.

Conditions in Hungary compelled Russia to be counterrevolutionary. Conditions compelled Hungarians to be revolutionists. Yet an hour before the revolution began nobody
knew it would. Certainly Ernoe Geroe, the first Communist
party secretary of Hungary, suspected no trouble, for he was
in Yugoslavia from October 15 to 23, dining with Tito and
going to the opera. Prime Minister Hegedues and most of
the leaders of the party and government were there with him.
They returned to find Budapest in turmoil.

During their absence newspaper attacks on Rakosi multiplied; Moscow had retained him in power too long. By in-
ference, these strictures were aimed at Geroe, a lesser Rakosi.
In the same period the Communist party restored Imre Nagy
to membership and he again appeared in public. Simultaneously resolutions were adopted by factories and universities demanding Nagy's return to office. Workers also asked

for higher wages, peasants for the abolition of compulsory deliveries of farm produce to the state at low prices.

October 20, 21, and 22, Hungary listened to the radio; western stations, Polish stations broadcasting in Hungarian, and Hungarian stations as well were telling the story of Russia's near-intervention in Poland and Gomulka's victorious bloodless revolution. Anti-Stalinist (anti-Geroe) elements had apparently won control over *Szabad Nep,* the chief party daily, and over Radio Budapest. They commented enthusiastically on Polish events.

At 9 A.M. and again at 10 A.M. on October 23, Radio Budapest announced a silent march of sympathy to the Polish embassy for 3 P.M. that day. . . . At 12:43 P.M. Radio Budapest announced that Minister of Interior Laszlo Piros had banned the procession. At 1 P.M. Radio Budapest announced that the Petoefi Club had met and adopted a resolution urging an immediate session of the party's Central Committee to reorganize the government and bring Nagy into it; the expulsion of Rakosi from the positions he still held; a revision of the party's attitude to art; and "complete equality" with the Soviet Union with a view to ending Russia's monopoly use of Hungarian uranium. . . . At 1:23 P.M. Radio Budapest announced that Piros had lifted the ban on the pro-Polish demonstration, and that the Hungarian Young Communist League would participate. . . . Later in the afternoon a great multitude of workers, students, Young Communists, and hundreds of Hungarian army officers, carrying Polish and Hungarian flags, filed past the statue of Polish General Bem who fought against the Russians and Austrians in the Kossuth revolution, and cheered as they reached the Polish embassy. At 4 P.M. they stopped before the statue of Sandor Petoefi, wreathed it with flowers, and listened to Imre Sinkovits, an actor, recite Petoefi's poem, "Rise, Hungarians." Addressing the marchers who gathered around him in a giant circle, Peter Veres, president of the Hungarian Writers Union,

enunciated a political program: national equality and independence [in other words, freedom from Russian domina-
tion]; management of factories by workers and specialists,
revision of the wage system, and abolition of norms; freedom
for peasants to leave collectives and abolition of compulsory
deliveries to the state; elimination of the Rakosi clique [a hint
to Geroe to go]; the return of Nagy; free and secret elections
to Parliament. Veres's words were broadcast by Radio Budapest. . . . At 6:30 P.M. Radio Budapest announced that the
Politburo had met and convened the Central Committee for
October 31, to reorganize the party and government. . . .
At 7 P.M. Geroe, back from Yugoslavia that very day, broadcast over Radio Budapest.

His speech was fateful, fatal. Ill-informed, insensitive, or
inflexible, or all three, or instructed by the Russians, he made
a harsh, Stalinist statement: ". . . we want a socialist democracy and not a bourgeois democracy . . . our working class
and our people jealously guard the achievements of our people's democracy and will not allow anyone to touch them
. . . The main purpose of the enemies of our people today is
to undermine the power of the working class . . . to shake
the people's faith in their party . . . to try to loosen the close
and friendly ties between our country . . . and the other
countries building socialism, particularly between our country and the Socialist Soviet Union . . . They heap slanders on
the Soviet Union. They assert that our trade with the Soviet
Union is one-sided and our independence allegedly has to
be defended not against the imperialists but against the
Soviet Union. This is a barefaced lie . . ." and so on and so
on in the same' tone.

As he spoke, a second demonstration, one hundred thousand strong, was marching through the streets of Budapest.
Infuriated by Geroe's declarations, students stormed the radio
station. AVH (secret-police) guards, apparently fearful of being overwhelmed, threw some tear gas and fired into the

crowd. Men and women were killed. Demonstrators again rushed the station and were again driven back with losses. They turned away and assaulted the Communist party headquarters, Radio Kossuth, railway stations, the telephone exchange, the central telegraph, and military schools and barracks. They appear to have captured the Military Academy (or it surrendered to them), for thereafter they were well supplied with machine guns and rifles. They definitely seized the building of *Szabad Nep*, the party daily; this was later admitted by Radio Budapest.

Geroe summoned Soviet tanks that very evening. From windows and roofs, from behind doorways and trees, youths and workers heaved gasoline-filled bottles at the big T 54 Stalins. The tanks replied. Fighting continued all night.

Thus began Hungary's October. It differed from Poland's October because from the first hour blood was sprayed on the fires of nationalist passion. That made it difficult, or indeed impossible, to control. It evolved quickly, therefore, from a national Communist revolution to a democratic revolution.

CHAPTER 21

The Diary of a Revolution

October 24, 1956. "Attention! Attention! We repeat the announcement. Imre Nagy has become the new Prime Minister . . ." That was the official Radio Budapest at 7:13 A.M.

Instead of waiting till October 31, as agreed, the Hungarian Communist party's Central Committee met the evening of the first day of the revolution, October 23, and elected Nagy Premier and member of the Politburo. It also dismissed a number of Rakosi men from the leadership and introduced a large number of Nagy men into it. Among the latter was Janos Kadar, arrested in 1951, tortured (teeth knocked out, fingernails pulled off), and released by Nagy in 1953.

But Geroe remained first secretary of the party.

"Attention! Attention!" Radio Budapest calling at 8 A.M. "The dastardly armed attacks of counterrevolutionary gangs during the night have created an extremely serious situation. The bandits have penetrated into factories and public buildings and have murdered many civilians, members of the national defense forces, and fighters of the state Security organization. The government was unprepared for these bloody dastardly attacks and therefore applied for help, in accordance with the terms of the Warsaw Pact, to the Soviet formations stationed in Hungary. The Soviet formations, in compliance with the government's request, are taking part in the restoration of order."

Twenty minutes later the Minister of Interior decreed a curfew until 1 o'clock that afternoon. Industry, transportation, and communications were paralyzed. Soviet tanks and Hungarian AVH policemen engaged armed rebels in Budapest streets, and both sides suffered heavy casualties.

Prime Minister Nagy addressed the nation at 11 A.M. and promised an amnesty to all insurgents who laid down their arms by 1 P.M. He dedicated himself to "Socialism . . . corresponding to our national characteristics" and "radical improvement of workers' living conditions."

Seven minutes after one the deadline for the surrender of arms was extended from 1 to 5 P.M. "Women," the official radio announcer cried, "do not let your husbands run into deadly danger . . . Mothers, do not let your sons go into the streets where they face deadly gun barrels."

At 5:48 P.M. Radio Budapest mentioned the name of a young man, seventeen years old, whose mother had had a nervous breakdown when she heard he was fighting. "If he wishes to see his mother alive he should go home immediately." Street battles continued all day and all night of the second day of the revolution.

October 25. The government radio claimed that the rebels had been suppressed and Soviet troops were "mopping up" the last pockets of resistance. Nevertheless, Colonel General Istvan Bata, Minister of Defense, broadcast several appeals that day to "members of the army, who, for one reason or another, have been separated from their units," to return to barracks. Later it became known that Hungarian soldiers had joined the rebels, some with their tanks, Soviet-made tanks, so that now it was Russian tanks manned by Hungarians versus Russian tanks manned by Russians. Occasionally Soviet crews surrendered their tanks to the rebels.

At 11:33 A.M. a communiqué from the Politburo announced that Geroe had been dismissed as first secretary and succeeded by Kadar.

Kadar then came to the microphone, referred to the government's desire for "an equitable and just settlement" with Russia, and spoke of "the grave situation in which we are involved."

Nagy followed him. "As Premier," he said, "I wish to announce that the Hungarian government will begin talks with the Soviet Union . . . concerned with the withdrawal of the Soviet forces stationed in Hungary. These talks will be carried out on the basis of equality and national independence . . ."

But is there not a contradiction here? If Hungary was equal and independent, talks were unnecessary. Nagy could simply ask the Soviet forces to leave.

Budapest, a city of 1,750,000 (approximately one-fifth of Hungary's nine million inhabitants), rocked with constant fighting. The 2 P.M. to 9 A.M. curfew notwithstanding, people filled the streets heedless of bullets, unmindful of repeated radio appeals to stay home. The tanks did not terrify, the government's authority had vanished.

October 26. The revolt now spread to the provinces. At ten minutes past midnight Radio Free Miskolc went on the air. Speaking for the newly formed revolutionary workers' council of greater Miskolc, a town of over one hundred thousand persons in northeastern Hungary near the Czechoslovak border, it demanded the immediate departure of the Soviet army, the formation of a new government, and the right to strike.

At 1:20 A.M. a representative of the Ministry of Interior in Baranya County (southwestern Hungary, near the Yugoslav frontier), speaking over Radio Pecs, said "there is no such thing as a revolutionary committee. What happened is this. One or two irresponsible elements, posing as a revolutionary committee, broke into the studio in the evening hours and had an announcement read." But at 10:45 A.M. rebels were broadcasting over Radio Pecs.

Rebels also captured Radio Nyiregyhaza near the Rumanian and Soviet boundaries, and at 5:30 P.M. asked the Budapest government to act "without subterfuge, sincerely in the spirit of humaneness, and in the interest of our people . . ."

October 27. The situation was bewilderingly fluid. Radio stations changed hands repeatedly, attacking the government in the morning, supporting it in the afternoon, attacking it in the evening. Insurgents seemed to control most of western Hungary. Soviet troops were invading the area. A general strike, however, hampered their movements. The regular Hungarian army was either passive or sympathetic to the revolutionaries. Only AVH Security formations acted as Soviet auxiliaries.

From the first day of the revolution, rebels made the AVH secret policemen the special target of their fury and guns. Remarkable, and terrible, pictures were taken by *Life* magazine photographers of disarmed AVH officers, death in their eyes, being shot at close range by insurgents after their Russian-style epaulets had been pulled off and women had spat in their faces. Other Security policemen were hanged head down. The only thing to be said in explanation, if not apology, is that persons who themselves court death with baffling abandon, as did the rebels facing mammoth tanks and seasoned soldiers, attach little value to the lives of their enemies. The secret police were vigorously hated as the symbol and support of a detested imported regime; and, at the first opportunity, the people brutally made them pay for the massacres and tortures of innocent citizens by the agency to which they belonged.

Likewise Communist books were burned by Hungarian insurgents. This appears illiberal. Actually, if the action was at all rational, it need not have been an expression of intolerance. The rebels were not infringing the freedom to read.

They were destroying the literature with which a state monopoly had flooded the land. Private organizations or a Communist party competing with other parties could publish without hindrance.

Impassioned Hungarians retained a sense of humor; when Radio Budapest stated that the military would fire on any assembly of four or more persons, they commented, "Proletarians of the world unite, but not in groups of more than three."

At 6 A.M. Radio Budapest appealed for peace: "Enough bloodshed. Enough ransacked streets. We would love to know whether our children, our relatives, are still alive." Boys of fourteen, fifteen, sixteen, and older, were ambushing Soviet tanks in the streets of Budapest all night. Mr. Victor Zorza, *Manchester Guardian* expert on Soviet affairs, in Hungary at that time, spoke to a mother of one of these seventeen-year-old student rebels. "He came home," she said, "during a break in the fighting to get his first hot meal in three days. 'Don't go back, my little son,' I said to him. 'I wouldn't stop you, I really wouldn't, if there were any hope that we may win. But there is no hope for us, there is only death for you if you go, my little son.'

"'There is hope in death, little mother,' he replied.

"That night he was shot dead."

The streets of Budapest were littered with dead, including the dead bodies of Soviet tank crews lying beside their burned-out, thirty-six-ton monsters. Inferior in equipment and training, but armed with patriotic zeal, the teen-age Hungarians fought without regard to self or mercy, and many a sad Russian mother now mourns the loss of a son who might have been obeying dictators' orders against the dictates of his own heart. Though the tanks were mammoths, the human beings inside were afraid and they usually moved in bumper-to-bumper convoys to protect one another. Whenever Hungarians fired on them from an apartment house the Russians

threw streams of shells into it, killing people and kindling
hate. It was a vicious circle of violence.

Often in those agitated and tragic days, youthful groups of
fighters sent runners to the Writers Union for advice. The
writers decried personal vengeance. The Writers Union became a kind of staff where resistance units learned what was
going on. Prime Minister Imre Nagy frequently consulted
the Writers Union by telephone, particularly Peter Veres
and Gyula Hay.

The puzzled government announced changes in its composition. The reconstituted cabinet consisted of twenty-one
Communists and six members of the disbanded Small Holders party. Of the six, several had collaborated with the Communists; only two were independents: former President of
the Republic Zoltan Tildy, and Bela Kovacs, general secretary of the Small Holders party, who was arrested on February 26, 1947, and transported to Siberia where he remained
until, a broken man physically, he came home to Hungary in
1954. The government was not really new.

The day this government came into being, the day Radio
Budapest said, "Enough bloodshed," AVH troops broke into
a building in Magyarovar, a town near the Austrian frontier
held by rebel students and workers, and machine-gunned
eighty-six of them. A grizzly photograph of the corpses
massed on the floor was circulated throughout Hungary.

At 2:35 P.M. Radio Free Miskolc stated that the workers'
council and students' parliament had been in control of the
peaceful town for forty-eight hours. The garrison and police
were supporting the workers.

Later that afternoon Radio Free Pecs announced that the
army garrison was siding with the rebels: "We are also sons
of workers, of miners, peasants, and intellectuals." Western
Hungary remained in insurgent hands.

Radio Free Miskolc at 10:45 P.M.: "The Hungarian people
have lost confidence in the Imre Nagy government . . . So-

viet troops should stop fighting as soon as possible and leave
Hungary . . . Blood has run in rivers and the bitterness of
the people turned into a revolutionary rage. Should Russia
again fling Hungarian liberty in the mud as she did in 1849?"

No newspapers were printed in Budapest on October 27.

October 28. Radio Budapest reported Soviet casualties during the night. Much fighting centered around the Kilian Barracks, where General Paul Maleter of the Hungarian army
commanded the revolutionists. Radio Budapest at 10 A.M.:
"Attention! Attention! A message to the resistants in the
Kilian Barracks and the [nearby] Corvin District. This message is sent by two intermediaries: 'We have transmitted your
answer to the commanders of the Soviet and Hungarian
troops. They consider your conditions unacceptable. In their
opinion the new Hungarian government . . . represents the
interests of the whole Hungarian people . . .'"

The Kilian Barracks continued to resist.

Soviet soldiers were reported deserting to the rebels. Photographs taken in Budapest show Russian tanks burning in the
streets.

Much depended on who was at the microphone. A com-
mentator on Radio Budapest at 1:25 P.M. said, "The true
reason for the recent dramatic events is the eight years of Stalinism, the unrestricted fury of despotism . . . So—one may
ask—what was the actual reason for the warfare of the last
days in Budapest? Delay, temporizing. The failure to understand the real, concrete situation as it was, the disregard of
the will of the people . . ."

Radio Free Gyor near the Austrian border reported that
the local Petoefi Club, the miners, and the Writers Union
were demanding "that Imre Nagy call on the Russian troops
to begin their withdrawal from Hungary carrying white flags
. . . How do the miners regard the future? The future social
system of Hungary shall be decided by free elections. We
do not object to the Communist party standing with the other

parties . . . Until these demands are met the miners of Selinka and its district are not prepared to produce a single spadeful of coal."

Later the same station broadcast a message from the army garrison of Gyor: "Workers of Gyor! We, the soldiers of the Gyor garrison, support your justified demands . . . Fight with us for an independent Hungary." Much of the nation's army had gone over to the rebels.

Provincial workers' councils were communicating with one another by telephone and wireless. For instance: "The National Council of Komarom informs Hegyeshalom [close by the Austrian border] that the road is clear until Esztergom . . ."

That afternoon Premier Nagy bent to the popular storm and made a conciliatory speech full of promises. The rebel Radio Free Miskolc quoted copiously from it but added, "We are only partially satisfied." Why? "The people of Borsod County want not only that Soviet troops withdraw from Budapest but that they withdraw completely from Hungarian territory and go home."

A huge gathering of citizens, using ropes, pulled down a giant statue of Stalin in Budapest and shouted joyously as it crashed and broke in pieces. The massive head remained whole.

Monday, Tuesday, and Wednesday, the last three days of October, 1956, represent one of the great climaxes, perhaps the greatest, of the Hungarian revolution. For in those three days, the revolution revealed its true strength; it grew so strong, both in support and in political logic, that it won the Nagy government over to its side. Nagy, the Communist, joined the revolution. That produced a crisis in Hungary's relations with Russia, provoked furious Russian reprisals, and set the pattern for the future.

October 29. An article by Ferenc Molnar in the *Szabad Nep,* official Hungarian Communist party daily, was a straw in the new wind. It answered and condemned an editorial in the Moscow *Pravda* entitled "The Collapse of the Adventure Directed Against the Hungarian People." Mr. Molnar maintained that the events of the past week were not an adventure nor had the effort collapsed. "The slogans of socialist democracy, not those of reaction and counterrevolution," Mr. Molnar stated, "were the loudest. The insurgent people of Pest and Buda want freedom and a life . . . without fear or terror. They want more bread and national independence. Is this what *Pravda* calls an adventure? . . . Something really did collapse and that was the rule of the Rakosi-Geroe clique." It was not necessary for Molnar to tell *Pravda* that Rakosi and Geroe were Moscow men.

People had been tearing out the red star which the Communist regime placed in the center of the red-white-green national flag. They resented the red star and the Russian-style shoulder boards on military and police uniforms. Now the government ordered ribbons with the national tricolor worn on military caps. The Minister of Interior declared the AVH Security force dissolved.

Radio Free Gyor, at 8:25 A.M., thanked the army for liquidating the Security police.

Radio Free Miskolc at 11 A.M.: "Attention! Attention! This is an appeal from the Debrecen Hospital: We need . . . iron lungs urgently because the one we have is out of order."

Radio Budapest at 2 P.M.: "The Executive Committee of the Budapest City Council has decided to rename Stalin Street, The Street of Hungarian Youth; from now on Stalin Bridge will be called Arpad Bridge, and Stalin Square will be Gyorgy Dozsa Square."

Same station, at 3:57 P.M., repeated the government decision to abolish the AVH and all police units "with special privileges."

At 12:15 P.M. Radio Free Gyor said, "Today we are informed . . . that Soviet units have begun to leave the capital

and are marching to . . . Lake Balaton . . . their military
base." Radio Budapest, however, had contradictory news at
4:17 P.M.: "In accordance with an agreement reached with
leaders of the Budapest resistance groups, the insurgents are
beginning to hand over their arms to Hungarian troops re-
lieving Soviet units. Within twenty-four hours after they
hand over their arms, the withdrawal of Soviet units from
Budapest will begin." The conditional withdrawal, then, had
not yet begun. If Radio Budapest was correctly informed, the
Soviet military were relinquishing their guard duty to Hungarian soldiers but did not intend to quit the capital city until
the rebels had disarmed themselves. The rebels, it is known,
hesitated; they suspected a trap.

Radio Free Miskolc, at 1 P.M.: "We wish to inform you that
today's funerals are taking place from 11 A.M. to 3 o'clock . . .
Tomorrow funerals will begin at 2 o'clock." At 1:15: "Bloody
fighting continues." The workers' council of Borsod County
dislikes the composition of the new Nagy government and
demands that Soviet troops be withdrawn immediately, "not
only from Budapest and not to their bases but from our country." At 1:40: "Attention Debrecen Hospital! Attention! Munich has heard the broadcast . . . asking for iron lungs.
Munich . . . is doing its utmost to forward . . . the lungs
from Germany."

October 30. Out of the welter of blood and the confusion
on the ground and in the air waves a simple fact emerged:
Hungary wanted freedom from Russia and freedom from dictatorship. Prime Minister Nagy drew the conclusion and
made a momentous declaration. Speaking on Radio Budapest
beginning at 1:28 P.M. he said: "Hungarian workers, peasants, intellectuals. As a result of the revolution . . . and the
mighty movement of the democratic forces, our nation has
reached the crossroads. The national government, acting in
complete agreement with the Presidium of the Hungarian
Workers party, has arrived at a decision vital to the nation's

life . . . In the interests of further democratization . . . the Cabinet has abolished the one-party system . . ."

This was the turning point in the history of the revolution. Instead of the Communist party monopoly, Nagy stated, there would be "democratic cooperation of the coalition parties." He then announced a new national government including himself, Zoltan Tildy, Bela Kovacs, Janos Kadar, Geza Losonczy, editor of *Magyar Nemzet*, Ferenc Erdei, and persons to be appointed by the Social Democratic party.

"The national government," Nagy continued, "appeals to the headquarters of the Soviet Command to begin the immediate withdrawal of Soviet troops from Budapest. At the same time we wish to inform the people of Hungary that we are going to request the Soviet Union to withdraw all Soviet troops from Hungary."

(It follows that the Soviet evacuation had not yet commenced. It also follows that the talks which, on October 25, Nagy promised to initiate with Russia had either not started or had failed to lead to the withdrawal of the Soviet army.)

"In the name of the national government," Nagy continued, "I wish to declare that we recognize all the autonomous democratic local authorities which were formed during the revolution, that we rely on them for support." This was a reference to the district workers' councils and students' parliaments. Nagy did not regard them as counterrevolutionaries or bandits.

At 5:30 the Minister of Defense announced that "the Commander of the Soviet troops having agreed, all Soviet troops stationed in Budapest begin their withdrawal on October 30 at 3 o'clock and, according to plan, the withdrawal will be completed by dawn of October 31, 1956."

But exactly fifteen minutes earlier, Radio Free Miskolc, not far from the Soviet frontier, said, "Just now it has been announced from Kisvarda that . . . many thousands of tanks . . . are pouring into our country . . . Motorized infantry

is advancing to Nyiregyhaza. New Russian units! Marshal
Zhukov, do you know of this? You must know . . ."

The departure of some Soviet troops from Budapest did
occur on October 30. They were apparently regrouping in a
circle around the capital.

October 31. At 1:15 A.M. the Hungarian air force publicly
threatened to bomb the Soviet army if it did not leave the
country.

Later that morning Premier Nagy made known that Cardinal Mindszenty, the Catholic primate arrested in 1948, had
been released; "the accusations leveled against him . . . were
unjustified."

At 8:08 A.M. Radio Budapest corrected its earlier statement
that the Soviet forces had left Budapest. Soviet tanks, it said,
were still stationed in front of the Ministry of Defense, the
Ministry of Interior, and the Soviet embassy. (According
to rumor, Moscow Presidium [Politburo] members Mikoyan
and Suslov had been in Budapest, probably at the embassy,
for some days.) At 10:10 it asserted that Soviet tanks were
in position in front of the Parliament building, the seat of
government.

At 11 A.M. the station quoted the text of a Soviet government declaration published in the Moscow morning press
of October 31: "The Soviet government has instructed its military command to withdraw military formations from Budapest as soon as the Hungarian government considers it
indispensable." This sounded ominous. Withdraw only from
Budapest? The Hungarian government had already urged
withdrawal from the entire country. "At the same time," the
declaration continued, "the Soviet government is ready to enter into negotiations with the government of the Hungarian
People's Republic and with other governments which are
party to the Warsaw Pact regarding the stay of Soviet troops
in Hungary . . ." This made withdrawal from Hungary con-
tingent not on whether the Hungarian government "considers

it indispensable" but on the views of Russia and Russia's satellites, and opened up the prospect of prolonged and perhaps
futile negotiations. The Soviet government's declaration,
drafted on October 30, at the latest, did not indicate any intention of taking its army out of Hungary and did not suggest
that Moscow had ever had any such intention.

That afternoon Prime Minister Nagy, addressing a mass
meeting at the Kossuth Memorial, affirmed that it was not he
who had requested aid from the Soviet military. He hinted
at Geroe as the culprit.

November 1. At 7:55 A.M. Radio Budapest, now rechristened Radio Free Kossuth, gave currency to a report that
Geroe, ex-Prime Minister Hegedues, and ex-Minister of Interior Laszlo Piro had fled to Russia.

New newspapers began appearing. Free trade unions came
into existence. New political parties were being organized.
The National Peasant party changed its name to Petoefi party
to "express its hostility to the years of tyranny."

Now came the second turning point: in the afternoon Premier Nagy called on Soviet Ambassador Andropov to tell him
that "the Hungarian government had authoritative information regarding the entry of new Soviet military units into
Hungary." He protested and demanded their withdrawal
without delay. He also told the ambassador that "the Hungarian government is giving immediate notice of the ter-
mination of the Warsaw Pact and is declaring Hungary's
neutrality."

This crucial, historic move made, Nagy informed all diplomatic missions in Budapest of the contents of his talk with
the Soviet ambassador. He next telegraphed the same data
to the secretary-general of the United Nations and requested
that the Hungarian question be placed on the agenda.

Having had enough, Hungary wished to retire from the
Soviet empire and assume the status of a neutral. Neighboring
little Austria, long occupied by the four great powers because

of Russia's refusal to get out, had ultimately turned that refusal into consent and was prospering in her neutrality. The
example whetted Hungary's appetite for similar treatment.

But Austria had never been a Soviet colony, and her neutrality brought Russia certain advantages. The neutrality of
Hungary would be a complete loss to Moscow, a setback to
Russian power, a proof that Communism had been rejected
by a nation which experienced it. Hungary, democratic and
independent, her defection unpunished, would be a herald
of freedom crying "Liberate Yourselves" to the remaining victims of Kremlin totalitarianism.

The odds were against Hungary's success. Kadar saw this
and made an equivocating speech in the evening. But Nagy
saw that the alternative to a desperate stab for neutrality and
democracy was to become a Muscovite quisling, a traitor to
Hungary scorned by Hungarians.

The choice (and the struggle) in Hungary was never
between Communists and anti-Communists. Persons calling
themselves Communists stood on both sides of the barricades.
The protagonists were Russia and Hungary. A few Communists, recognizing that no Communist regime could endure in
Hungary without a dictatorship backed by Soviet arms, gave
their first loyalty—as ever—to Moscow; the majority of party
members, realizing that Russia had perverted their early
ideals, and infected with the zeal of the fighting students and
workers—in whom, for the first time, they saw the true revolutionary spirit—preferred to lose their privileged political
monopoly but win a chance in the democratic lottery.

For Russia the choice was much simpler: to be or not to be
in Hungary.

At 10:30 P.M. the Soviet embassy announced that the air
fields of the Hungarian air force had been surrounded by Soviet armor "to secure the air transportation of families of Soviet troops stationed in Hungary." The Hungarian air force
replied that it "is ready, in full complement, to defend itself

against overwhelming odds." But the Nagy government forbade shooting.

November 2. Nepskarat, the new daily of the Hungarian Free Trade Unions, wrote, "As of today, we are no longer the tool of colonialism disguised as socialism, nor a figure on the chessboard of any conqueror." The Ministry of Education issued the following directive: "All history books used at present in general and secondary schools are to be withdrawn. Soviet literature is no longer to be taught. The compulsory study of Russian is to cease. The Russo-Hungarian Maxim Gorki School is to close . . . Religious instruction is to be given to those who ask for it."

Hungary was doomed. The Russians would not tolerate her release into such freedom.

November 3. An ominous political silence brooded over Hungary. Additional Soviet armored units equal, it was said, to the strength of the Hitler panzer divisions which invaded Russia in 1941 rumbled over highways and fields taking up aggressive positions. Russian infantry retook the Kovagoszollos uranium mine from the rebels.

November 4. Radio Free Kossuth, 5:20 A.M.: "Attention! Attention! Premier Imre Nagy will address the Hungarian nation."

"This is Imre Nagy speaking. Today, at daybreak, Soviet troops attacked our capital with the obvious intent of overthrowing the legal democratic Hungarian government. Our troops are in combat. The government is at its post. I notify the people of our country and the entire world of this fact."

Imre Nagy's words were repeated in English, Russian, and French translation.

Moscow was carrying out the death sentence it had passed on Hungarian democracy and independence.

CHAPTER 22

The Tanks That Failed

Hungary's body was crushed; her spirit soared. One by one, in the week after November 4, the provincial rebel radios, their voices weaker by the hour, faded out. "Help, Help, Help," they called to the West, "SOS, SOS, SOS, send medicines, send arms." Then silence.

Prime Minister Nagy fled to the Yugoslav embassy in Budapest, whence, by a ruse, the Russians abducted him to Rumania. Kadar became the Kremlin's little prisoner-king of Hungary.

Despite hopeless odds, sporadic fighting continued for weeks. *Nepszabadsag,* the rechristened Hungarian Communist party daily, reported, for instance, that on December 13, in Miskolc, "the counterrevolutionaries opened fire on Red Army forces, and this had to be returned by the Soviet troops." The article also referred to the distribution of "Fascist leaflets." The same day Radio Kossuth said several villages in Bekes County "suddenly became more restless." In Debrecen, according to official Budapest sources, demonstrators burned an issue of the local newspaper. Guerrilla fighters made hit-and-run sorties from hills, bogs, and woods.

But the end of the organized, continuous armed struggle was only a beginning. There followed a glorious phase in which the Hungarian people said no to the military victor.

It was an active negative, it was not passive resistance but positive disobedience.

Jeno Ungvari, in "A Letter from a Sad City" to the Polish Communist *Trybuna Wolnosci* of December 2, 1956, wrote, "Last week we witnessed a kind of struggle against the government by means of typed and written and mimeographed leaflets on walls, fences, and poster columns . . . This was an obvious display of loss of confidence in newspapers. The people did not read newspapers but only leaflets. . . . It is to be deplored," the Polish author added, "that thousands of the best sons of their motherland, thousands of revolutionary youths, go to Austria . . ." They too were saying no.

Napoleon is reported to have declared, "You can do anything with a bayonet except sit on it." The Russians will sit in their tanks, but tanks cannot plant potatoes, win arguments, dig coal, or run factories or trains. The Kremlin and its Hungarian quislings are endlessly powerful, yet powerless in the face of the people's will power.

When the fighting was over, government militia occupied factories. Workers said they could not work in the shadow of guns. When Kadar tried to suppress the workers' councils, they organized a forty-eight-hour general strike which brought all of industry's wheels to a halt. Factory workers' councils were united in district councils, and the districts had a secret national organization. The government arrested its leaders. The workers struck again and announced they would not return to their benches until the leaders were released. The working people cannot strike forever, but they can strike whenever they wish, and the government is unable to stop them.

Peasants have left the involuntary collectives and formed similar revolutionary councils.

These workers' and peasants' councils are soviets. Soviet is the ordinary Russian word for council. They sprang up in Russia early in 1917, when they were democratic institutions.

Subsequently the Communists seized control of them. As a result, the government which, in theory, was based on those soviets, ultimately became in fact a Communist party dictatorship and a Soviet government in name only.

Forty years later, this so-called Soviet government of Russia suppressed real soviets in Hungary.

Before his successful coup in November, 1917, Lenin, having satisfied himself that Communists would enjoy a majority in key soviets, cried, "All power to the soviets." They indeed had a tremendous following. Lenin, with demonic delight, characterized the then existing situation as "dual government," which really meant no effective government. The conventional Provisional or Kerensky government exercised only nominal power because the soviets, with their large popular support, obstructed or vetoed its actions. Out of this chaotic competition, Lenin forged the revolution.

"Dual government" is the closest description of the Hungarian situation. Conditions are never exactly analagous, and the country-wide presence of a huge foreign army of occupation makes Hungary today very different from the Russia of 1917. But the essence is similar: the Hungarian government is a hollow reed, the soviets have solid backing. Workers and peasants take orders from their soviets and grudgingly obey Russia's unhappy proconsul when privation leaves them no alternative. Their chief remaining weapon is their labor and they yield the smallest possible fraction of it to the enemy. To embarrass him the nation sacrifices its own necessities. Defeated in war, the country continues the war with other means and with a civil courage which is a rare commodity in the modern world but which Hungary possesses in abundance.

Unwilling to recognize her government and unable to overthrow it, Hungary has resorted to limited self-rule and voluntary self-denial. There is in Hungary a government without a people and a people without a government.

Shifting prime ministers in Budapest will not solve this

problem. A puppet by any other name is still a Kadar. Without tanks he falls—unless he deserts to the soviets, if they will have him.

Moscow will try to rule Hungary by terror and concessions. It has already made concessions and will make more. But concessions win no converts, for the people are not seeking gifts from the conqueror; they eagerly desire his early departure in the company of his Hungarian agents.

Russia's problem in Hungary is insoluble. Frantically, Quisling Kadar denounces Imre Nagy, the writer Gyula Hay, and other prominent Hungarian revolutionaries as traitors. National Communism, he said on January 30, 1957, is "the twin brother" of national Socialism or Nazism, which the imperialists, he declared, invented in the 1930's. Nobody pays any attention to what Kadar says. The official Budapest daily, *Nepszabadsag*, of February 23, 1957, printed an article by Istvan Pinter, who tells of a discussion he had with a seventeen-year-old boy. "Naturally you are going to stuff me with Marxist arguments," the boy asserted defiantly. ". . . there is no good trying. You will not convince me." The Hungarian universities, closed on the first day of the revolution—October 23, 1956—were not reopened until the second fortnight of February, 1957. The moment classes resumed the secret police resumed its persecution of students. Radio Budapest announced on February 23 that the police had searched the Technical University of Miskolc, found arms, ammunition, and anti-government leaflets, and arrested several students. Despite tightening terror against students, workers, intellectuals, and peasants, it is the authorities who are afraid. They have reason to be. They sit in the crater of a smoking volcano.

Moscow's weakness in Hungary is that it has only power. The Russian tank carries cannon but no ideas, ideals, or ideology. Like the remote rulers that dispatched it, it is an instrument of cold power. It can suppress, repress, oppress, but it cannot govern because it has no access to the minds or hearts of the Hungarian people.

The tanks have failed. Hungary taught the Kremlin the limitations of force. Communism has failed. Stalin emptied it of content and made it as hollow as a tank. It attracts neither young nor old. Russia's hold on Hungary remains precarious and the Hungarian situation remains revolutionary.

CHAPTER 23

Russia in Retreat

The Moscow monolith is split. The so-called Communist world (for there is no Communism in it) is surely unlike its former cohesive self when Poland applauds as revolutionists those whom Russian tanks shoot down as Hungarian "Fascists," and when Poland herself is attacked for disloyalty to Moscow by East German and French Communist leaders after she has received welcome expressions of sympathy from Red China and from Tito who is flagellated by Bulgarian, Czechoslovak, and Albanian Communists and—sometimes politely, sometimes rudely—by Moscow.

The iron curtain has been breached not by the West but by anti-Russian rebels on the other side. Polish newspapers tell the truth about Poland and Hungary, and Soviet citizens queue in Russian cities to read them for facts which their own distorting press suppresses. Polish and Hungarian students have been sent home from Soviet universities because they know what happened in their own countries and share the information with Russian friends. Czechoslovakia has stopped the distribution of newspapers from Poland; French Communists complain that events in Poland are "upsetting" the French workers; and the East German government, reversing the earlier practice, now requires Polish citizens entering its territory to obtain a visa and fill in a form giving the names of the persons they intend to see.

The real subversives are within; even the Stalinist methods employed in Hungary cannot eradicate them. Communism breeds its own troublemakers and gravediggers; the most tenacious foreign agents could not do nearly so well.

Instead of serving as an intellectual *cordon sanitaire* to keep out western thoughts of freedom, the rebellious satellites are infecting their neighbors and the vast eastern hinterland behind them with ideas of insubordination, hopes of democracy, distrust of Marxism, and doubts about the ultimate world triumph of Communism. On both sides of the iron curtain fewer persons regard Communism as the wave of the future; far more identify it with an ocean of terror. Russia's imperial conquests during the Second World War actually diminished the attraction of Communist teachings. The sword in the right hand destroyed the book in the left.

Now the sword is blunted. Russia did not acquire her satellite colonies for national defense purposes. Soviet imperialism was rather the result of (1) the opportunities offered by the 1939 pact with Hitler and the consequent hostilities, (2) the need to substitute the strong intoxicant of Russian nationalism for the diluted potion of Communism. But once annexed, the satellites were put down in Moscow's ledgers as a military asset. Frightened by the Kremlin's "peace" campaigns, and acting on its instructions, the satellites ruined their economies to reinforce their armies. Thereupon defense ministries in Europe and America employed mechanical brains to calculate the number of satellite soldiers and weapons Russia could put in the field against them. Today, largely due to events in Poland and Hungary and their repercussions beyond, the satellite armies can be written off as unreliable. In case of war, indeed, Russia would have to station a large portion of her own forces in the satellites to keep them from throwing off the heavy red yoke.

Nor can the Moscow marshals and generals be happy about stationing their troops in a sea of hate in Poland or using them to kill Hungarian civilians. The business of a soldier is to fight soldiers, and any other duty is demoralizing. Prime Minister Jawaharlal Nehru, who sent Mr. K. P. S. Menon, his Moscow ambassador, and Dr. J. N. Khosla, his Prague envoy, to investigate conditions in Hungary, told the Upper House of the Indian Parliament on December 13, 1956, that 25,000 Hungarians and 7000 Russians had been killed during the uprising. Neither cautious estimate could bring comfort to Marshal Zhukov. Both casualty lists might have been still longer but for the Kremlin's fear of driving more Hungarians into a suicidal frenzy and more of its troops into the camp of revolution. The *Great Soviet Encyclopedia's* article on Hungary states that in 1849 many Russian soldiers deserted to the Hungarian side. Those soldiers were, in their majority, marauding Cossacks and unlettered muzhiks, whereas today's Soviet army, especially the technically trained tank corps, has gone to school, has been stuffed with history, and knows that what it saw in Hungary was a real revolution such as they had studied in their Bolshevik textbooks at home, only this time it was directed against their country. Crushing it must have been a repugnant and depressing duty. Face to face with workers in overalls and teen-age student boys and girls the Russian soldiers cannot have believed the Soviet propaganda about foreign spies and Fascists, and if a number went over to the revolutionists to prove their loyalty to revolution one would not be surprised. There is at least one documented instance, quoted in a *New York Times* dispatch from Vienna dated February 24, 1957, of a combat troop which consisted of seven T 34 tanks and thirteen other vehicles which joined the Hungarian rebels.

Like so many classic empires before it, the Russian empire too has become an economic as well as a military liability. Immediately after World War II, the Soviet government engaged in the most merciless exploitation of its satellites. This was one of the reasons for Yugoslavia's defection in 1948. Russia's robbery of Polish coal, data on which have now been released by the Polish authorities, is another documented example. Not only did Moscow gouge the satellites in its own trade with them but it insisted on acting as their middleman—at a profit—with third parties. Uranium imperialism was an additional vicious aspect of Russian exploitation. In East Germany, Czechoslovakia, Rumania, and Hungary, Moscow seized the uranium deposits, worked them as a secret monopoly, and carried the product to the Soviet Union.

Wherever possible the draining of the satellites for the enrichment of the mother country still continues, but in most places it has already continued so long that the law of diminishing returns has set in. Dire poverty grips the subjugated peoples, and, in Poland and Hungary, it has led to revolt. Even the diminishing returns have ceased, and Russia was forced to reverse the flow and return to the satellites a part of what it had extorted. Moscow has given loans to Poland and East Germany, and sent food to Poland, Hungary, and Rumania, which in their pre-Communist days, before collectivization injured their farms, were self-sufficient in food and sometimes exported it. Increased Polish political independence, moreover, has enabled the Warsaw government to eliminate Moscow as a commercial intermediary. Thus, in 1956, Poland delivered to Finland nine million dollars' worth of coal, but payment was in the form of Russian goods which were objectionable to Poland alike as an indication of subservience and because of their high cost and low quality. In 1957, Poland is dealing with Finland directly.

Poland's greater economic independence, though limited, has struck the Russian empire a serious blow. In December, 1956, Poland drastically cut her coal shipments to Russia, East Germany, and Czechoslovakia on the ground that she wanted to sell it to western countries for hard currency instead of to Communist countries for goods. As a result the Soviet Union undertook to send some of its own coal to East

Germany and Czechoslovakia. But these two nations, realizing that the supply would be inadequate, reduced their industrial goals. "We have to solve the coal problem out of our own resources," the East German government stated in January, 1957, and, knowing that this was impossible, it ordered zone-wide retrenchments. The same number of dwellings, it decreed, must be produced "with less steel and less cement." In these circumstances, the same number of dwellings will certainly not be produced—and the quality of those built will suffer. Economic shortages everywhere in the Soviet empire are becoming a regular Kremlin nightmare, and the trouble must grow as the people cry out for a better life.

Poland and Hungary are special economic problems to Russia. Unless the Polish government receives hundreds of millions of dollars in foreign aid it may not be able to maintain order in the country or itself in power. A sum of this magnitude, however, would reduce the Soviet population's living standards and hobble Russia's economy. On the other hand, the Kremlin objects to western aid to Poland because it might push her farther away from Moscow and Marxism. But a Russian dog-in-the-manger attitude (neither giving adequately nor letting others give) would release a Polish roar of protest.

The Kremlin's dilemma in Hungary is still more baffling and seems to have caused dissension in the Soviet Union's collective directorate. In the foreseeable future the Hungarians are unlikely to work hard enough to revive their national economy or make it viable. Russia, consequently, must either support millions of Hungarians or deport them. It could do both. But whether helpful or harmful, anything it does will be resented and rewarded with nationalistic hostility.

Other imperialisms have faced similar contradictions before. But Communism compounds them. It multiplies the irritation of foreign domination by the disaster of an irrational economic system and total loss of liberty. In all the satellites, therefore, and notably in Poland and Hungary, Moscow has to contend with anti-Communism plus anti-Russianism. There is little prospect that the brittle Kremlin administrators will learn to cope with their manifold colonial difficulties.

Can Russia cut her losses and cut the satellites loose? Soviet economists must by now have discovered that the imperial cornucopia they dreamt of has turned out to be an empty bag. Nevertheless, uranium is as indispensable to the Russians as oil to western Europe and, for some strange reason, those who have once been owners are reluctant to become mere buyers or unprivileged concessionaires. But the longer Moscow holds the satellites the more hatred it will generate and the worse will be the terms of its trade relations with a liberated eastern Europe.

The Russian military share the economists' disappointment. The expected manpower bonanza of the satellites with their hundred million inhabitants (added to Russia's two hundred million) is a joke. But the generals are probably not eager to abandon territory bought with the blood and bones of their soldiers. Or are their ideas so antiquated as to lead them to think that the width of the satellite belt would be decisive in the age of rockets and air warfare?

Whatever the sentiments of the economists and the military, the decision lies with the politicians and with a few marshals, notably Zhukov who has achieved a pre-eminent political position—witness, among other things, his official visit to India late in January, 1957.

Kremlinology, that dark and dubious science which seeks to determine how what Kremlin leader thinks this evening or will think tomorrow evening, is hardly as good a guide to the future of Soviet imperialism as logic and historic precedent. Russia can (1) try to use the power of her army, secret police, and stooges to hold the satellites in silent subjugation no matter what the cost; (2) try to win popular assent in the satellites by offering economic concessions, making military occupation as invisible and painless as possible, and granting the reshuffled satellite regimes a semblance or modicum of independence in domestic and foreign policy-making; (3) propose the withdrawal of her armed forces from Poland, Hungary, East Germany, Rumania, Bulgaria, and Albania, or from one or two or three of them in return for the retirement of American military units from Europe and of western military units from Germany, and then the establishment of a neutral buffer zone between West and East.

Choices number one and two are certain to fail in a maximum period of five to ten years, probably less. The day of empire is done in Africa and Asia; it is sure to end soon in Europe. Naked force is self-defeating in a colony and would, in time, react badly on the Soviet public. Apparent self-government and economic gifts may delay the hour of departure but, judging by broad experience elsewhere, there is no substitute for full national freedom. Subject peoples have very good vision for deception.

Choice number three tempts Moscow. It is good business and politics to sell nothing for something. If Moscow finds that it must draw back its armies from the satellites why not do so in exchange for the retirement of western armed forces from Central Europe and the resulting disruption of NATO? That would be an excellent bargain for Russia. Would it be wise strategy or sensible policy for the West?

No American or western troops could be stationed in a neutralized Germany. This would leave Europe exposed to Russian aggression or pressures. At present the presence of United States armed forces in Germany which would be involved the moment a Russian army crossed on to German territory is a deterrent to Soviet attack and therefore a guarantee of world peace. No United States commander would agree to Belgium and Holland as an alternative station to Germany, because those countries offer too narrow a terrain for defense and maneuvering. The American army might be unwelcome in France and Britain (it is welcome in Germany

where, in the absence of an adequate German defense establishment, the people regard it as their protector). Even if the
American army remained somewhere in Europe its retirement
from a neutralized Germany would create a tempting power
vacuum in Germany. Historically Russia is the great vacuum
filler.

American military aviation based on Britain or the Continent is not the same thing as American soldiers in Germany,
for the point is not primarily to be able to repel an attack but
to prevent it, and the American army in Germany serves notice on the potential aggressor that the United States would
automatically go to war in the event of an invasion of Germany.

Pulling back the American army to the fringes of the European continent or, most probably, to the United States
(in case Germany were neutralized) raises the question of
whether the United States—or any nation which is not the
actual victim of attack—would, in the atomic-hydrogen age,
involve itself in war and thereby invite the big bombs on its
head. There is a possibility, indeed a likelihood, that such a
prospect would arouse all the Munich-appeasement instincts
of self-preservation and conduce to inertia and isolationism.
The same can be said of an international guarantee of the
neutrality of Germany and of the entire projected neutral
zone across Europe. Would the United States or England or
France precipitate a world war if Russia, having evacuated
Rumania, sent her army back into it at the invitation of the
Rumanian government? The tendency would be to ask:
Where is Rumania? or: Why ruin civilization for the sake of
some unknown and inaccessible country?

The neutralization of Germany and the withdrawal of
NATO from German soil would ruin NATO, and the Euro-
pean continent would lie exposed. That can be no service to
Russia's present satellites. They would still shudder under the
Muscovite shadow without real freedom. If Russia were the

only great military power in Europe, the entire continent would fear her and bow to her. Germany especially would be in danger of slipping into the Soviet orbit.

The western powers are under no moral obligation to pay for a Soviet military retreat from the satellites which merely prolongs their agony and perpetuates the menace of Russian imperialism in Europe. It is neither Christian nor Gandhian to help the evildoer commit more evil deeds. Peace and security depend on the recession of Russian imperialism (and of all other imperialisms). It is better that this process should ripen from within as a result of the heat of popular displeasure. A diplomatic bargain is no substitute for the inevitable, natural evolution of national freedom.

Retreat from empire would relieve Russia's economic strain, reduce her heavy armaments outlays, improve her relations with the rest of the world, and reduce the present high cost of her foreign policy. The Soviet population would be grateful for the resulting rise in living standards.

The loss of empire could also bring the Soviet Union a greater measure of freedom. The present possibility is that the suppression of rebellious satellites will stimulate murmurs of dissent in Russia and thereby induce suppression at home. A hard policy outside conduces to a hard policy within, whereas the liberation of the satellites should mean more liberty for the motherland. Indeed this may be the chief argument of some Soviet leaders against disinvolvement in empire. They could contend that it might initiate the long process of the dismantling of the dictatorship. Anti-imperialism always aims at double-edged benefits: for the colonies and for the imperial power. Freedom granted to one hundred million persons just across the Soviet frontier is bound to have a salutary effect on the civil rights of those within.

No matter how Russia's satellites win national independence there is no doubt that they will. Russia cannot win in Europe. Russia cannot advance in Europe. She appeals only to Middle East despots or to others in that region who, crazed by hate, are ready to forego personal liberty. Even they will learn that behind the red mask of Communism lurks the imperial lust of Russia.

The millions in France, Italy, and elsewhere who vote Communist are not usually pro-Communist or disloyally pro-Russian. They vote against their unhappy conditions. (1) They should find more effective and more dignified ways of protesting. (2) Their lot should be improved. Hungary showed them and many European and American intellectuals the hollowness of the Communist idol. Indeed, Hungarian and Polish developments have cured the color blindness of numerous Asians and Africans who in their preoccupation with white imperialism could not see the virulent red variety. Before Russian imperialism is vanquished more persons with defective political vision will see better.

Once the truth is known Russia will be recognized for what she is: a strong power seeking power for herself at the expense of others. The others, in union, will defeat her. Freedom must win. It is only a matter of time, and the value of time depends on what we do with it—and with ourselves.

Index